45.00

D0208170

Privacy as a Constitutional Right

PRIVACY AS A CONSTITUTIONAL RIGHT

SEX, DRUGS, and the RIGHT to LIFE

DARIEN A. McWHIRTER and
JON D. BIBLE

QUORUM BOOKS
New York · Westport, Connecticut · London

Library of Congress Cataloging-in-Publication Data

McWhirter, Darien A. (Darien Auburn)
  Privacy as a constitutional right : sex, drugs, and the right to
life / Darien A. McWhirter and Jon D. Bible.
    p.   cm.
  Includes index.
  ISBN 0-89930-638-1 (alk paper)
  1. Privacy, Right of—United States.   I. Bible, Jon D.
II. Title.
KF1262.M45   1992
342.73'0858—dc20   91-47986
[347.302858]

British Library Cataloguing in Publication Data is available.

Copyright © 1992 by Darien A. McWhirter and Jon D. Bible

All rights reserved. No portion of this book may be
reproduced, by any process or technique, without the
express written consent of the publisher.

Library of Congress Catalog Card Number: 91-47986
ISBN: 0-89930-638-1

First published in 1992

Quorum Books, One Madison Avenue, New York, NY 10010
An imprint of Greenwood Publishing Group, Inc.

Printed in the United States of America

The paper used in this book complies with the
Permanent Paper Standard issued by the National
Information Standards Organization (Z39.48-1984).

10 9 8 7 6 5 4 3 2 1

To the memory of
Justice Louis D. Brandeis
and
Justice William O. Douglas
who occupied the
privacy seat on the
United States Supreme Court
for over half a century

Contents

Preface   ix

1. Introduction   1

Part I: The Foundations of Constitutional Privacy

2. The Historical Foundation: From Hittites to Puritans   17

3. The Philosophical Foundation: From Natural Law to
   Natural Rights   33

4. The Constitutional Foundation: From Natural Rights to
   Substantive Due Process   59

5. The Common Law Foundation: Creating the Right
   to Privacy   75

Part II: Constitutional Privacy

6. Creating Constitutional Privacy   91

7. Sex and Marriage   107

8. Life and Death   127

9. Mind and Body   137

Part III: Beyond Constitutional Privacy

10. Who Owns History?   153

11. State Constitutional Privacy   173

12. Conclusion   181

     Appendix   189

     Index   195

Preface

This book is about constitutional privacy. In a nutshell, this term has to do with the extent to which the United States Constitution protects people from unreasonable intrusions into their private lives.

In October 1991, with the appointment of Clarence Thomas to the United States Supreme Court, the last truly liberal justice (Thurgood Marshall) had been replaced. The United States thus will end the twentieth century as it began, with a Supreme Court significantly more conservative than the average American. How this will affect the constitutional right of privacy that the Supreme Court recognized in 1965, and particularly the right to an abortion, remains to be seen. It is generally thought—feared in some quarters, hoped in others—that the new Court will limit the right, if not eliminate it altogether.

The purpose of this book is to explain the development and nature of the constitutional right of privacy. Fundamental concerns over morality, the separation of church and state, and the inherent power of government over our lives are implicated by this right. Other issues raised are whether consenting adults may engage in intimate sexual conduct without government supervision; whether women, including minor females, may obtain an abortion; and whether people should be left free to end their lives when and under what conditions they please. These issues and others discussed in this book are of fundamental importance to many people in America.

What appears in this book is, of course, the responsibility of the authors. We wish, however, to thank in particular Mr. Edward Cavazos, a law student at the University of Texas School of Law, who assisted in the preparation of parts of this book.

Privacy as a Constitutional Right

1

Introduction

"It's none of the government's business." How often has that phrase been heard in America? Yet the idea that some things are "none of the government's business" is of recent origin. Four thousand years ago in the first Hittite and Babylonian law codes everything was subject to the law. During the second episode of Masterpiece Theater's *I Claudius*, the Emperor Augustus explains to the young men of Rome why he found it necessary to pass a law requiring them to marry. The Empire needed new Roman citizens and it was their duty to provide them. As this book is written, it is illegal for a Chinese couple to have more than one child, and forced abortions are used to assure that result.

For most of the last 4000 years laws came from a king who ruled by divine right (or was himself divine). With little or no distinction between the realm of law and the realm of religion, anything was fair game for the workings of the law. At the same time during those 4000 years the idea of the "individual" developed as both a legal and social concept.

During the Reformation, the idea of individual worth expanded. Individuals were by then considered to be capable of conversing with God without the aid of a priest and of reading the Bible for themselves. Similar ideas moved into the political arena, particularly in England. The Magna Carta signed by King John in A.D. 1215 granted certain rights to all free men, not just aristocrats. For example, free men could only be imprisoned or exiled upon the "legal judgment of their peers" (trial by jury), and all free men had the right to come and go in time of peace except outlaws and prisoners.

With the abdication of James II and the ascension to the British throne of William of Orange, the British Parliament passed the Bill of Rights of 1689. This Bill of Rights stated that only Parliament had the power to pass laws and levy taxes. It also confirmed certain rights of the citizens such as the right to petition the king and the right of Protestant subjects to bear arms for their defense.

By the American Revolution, the idea that citizens had rights which governments could not infringe was firmly established. With the writing of the United States Constitution in 1787, the question of whether a fundamental charter of government should also contain a list of specific rights became of penultimate importance. Although the original authors had no intention of placing a "bill of rights" in the document, Thomas Jefferson, Patrick Henry, and others felt that a document which granted power should simultaneously limit that power. Others argued that if such a bill of rights only contained certain specified rights, other rights not on the list would be lost forever by their omission. Those demanding a set of specific rights won out and a bill of rights (the first ten amendments) went into effect in December 1791.

Over the last two centuries a debate has raged concerning the extent to which the Bill of Rights protects rights other than those listed in its specific provisions. The decision by the U.S. Supreme Court that the Fourteenth Amendment makes most of the provisions of the U.S. Bill of Rights applicable to state and local governments as well as the federal government has made this debate more complex. As the U.S. Supreme Court has become increasingly conservative, another factor has been the emergence of state courts willing to interpret state constitutional provisions more broadly than the U.S. Supreme Court interprets similar provisions in the U.S. Constitution. Given that many state constitutions contain a more extensive list of "rights" than the U.S. Constitution, this raises many possibilities for the expansion of individual rights in the United States.

During the first century of constitutional interpretation a number of fundamental rights became part of the general vocabulary, including the right of free speech and the right to assemble. In 1890 another potential right was added to the list: the right to privacy. This new right was first mentioned in an article entitled "The Right to Privacy," published in the *Harvard Law Review* and written by two Boston lawyers, Samuel Warren and Louis D. Brandeis (later a Supreme Court justice). Their concern was not with invasions by government but with invasions by the press into the privacy of individuals. They argued for the right to sue these insensitive newspapers for damages. Over the next century this right to sue for invasion of privacy expanded and ultimately came to influence interpretations of the Constitution as well.

In the 1990s a number of issues have arisen that are said to involve the constitutional right to privacy. These include issues relating to sex, drug use, and abortion. Before these issues can be discussed, a number of fundamental concepts must be examined. Throughout this book the discussion turns on the concept of "rights." Do people in the United States have a "right to privacy?" It is important, however, to realize that this concept of "individual rights" is relatively new. It was unknown to both the Greeks and the Romans and rose as a legal concept only when the worth of the individual increased during the Reformation. At the same time "rights" only make sense when they are opposed to "power." Rights are a limit on power, particularly the power of the state to affect individuals, and therefore only came into existence when the world recognized that there can be limits on governmental power.

POWER VERSUS RIGHTS

Until the American Revolution, discussions of the interplay of power and rights assumed that power came first. A king had conquered a territory and had total power over it. He could kill or enslave everyone within the kingdom. Everything from the deer in the forest to the water flowing in the rivers was thought to belong to him. The king then granted certain rights to some individuals living in the territory. He might grant to one the right to hunt deer in a particular forest, to another the right to control everything and everyone in a particular area (to "own" the land), and he might grant a set of rights to a group of individuals such as the inhabitants of a town (a town charter). English law developed guiding principles to use in interpreting these "grants" by the king. The fundamental rule of interpretation was that the king probably intended to give away as little as possible. If it was not clear from the language of the deed or charter, the assumption was that the recipient of the king's largess got less rather than more. For example, if the deed said "I grant this land to Bill," the English judges assumed that Bill had been given the land to use during his lifetime and that upon his death the land would revert to the king, not be inherited by Bill's heirs. If the king had meant to give the land to "Bill and his heirs" he would have said so. That is why even today in the United States, most deeds say the land is being granted to "Bill and his heirs" to clarify that Bill has full title and may do with the land whatever he wishes.

Given this ancient way of viewing grants by a king, the interpretation of the English Bill of Rights was that the king had total power except for whatever rights he granted to the people. The lawyers who were part of the American Revolution made a similar assumption. They assumed that at the moment of revolutionary victory, before the creation of any legitimate state governments or a national government, each individual in the society (each adult, white male that is) was all powerful and completely free. These citizens at that moment possessed all the rights and powers imaginable, from the right to speak their mind to the right to kill their neighbors. There was no "law" over them. These all-powerful individuals then formed governments. If the same assumption is made about them and their grant of power to those governments that was made for the English king, it must be assumed they granted only limited powers to those governments and reserved to themselves as many rights and powers as they could.

Using this concept to interpret the U.S. Constitution, for example, one would assume that in 1792 the federal government had only those powers granted by the document, such as the power to coin money and regulate interstate commerce. One would also assume that the Bill of Rights constituted a "reservation" of certain rights by the citizens out of their original state of "total rights and powers." Since "the people" stood in place of "the king" by right of conquest (or by right of successful revolution) any doubts concerning what powers and rights they reserved must be decided in their favor. To make this clear, the Ninth Amendment states: "The enumeration in the Constitution, of certain rights, shall not be construed to deny or disparage others retained by the people." During the twentieth century the question of what "unenumerated rights" were actually retained by the people would become of paramount importance. Specifically, did the people retain some general right to privacy, and if they did, what does this right encompass?

THE RULES OF STATUTORY CONSTRUCTION

Throughout this book, the question will be asked how the U.S. Constitution should be interpreted. Since the United States was the first nation founded on a written constitution, the question of how such a fundamental charter should be interpreted was a new one for American judges who turned to the ancient rules of statutory interpretation for guidance. These rules are few and generally make intuitive sense.

1. The Plain Meaning Rule

The first rule of statutory interpretation is that if the exact meaning of a statute can be determined by looking only at its words, that is how the statute should be interpreted. The whole idea of a "government of laws and not of men" is that, in theory, citizens should be able to go to the statute books and read the law for themselves.

2. The Intent of the Legislature Rule

If one cannot tell from the "plain words" what a statute means, one should try to ascertain the "intent" of the people who wrote the law and then interpret the statute in light of that intent. Was there a particular problem the authors were trying to solve or a particular incident that prompted the enactment of the statute? Did the legislative committee that reported to the legislature as a whole prepare a report on why the legislation was needed and what it was expected to accomplish? If the inquiry into plain meaning provides the "letter" of the law, the inquiry into intent provides its "spirit."

3. The Words in Context Rule

The same word can have very different meanings depending on the context. Take the word "light," for example. If the discussion is about vision, light refers to the rays of the sun, but if the discussion is about beer, light means low in calories (it may or may not mean "less filling").

4. The Specifics Reveal the General Rule

Often a statute will use a term that is capable of many interpretations and is followed by a list of specific items that the legislature intends to include in that general concept. The list can be used to clarify the general term and to determine what other items, not mentioned, should be included in the list. For example, suppose a statute says teachers may be dismissed during the school year if convicted of a "crime of moral turpitude," and then lists examples such as "rape, theft, and murder." Is running a red light a "crime of moral turpitude?" This certainly does not seem to be the kind of offense the legislature had in mind.

5. The Inclusion of One Excludes the Other Rule

Judges assume that if a general category is limited in some way, the legislature intended that limitation to have meaning. For example, if a sign on the cash register says "no personal checks accepted" this rule of interpretation would say that this business will cash payroll checks because payroll checks are not "personal" checks. If the business intended not to cash all types of checks, the sign would say "no checks accepted." By limiting "checks" to "personal" the business must have intended to accept other types of checks not in this particular subset of the universe of checks.

STRICT CONSTRUCTION OF A CONSTITUTION

During the last 200 years a number of justices of the U.S. Supreme Court have urged that these and other more technical rules of statutory construction be followed when interpreting the U.S. Constitution. This has never been the view of a majority of the justices, however. While they recognize that these rules help, they also note that the interpretation of a constitution and a statute are very different tasks. If they misinterpret a statute the legislature can always amend it to correct their mistake, but the Constitution is not so easily amended. Also, constitutions are intended to last for centuries and to apply to very different societies. This requires a recognition that the Constitution is more an embodiment of general principles than a statement of specific rules. This is particularly true of the U.S. Constitution, which is shorter than most state constitutions and has lasted longer with fewer amendments.

Take the Eleventh Amendment for example. It says: "The Judicial power of the United States shall not be construed to extend to any suit in law or equity, commenced or prosecuted against one of the United States by Citizens of another State, or by Citizens or Subjects of any Foreign State." The question is: does this amendment prevent citizens of a state from suing their own state in federal court? The answer by strict construction has always been NO.

The plain meaning rule says look to the words themselves. The amendment speaks of "citizens of another state" and "citizens or subjects of any foreign state," but it does not include "citizens of the state being sued." Also, if the people who wrote and voted on this amendment had intended to include everyone, why did they mention only these two groups to the exclusion of "citizens of the state being sued?" As for the intent of the authors, this amendment came about because of a specific incident. Someone from South Carolina sued the state of Georgia in federal court. The injury to be corrected was a specific one, the humiliation of being dragged into federal court by a "foreigner." Another rule of construction in American law is that any rule that limits the right of people to seek redress of their grievances in a court should be construed as narrowly as possible. The fundamental rule of construction discussed above, that the people are assumed to give up as little of their powers and rights as possible, would also support this interpretation.

These arguments have been made several times to no avail since the Eleventh Amendment went into effect in 1798. A majority of the U.S. Supreme Court has always interpreted the amendment to preclude citizens of a state from suing their own state in federal court. Despite all the "strict construction" arguments to the contrary, the justices decided that the amendment stands for the general principle that states cannot be sued in federal court.

HYPOTHETICALS AND THE CHAIN OF HORRORS

This book will also use another tool that lawyers use to reason about the law: the use of hypothetical situations. The utility of discussing situations not currently before the court lies in trying to predict the long term effects of a particular decision. This book deals with the question of where to draw the line between the right of the majority in a democracy to make laws and the right of individuals and minorities to live their lives as they see fit without government interference. At present, in the United States, there are states ruled by Protestant, Mormon, and Catholic majorities. It is no coincidence that the two strictest abortion laws passed in 1991 were in Utah and Louisiana (Mormon and Catholic states respectively). Before deciding that certain issues should legitimately be left to the majority in a state, it might be useful to ask if the justices would feel the same way if a state where a majority of the citizens are Islamic Fundamentalists, Chinese Communists, or John Stuart Mill-type agnostics is imagined.

The use of hypothetical situations often leads to what lawyers call "the great chain of horrors" argument. This argument simply says that if the judges rule a particular way, a series of decisions and events might follow leading to an ultimately "horrible" result.

The use of these arguments can be illustrated with a simple "what if." What if the U.S. Supreme Court decides to get out of the abortion regulation business and leaves it up to the states to decide if and when a woman can have an abortion? While a Catholic or Mormon state might use this power to prevent most abortions, a state run by Chinese Communists might use it to "require" women who are pregnant and already have the legal limit of children to have abortions. Given that possibility, is the Court really ready to give up all control over this area? On the other hand, if the Court says a state may prevent but not require abortions, is it not simply siding with one religion or ideology against another?

COMMON LAW VERSUS CONSTITUTIONAL LAW

The United States inherited much of its law from England. The law that sets out rules for resolving disputes between individuals is called the "common law." This law was essentially made by judges ruling in cases not governed by a constitutional or statutory provision and by other judges who followed the precedent of past decisions in similar cases. In a sense, every state (except Louisiana which inherited its basic law from France and Spain) began with the common law of England and has over time altered that law to fit its particular circumstances.

The federal government did not inherit the common law; rather federal law flows from a written constitution and written statutes. While federal judges may look to the common law to help understand the meaning of particular terms, they may not "incorporate" common law principles into the U.S. Constitution or federal statutes unless they conclude that was the intent of the authors.

A state supreme court, on the other hand, is not so restrained. Because state supreme courts are the final arbiters of the meaning of both the state constitution and the content of the state's common law, they are free to base their decisions on either one. For example, a state supreme court can decide that a person has a "right to die" under the state constitution or because the state common law provides such a right. The U.S. Supreme Court can only find a right to die in the U.S. Constitution.

NATURAL LAW AND NATURAL RIGHTS

Any discussion of the fundamental principles of American law must deal with the concepts of natural law and natural rights. While many people use these two terms interchangeably they do not mean the same thing. Both natural law and natural rights are invoked in the Declaration of Independence. The Declaration begins by saying that it had become necessary for the thirteen United States of America to "assume among the powers of the earth, the separate and equal station to which the Laws of Nature and of Nature's God entitle them." It goes on to say:

We hold these truths to be self-evident, that all men are created equal, that they are endowed by their Creator with certain unalienable Rights, that among these are Life, Liberty and the pursuit of Happiness.—That to secure these rights, Governments are instituted among Men, deriving their just powers from the consent of the governed.

The concept of natural law was invoked to make clear what kind of powers the new nation would have, namely all the powers other nations have and have always had. In a sense, the concept of natural law clarified that the definition of the new nation would be like all past independent nations of which history provides hundreds of examples. It would not be a "colony" of England or part of a "federation" with England, but rather would be equal to England.

The natural rights concept established that the citizens of the new United States would have the right to life, liberty and the pursuit of happiness. This suggested that there would be a "natural" line between the powers of government and the rights of citizens. The last two hundred years have been spent trying to decide where that natural line is.

PRIVACY IN AMERICA

That Americans have always had a greater concern with privacy than their European ancestors is demonstrated by a thousand incidents of history. To mention one, after the United States purchased the territory of Louisiana thousands of people from Kentucky floated down the Mississippi river to take up residence in New Orleans. These supposedly primitive Kentuck people were appalled by the architecture they encountered. The homes required people to walk through a bedroom to get to a living room, and in many cases the stairways joining sleeping and living quarters were outside the houses for everyone to see! The new Americans soon built homes with hallways and indoor stairways, even though by European standards such things were considered a waste of indoor space.

Other examples abound. Americans excelled at building fences and invented both barbed wire and chainlink. When railroads became the rage it was an American who came up with the private Pullman compartment. In America even the cheapest motel provides each room with a "private" bathroom; indeed, many Americans consider the lack of such "private" facilities the worst part of travel in Europe. When Americans felt they could not get enough privacy in either small towns or cities, they invented suburbs. In short, Americans have a significant concern with privacy and in many cases have made sacrifices to satisfy this desire to "be let alone."

SEPARATION OF CHURCH AND STATE

The United States was founded on the principle of the separation of church and state. There had never been a "secular" state before; indeed, throughout history state and religion had been two sides of the same coin, each working to support the power of the other. America owes that separation to one man more than any other, Thomas Jefferson. Jefferson authored the Virginia Bill for Establishing Religious Freedom. He considered it and the Declaration of Independence to be his two greatest writings. Although the bill was introduced in 1779, it was not passed by the Virginia legislature until 1786 (for a copy of the original text see the Appendix). Jefferson described the fight for passage as his "severest contest," believing that freedom of religion was among the "natural rights" on which government could not infringe.

It was to a great extent because of Thomas Jefferson and his victory in Virginia that the First Amendment to the U.S. Constitution prohibits the "establishment of religion" and governmental interference with the "free exercise" of religion. Of course, these phrases are easy to say and difficult to define. While it is clear that the prohibition of an "established" church would prevent government from imposing a tax to support a particular church, what if government wants to provide a religious school with free textbooks or build a building on the campus of a religious college? These kinds of questions have been very difficult for the U.S. Supreme Court. What does the right to freely exercise one's religion mean? Does it mean only the right to "believe" whatever one wants about issues such as the existence of God, or does it also protect the right to act on those beliefs and do whatever one believes God wants, whether that includes smoking peyote or having four wives? It seems clear, reading the Virginia Bill for Establishing Religious Freedom, that it protects "freedom of belief," not "freedom of action," but the First Amendment of the U.S. Constitution is not so clear.

Although many would object that it is useless to be allowed to profess a belief if acting on it is prohibited, the problem with holding that the "free exercise" clause protects behavior is obvious. If the Court were to rule that the members of a particular religion could not be prosecuted for smoking peyote as part of their religious ceremonies, people would be encouraged to join that sect in order to smoke peyote without prosecution. This would be a kind of "establishment" of religion, and it would also violate the principle of equal protection by providing a privilege to one group that is withheld from others.

While it has been argued that allowing the majority to pass laws imposing its morality on the rest of society violates the separation of church and state, the U.S. Supreme Court has never seen it that way. If a particular "behavior" is to be declared beyond the reach of the democratically elected majority, there must be some basis for this conclusion other than the desire to keep the church and state separate.

THE U.S. SUPREME COURT

While every set of Supreme Court justices has been unique, it is fair to speak of "periods" of the Supreme Court. The pre–Civil War period runs from the swearing in of the first chief justice, John Jay, in 1789 to the end of the Civil War. Two of the most famous decisions of that period are *Marbury v. Madison* and *Dred Scott v. Sandford.*[1] *Marbury* established the principle that the Court may declare unconstitutional statutes passed by Congress or the states. *Dred Scott* declared the Missouri Compromise unconstitutional and made the Civil War all but inevitable.

The post–Civil War period runs from the end of the Civil War to 1905. During that period the Court used its power not to declare statutes unconstitutional, but to interpret them narrowly to avoid coming to grips with constitutional questions. It would take the Court many decades to forget the terrible result of *Dred Scott.*

The Court that sat from 1905 to 1937 is often called the Lochner Court after the famous decision in *Lochner v. New York* handed down in 1905.[2] There the Court struck down a New York law that limited bakers' working hours to sixty a week and ten a day, the majority concluding that this arbitrarily interfered with the "liberty" to contract enjoyed by both employers and employees and protected by the Fourteenth Amendment. It was the Lochner Court that struck down much of the New Deal legislation and led Franklin D. Roosevelt to propose a change in the number of Supreme Court justices in order to get around this roadblock. This proved unnecessary when one justice changed his mind in 1937 and five to four against the New Deal became five to four in favor. Soon after this change several justices retired and Presidents Roosevelt and Truman eventually appointed a completely new group of justices.

The Court from 1937 to 1953 can be called the New Deal Court. It stood for the proposition that government, particularly the federal government, should be given a great deal of freedom to solve social problems and to regulate business. At the same time this Court did not declare the Fourteenth Amendment to be meaningless; instead it concluded that what the amendment really did was make the Bill of Rights applicable to the states as well as the Federal government. State statutes could now be struck down for violating the U.S. Bill of Rights.

In 1953, President Eisenhower appointed Earl Warren to be Chief Justice, beginning a decade and a half considered the most liberal period in the Court's history. Separate but equal schools were declared unconstitutional and the rights of criminal defendants were expanded. In 1962 the Court outlawed prayer in the public schools and billboards appeared calling for Earl Warren's impeachment.[3]

In 1969, President Nixon appointed Warren Burger as Chief Justice sparking an era of compromise among liberal, conservative, and moderate justices on fundamental issues such as abortion and civil rights. In 1986 Justice Rehnquist was elevated to the post of chief justice and an age of greater conservatism began. As this book is written only Justices Blackmun, Stevens, and White are left from the days of compromise. They would have been classified as moderates during the Burger era. The two liberal justices, Brennan and Marshall, have retired, and with the appointment of Clarence Thomas in 1991 to replace Justice Marshall, Presidents Reagan and Bush have been able to appoint a conservative majority to the Court.

It is interesting that both the liberal Democratic Presidents Roosevelt and Truman and the conservative Republican Presidents Reagan and Bush stated that they wanted to appoint strict constructionists to the Supreme Court. Yet there have not been more than a few such justices on the Court during the last two centuries. Why? Because strong forces of law, logic, and policy work against the application of "strict construction" when it comes to the difficult issues of the day.

AMERICA'S TWO GREAT DILEMMAS

Throughout its history the United States has contained within its legal and philosophical system two great dilemmas. The first is the problem of creating a system that protects everyone "equally" when so many different groups exist within the society. The second is the problem of trying to separate state from church when history provides no guide for such a separation. Both of these dilemmas are invoked by the right to privacy. How can men and women be treated equally when only women get pregnant? Where is the proper line between issues of morality and law when most people in the society either profess a Christian faith or have been raised in a Judeo-Christian setting?

The dilemma of equal rights has resulted in both a civil war and a civil rights movement. The dilemma of creating a secular state has resulted in dozens of difficult Supreme Court decisions. The idea that decisions on privacy and abortion are simply changed when new justices with different philosophies are added to the Supreme Court calls into question for millions of Americans the legitimacy of the Court in a way that has not occurred in decades.

At the same time these two dilemmas more than any other invoke the concept of America. While they have caused the society much anguish and pain over two centuries they are fundamentally what the new experiment in individual liberty and equality called the United States of America is all about.

NOTES

1. 5 U.S. 137 (1803); 60 U.S. 393 (1857).
2. 198 U.S. 45 (1905).
3. Engel v. Vitale, 370 U.S. 421 (1962); School Dist. v. Schempp, 374 U.S. 203 (1963).

The Foundations of Constitutional Privacy

2

The Historical Foundation: From Hittites to Puritans

This book is concerned with how the legal system should treat issues such as adultery, incest, abortion, illegitimate children, sex, sodomy, marriage, divorce, homosexuality, prostitution, contraception, bigamy, and fornication. It has been suggested that some if not all of these issues are covered by the constitutional right to privacy. It has also been suggested that the right to privacy protects the "traditional freedom" to engage in some of these activities. The only place to find the extent of that traditional freedom is in history, particularly the history and traditions of the Indo-Europeans.

Most modern European languages are descendants of an ancient Proto-Indo-European language spoken in what is today southwestern Russia 7000 years ago. The speakers of this ancient proto-language and its early descendants such as Hittite, Sanskrit, Greek, and Latin had a culture that clashed with the established cultures of Europe, the Middle East, and India. In Europe the old culture was essentially destroyed and replaced by an Indo-European culture.[1]

Archaeologists hypothesize that organized farming began in what is today Western Syria about 12,000 years ago. This early farming culture spread to Egypt in the south, India in the east and throughout Europe as far as Ireland in the west over the next 5000 years. It can be hypothesized, though never proven because these people left no written records, that these early farmers had a matriarchal society in which priestesses ruled a society dominated by a religion that worshipped the sun-goddess.[2] In this society land and property may have passed from mother to daughter, not father to son, and sexual activity may have been seen as unrelated to the act of creating children. Children may have been viewed as gifts from the gods, and every birth may have been seen as an immaculate conception.

Marriages between brothers and sisters may have been common, perhaps even required by the religion (this kept property in the family). This practice of brother-sister marriage was still widespread in the Egyptian Delta during the time of Christ. The handling of snakes may have been an important part of their religious ceremonies (Christ preached tolerance of the snake handlers), along with the performance of sexual acts with animals. Rules against adultery may not have existed. Who cares who has sex with a woman if sex is unrelated to procreation and property passes from mother to daughter, not father to son? In other words, rules against adultery, incest, and sodomy may not have existed and these acts may even have been required by the religion of the sun-goddess.

Evidence suggests that beginning 7000 years ago patriarchal-warrior-nomadic groups began to appear in areas that had been controlled by the farming culture. Those who came to dominate the Middle East and North Africa spoke languages from the Afroasiatic language family. Egyptian is a branch of this language family as are the semitic languages of Hebrew and Arabic. The Indo-European language family came to dominate Europe as well as Iran and the northern half of India.

While the Egyptians were inventing hieroglyphics, the Sumerians in Mesopotamia were inventing cuneiform writing. This method of writing on clay tablets with a wedge-shaped stylus was taken over by the Akkadians (speaking an Afroasiatic language) after they conquered Sumer at the end of the third millennium.[3]

By the middle of the second millennium the Middle East was dominated by four empires: Egypt, Babylonia (southern Mesopotamia), Mittani (northern Mesopotamia and Syria), and Hatti (what is today central Turkey). While the Egyptians wrote with hieroglyphics, the other three empires used cuneiform based on the system invented by the Sumerians and developed further by the Akkadians. While the Babylonians spoke an Afroasiatic language, the rulers of Hatti and Mittani spoke Indo-European languages. Archaeologists have never discovered the ruins of the Mittanian capital of Washukanni, but they have excavated both Babylon and the capitol of the Hittite empire, Hattusa.

HAMMURABI'S LAW CODE

The Code of Hammurabi, written about 1750 B.C., is the oldest complete law code still in existence written in an Afroasiatic language.[4] The modern reader notices immediately that the punishment for many things was either death or disfigurement. The penalty for murder was death, as was the penalty for accusing someone of murder if the accused was not convicted.[5] Anyone accused of sorcery was plunged into the river. If he drowned the accuser got his property; if he lived, then the accuser was put to death and the accused got the accuser's property.[6] The penalty for theft was either immediate death or death if the accused could not pay the fine.[7] Altogether, out of 282 laws, the penalty was death in thirty-four laws and disfigurement in twelve. The Code of Hammurabi contains the basic concept of an eye for an eye and a tooth for a tooth.[8]

There were many laws dealing with what to do with the estates of men missing or killed in war.[9] Many also dealt with the leasing of property and the lending of money, as well as with real estate and trade.[10]

A wife caught in the act of adultery was put to death along with her lover.[11] A man who had sex with his daughter was sent into exile, while one who had sex with his daughter-in-law was put to death.[12] If a son had sex with his mother they were both burned at the stake.[13] There were no laws against sex or marriage between brothers and sisters. Generally women were not allowed to own land, but they could hold it for a time and then leave it to their children or brothers. There were a great many regulations concerning house builders, boatmen, and the hiring of oxen.[14] The wages of many occupations were set in the Code along with the price that could be charged for the rent of various animals as well as wagons and boats.[15]

Men and women could divorce each other, although it seems men could do it anytime they wished, as long as property was provided to support the children, while women who wanted a divorce had to be investigated and proven to not "be at fault." If they were at fault they were thrown into the river.[16]

There were a number of laws dealing with people who caused miscarriages. If a man hit a woman and caused the fetus to die he paid money to compensate the injured party. If the woman died they put the attacker's daughter to death as well, if the woman attacked was an aristocrat; otherwise, the attacker paid an extra amount depending on the class of the woman who died.[17]

Hammurabi's law code provides a summary of a patriarchal-warrior society. Land was owned by men, not women, and often came with the obligation to provide military service to the king. Adultery and incest across generations (father-daughter, mother-son) were not allowed, although there was no regulation of brother-sister incest or sodomy. Is this because these things were acceptable in the Babylonian Empire or because there were simply no people in the empire who would consider engaging in such activities? Perhaps people who considered such activities acceptable were allowed to engage in them as a kind of religious tolerance, but the laws against sorcery suggest some religions were not tolerated.

THE HITTITE LAW CODE

When scholars speak of the earliest example of "European" society they usually mean the ancient Greeks (500 B.C.) or perhaps the Greeks of Homer's epics (1200 B.C.) but there was in what is today central Turkey from 1700 B.C. to 1200 B.C. an empire ruled by people speaking an Indo-European language, the Hittites. To anyone familiar with later European society, there is much familiar about these Hittites. Like the Babylonians, they were patriarchal and warlike; unlike the Babylonians, their laws focused on compensating the victims of misdeeds, rather than on punishing the wrongdoer.

The Hittite law code is believed to have been written about 1500 B.C. as a revision of an earlier code.[18] Instead of being put to death, a killer had to pay damages. Instead of an eye for an eye and a nose for a nose, the Hittite law code called for a fixed amount of money for an eye or a nose with different amounts depending upon whether the victim was a freeman or a slave.[19]

A person who caused a miscarriage paid money to compensate for the loss. In the old version of the laws he paid a shekel for each month the woman had been pregnant before the miscarriage (half a shekel per month if she was a slave). In the new version the amount was simply set at twenty shekels if the woman involved was free and ten shekels if she was a slave.[20] Both men and women could obtain a divorce.[21] There were a number of laws dealing with how to treat children of marriages between slaves and free people and what happened when people eloped. There were also laws regulating land rent and the services that apparently went along with land ownership. Generally, the penalty for stealing was to pay back the value of the thing stolen and a fine, with the amount of the fine set in the Code.[22] There were also laws setting the legal rent for items such as axes, horses and oxen, as well as the proper wages for different kinds of work.[23]

Sorcery was not looked upon kindly. If someone killed a snake while "pronouncing another man's name" he had to pay one mina of silver (a large sum). If the person doing this was a slave he was put to death.[24] The prices of slaves were set in the Code depending on whether they were skilled craftsmen (ten shekels of silver) or bird-fanciers (twenty-five shekels).[25] The prices of many animals and products were also set by the Code.[26]

The laws at the end of the Code deal with sex.[27] It was a capital offense to "do evil" with a cow, a sheep, a pig, or a dog, but the Code specifically said there was no punishment for "doing evil" with a horse or a mule. It was also a capital offense for a man to "violate" his mother, daughter, or son; it was only a capital offense for a man to "violate" his stepmother if his father was still alive. A man was executed for cohabiting with free women who were sisters, or their mother. If he married a free woman and then "touched" her daughter, mother, or sisters it was also a capital offense, but if the women involved were slaves or foreigners there was no punishment. If a man "seized" a woman in the mountains he was killed, but if he "seized" her in her house she was killed. If a husband caught his wife with another man he could kill them both.

The Hittite law code contained rules concerning who married a woman if her husband died. First she went to one of his brothers. If none of the brothers could marry her, she went to his father. If he could not marry her she went to a son of one of his brothers.[28] Similar rules seem to have applied in Ancient Greece and Rome.

Except for the sexual crimes, the only other capital offenses for free men in the Hittite law code were rejecting the judgment of a judge or stealing a bronze spear at the gate of the palace.[29] These offenses were against the authority of the king and might be seen as akin to treason. The penalty for killing another person was the payment of one person (presumably a slave) if the killing was during a fight and four persons if the killing was not during a fight.[30]

Most of the capital crimes listed in the Hittite law code were sexual. Death came from adultery, sodomy with particular animals; and having sex with the female relatives of one's wife or cohabitant if they were free women. Death was also the punishment if a man had sex with his mother, daughter or son, although, as was the case in Hammurabi's code, there was no mention of sex or marriage between brothers and sisters. Why was there so much concern with people having sex with animals in the Hittite law code and none in Hammurabi's law code? Was it that the Babylonians were more tolerant of these kinds of practices, or that the Hittites actually had people in the Empire who engaged in such practices, perhaps on an organized basis as part of their religion?

It is interesting that the Code of Hammurabi calls for so many death and disfigurement penalties while the Hittite law code generally called for a monetary payment. Some might wonder what would happen in a legal system that made almost everything a matter of money if the offender did not have enough money. It was simple: He could always sell himself into slavery. The injured people were compensated and the offender was still alive to provide work for the empire.

The Hittite and Babylonian Empires were two ancient patriarchal-warlike societies of the type that came to dominate the western world.

Historians generally believe their morality was similar and did not look favorably on adultery, incest, or sodomy. Yet the only thing consistent about the two law codes is the punishment of a wife's adultery and incest across generations. In a society in which property and social standing were inherited by sons from fathers it makes sense that the state would be concerned with identifying the legitimate heirs. Adultery and incest across the generations would make this difficult and were therefore forbidden.

There were many similarities between the two law codes. Neither society seemed to enforce the rule of primogeniture (the oldest son inherits everything). There seemed to be an assumption that men would have only one wife but that there would also be illegitimate children. Divorce was allowed and suicide was not mentioned.

The ancient laws of both the Indo-Europeans and Afroasiatics were passed down through the millennia as these societies interacted with each other and the ancient goddess culture of old Europe. Over time different groups developed their own legal codes and religious practices but certain practices were generally forbidden by the religion if not by the laws: adultery, sodomy, and incest.

ANCIENT ATHENS

By the time Athens had its golden age it had been in contact with other societies for centuries.[31] Homer's *Iliad* suggests that people who killed other people in his time were expected to pay "blood money," but the penalty for murder was death during Athens' golden age. This was because Drakon wrote a law code for Athens that put the penalty for almost all crimes at death (we still call these kinds of penalties draconian). Solon revised the Athenian laws in approximately 600 B.C., eliminating most of the death penalties except for murder.

Under Athenian law bastard sons could be citizens but they could not inherit property. Solon revised the rules on slavery. People could no longer be enslaved for the nonpayment of debts and parents could no longer sell their children into slavery. If a man died, his property was divided among all his sons, not passed to only the oldest son. Women were prosecuted for adultery, but not men. The law required a man to divorce his adulterous wife. Divorce was easy for men: They simply sent the wife away and that terminated the marriage. Women, on the other hand, had to give written notice that they were leaving and that this constituted a divorce. It is not clear whether a husband could prevent a wife from divorcing him once this written notice had been given.

A dowry was not a gift to a husband but a fund to be used to help support the wife and to be inherited by her children. After a divorce the dowry went with the wife. If a woman died without children the dowry returned to her father's house.

The rules on marriage between relatives stated that a woman could not marry a direct ascendant or descendant (father, son) or her brother or half-brother by the same mother. She could, however, marry a half-brother by the same father or an adopted brother. While men and women could only have one husband or wife at a time, a man could have concubines.

Unwanted children were gotten rid of by exposure. While the father did not have the right to kill the newborn, he could place it in the wilderness to die. The presumption was that the infant was then in the hands of the gods who, if they wanted it to live, could take care of it. The legends of both the Indo-Europeans and the Afroasiatics contain stories of kings or heroes who were exposed as infants and grew up to be great men. Moses was exposed by sending him down the river in a small boat. Romulus, the founder of Rome, was exposed as an infant and supposedly raised by wolves. Oedipus was found and raised by a farmer so that he could become king and fulfill his destiny.

As for sexual offenses, seduction was considered worse than rape. This was because seduction meant the woman's mind had been corrupted as well as her body. Rape brought a fine paid to the state and an amount paid to the husband. A seducer caught in the act could be killed immediately by the husband; otherwise he was subject to fines and a variety of punishments the husband might choose short of bloodshed. A husband had to divorce a wife once she had been seduced and she could no longer attend religious ceremonies. People who brought people together for the purpose of seduction were put to death. Prostitution was legal. There are no records of laws concerned with sex between people and animals like those in the Hittite law code.

The penalty for cowardice was loss of citizenship; for treason or subversion of the democracy it was death. Intentionally causing a public body to make a wrong decision could also result in death. There were also a number of rules relating to religious practices that could bring death or exile to anyone who offended the gods.

Homosexuality appears to have been generally accepted in ancient Greece. K. J. Dover, in his book on the subject, says "overt homosexuality was already widespread by the early part of the sixth century B.C." in Greece.[32] There still exist a great many vase paintings that depict older men with young boys. Homosexual prostitutes could not hold public office but Dover says this was because it was generally believed that if men were willing to sell themselves they might be willing to sell out the interests of the state. Different Greek city-states held different opinions on homosexuality, with Sparta and Crete being famous for their tolerance of homosexual activity. According to legend, the army of Thebes had a special unit made up of homosexual lovers that formed the backbone of the army and died to the last man fighting the Macedonians.

Except for the concern of the Hittite law code with those who "did evil" with certain animals, the Hittite and Athenian laws were not very different. Adultery was forbidden along with marriage between close relatives. The concern seems to have been the regulation of the inheritance of property and citizenship status rather than a desire to control the sexual activities of the populace. The death penalty was reserved for those who threatened the existence of the state or violated the sacred religious rules.

ANCIENT ROME

During the early days of Rome the laws were unwritten and used mainly by the patricians to keep the plebeians in line. According to legend, in 462 b.c., the plebeian Terentilius proposed that a law code be published so everyone could actually read the laws. This ultimately resulted in the engraving of the laws on a set of twelve bronze tables. The laws of the Twelve Tables are believed to have been based on ancient Roman custom, although the laws drawn up by Solon for Athens may have been consulted. A complete text of the Twelve Tables has not survived to modern times. Just as with the ancient Athenian laws, the contents of the Twelve Tables are known from various statements about them in other texts.[33]

Under the authority of the Twelve Tables, people were sold into slavery if they could not pay their debts and children could be sold or put to death by their fathers. Men could divorce their wives by "turning them out." Children born more than ten months after the death of their supposed father were illegitimate. Property passed to the heirs according to rules set down in the laws. Later a will could be used to pass property any way the owner wished, but the legal heirs had to be mentioned in the will for it to be legal. Women could not own property on their own.

Apparently, very little warranted the death penalty under the Twelve Tables, but slander was one of those capital offenses. As was true under the Hittite law code, most offenses called for a monetary settlement paid to the victim, not an "eye for an eye." Murder was not a capital offense, but harvesting someone else's fields at night was. The same fate awaited anyone who intentionally burned down another's house or grain deposit. It was legally permissible for a homeowner to kill a thief who came in the night, but not one who came in the day, unless the thief fought back when caught; the thief was required to pay double the value of the goods stolen. Giving "false witness" could result in the guilty person being thrown from the Tarpeian Rock. Judges or other public officials who accepted bribes were also put to death.

Because the contents of parts of the Twelve Tables will never be known, it is difficult to say which topics were conspicuous by their absence. However, there is no record of laws relating to things such as adultery, incest, or sodomy.

ANCIENT GERMANIC EUROPE

Montesquieu spent a significant part of *The Spirit of Laws* discussing the early law codes of the Germanic tribes that settled in France after the fall of the Roman Empire. He was intrigued by the idea of paying "blood money" to compensate the relatives of someone who had been killed. He says there was a complication.[34] What if A killed B and paid the blood money, but the relatives of B would rather have their personal revenge instead? There was apparently nothing to keep them from killing A and then paying the same blood money back to A's relatives, who might be inclined to kill the killer of A and pay the blood money back, and so on. To avoid this result A could pay a fee, called the "fredum," to his king, count, or duke to buy protection. The amount of the payment was greater depending on the territory of the person providing the protection. Montesquieu believed this was the origin of the modern word "freedom."

Montesquieu was writing about the relationship between morality and law, but he could find little among the ancient Germanic law codes that spoke to this issue.

FEUDAL EUROPE

If there is in these ancient laws a basic Proto-Indo-European component concerned with issues of sex and morality, it is minimal and seems more concerned with acknowledging the legitimate heirs to property than with controlling the morality of the people. Adultery and incestuous marriage were generally forbidden. Over this basic legal-moral layer, a great deal was added by the development of feudal Europe after the fall of the Western Roman Empire. A major force in this process was the development of a medieval Roman Catholic religion obsessed with the idea of original sin.

The Indo-Europeans do not seem to have had the rule of primogeniture. This makes sense for a society in which the father's wealth consisted of cattle, sheep, and weapons. When the Indo-Europeans came to own land, usually after conquering existing settled societies as was the case for both the Hittites and the Germanic tribes that spread across Europe, issues arose that had not been a problem for a nomadic people. For the Franks who came into France the rule was still to divide up the empire among the king's sons.

Charlemagne (A.D. 742–814) marks an end and a beginning. He built an empire in western Europe and used force to bring Christianity to the heathens, causing many Saxons to flee to England in an attempt to preserve their ancient religion. In A.D. 797 the Empress of Constantinople deposed and blinded her son Constantine VI, causing the imperial throne to be vacant. In A.D. 799 the Pope was driven from Rome by the people, only to have his power restored by a Frankish army. At Christmas 800, the Pope crowned Charlemagne emperor of the reconstituted Roman Empire. The world seemed to stand on the brink of a new age of peace and progress, but this was not to be. In A.D. 843, the Treaty of Verdun divided the western Roman Empire among the three living grandsons of Charlemagne. Europe became even more divided and the real power fell to powerful aristocrats. The former freeholders became feudal tenants forced to seek the protection of their powerful neighbors. The feudal system had begun.

Feudalism lasted as a political-moral-religious-legal system in Europe until the eighteenth century. It was built on the idea of contractual obligations between lord and vassal, duke and king. These were dangerous times. The Vikings raided with impunity. There were constant threats from the Moslems in Spain and the Middle East as well as the tribes in the east. Feudal Europe developed its social-political system in an attempt to preserve what it believed to be civilization. The idea was to freeze society in place. With communication and transportation difficult the only way to assure a new duke or baron would come to power to hold the system together was to make these titles hereditary. To avoid division and chaos the rule of primogeniture was adopted. The oldest son would inherit everything: the wealth, the land, the title, the power. Rules against adultery became even more important as the legitimacy of each male heir in the chain of society could not be questioned without bringing the whole society to the brink of destruction.

On top of this feudal system was laid the theology of the medieval Roman Catholic church. Questions of life and death were to be decided by God, not man. Thus evolved rules against abortion or exposing infants (also, every person was needed to keep the society going). Religious dissent was not to be tolerated lest the whole system fall apart and bring about chaos. The task of both theology and philosophy was to justify the legitimacy of the social system and the one true faith.

ENGLAND

The feudal system was finally solidified in England with the conquest by William the Conqueror in A.D. 1066. The rule of primogeniture became the rule of inheritance and land was held from the king in return for various feudal payments and services. It had been the custom in Europe that as people moved from place to place they were subject to the law of their tribe, not the law of the land. This system was ultimately replaced by English common law, a law common to everyone regardless of their tribal heritage. The Anglo-Saxons had relied on trial by ordeal while the Normans had used trial by combat. Both systems eventually gave way to trial by jury.[35]

William owed his legitimacy to the fact that the pope in Rome recognized him as the legitimate ruler of England. In return William gave new powers to the Roman Catholic church in England. He set up ecclesiastical courts, headed by bishops, and put issues such as inheritance of personal property, marriage, legitimacy, adultery, incest, and sodomy under their control. The church used whippings, fines, and penance to punish those who violated the moral code. The church was officially against capital punishment (only God can take a life) but it turned the other cheek when heretics and witches were burned at the stake. Whereas marriage had been a contract it became a holy sacrament. Whereas divorce had been possible, it became all but impossible, and remained so in England until 1857 despite the substitution of the Anglican church for the Catholic and the fact that the Anglican church came into being because of the desire of Henry VIII to receive a divorce. The church developed complex rules concerning whom people could and could not marry based on their degree of blood kinship.

About the only way to get a real divorce was to prove that one's spouse was not a true believer. This led many people to move from Protestant to Catholic, and vice versa, in an effort to justify divorce. Most people did not qualify for a real divorce and instead received a *mensa et toro*, a kind of legal separation during life with the marriage remaining for eternity. Bastards could not inherit property.

The rules on murder evolved from "blood-feud" to "blood-money" to capital punishment. The "blood-money" system was similar to the one that prevailed on the continent. An amount was paid to the relatives as compensation and another to the king for protection. A similar system applied to people who caused bodily harm. Once someone paid the fee they were "under the king's protection." Anyone who harmed them after that was subject to whipping, mutilation, imprisonment, or capital punishment for having violated the wishes of the king. English criminal law developed out of this system as more people were put "under the king's protection" for one reason or another. Eventually the old system of damages and fines faded away. Suicide brought a forfeiture of property and treason brought punishment worse than death (such as being drawn and quartered) as well as a forfeiture of property to the king.

While the king's courts were executing criminals the ecclesiastical courts were using whipping and fines to punish fornicators, adulteresses, and those who committed incest or bigamy. Some in England, particularly the Puritans, felt the Anglican church was too soft on these degenerates. When the Puritans found themselves in control of Parliament in the 1650s the ecclesiastical courts were all but abolished and moral crimes became crimes against the state. Adultery became a capital offense and conviction for fornication brought three months in prison. While the Puritans were bringing the power of the state to bear on immorality in England, the Puritans in New England were trying to accomplish the same goal in the New World.

AMERICA

Contrary to popular belief, the colonies did not accept English law wholesale. Many colonists came to America to get away from some aspect of the English legal system and it seemed to them ridiculous to impose the same evil on themselves in the New World. For example, most colonies rejected the rule of primogeniture. Property would be left by will, and if there was no will the children would inherit equally. Some southern colonies did have the rule of primogeniture until revolutionary war times and some northern colonies gave the oldest son a double portion because this practice could be found in the Bible. The idea that law should be guided by the Bible was common in the colonies as people felt they were moving past the law of man toward a law of nature and of God.[36]

The Puritans of Massachusetts felt that there should be no separation between church and state. The laws passed during the second half of the seventeenth century in Massachusetts viewed sexual crimes as more serious than crimes against property. Records suggest that there were fifteen executions in Massachusetts before 1660: four for murder, two for infanticide, two for adultery, two for witchcraft, one for buggery, and four for being a Quaker.[37] As this book is written, the penalty in Massachusetts for adultery is imprisonment for up to three years; for incest and sodomy the punishment is imprisonment for up to twenty years; while fornication is punishable by imprisonment for up to three months, just as it was in England under the Puritans over three centuries ago.[38]

The "Great Law" of 1682 passed in Pennsylvania contained elaborate provisions regulating sexual morality, but the penalties were less severe than in Massachusetts. The Quakers felt that being kicked out of the congregation was a severe punishment but as the size of the congregations dwindled some church leaders wished for another remedy. Today in Pennsylvania adultery is not a crime and the punishment for "voluntary deviate sexual intercourse" is up to two years in prison (it is a second-degree misdemeanor). The punishment for incest was raised to what it had been in the nineteenth century in 1989 when it again became a second degree felony punishable by up to ten years in prison.[39]

The attitude of the colonies toward divorce was similar to that of both the Catholic and Anglican churches: they were against it. There was no such thing as a legal divorce for many years in South Carolina, and in Georgia it required an act of the legislature. Adultery was the only ground for divorce in New York well into the twentieth century. Wealthy New Yorkers went to Nevada where a divorce could be had for a fee. Those who could not afford the trip paid people to lie in court to prove adultery and obtain a divorce.

South Carolina long prided itself for not having laws on such things as adultery and fornication. Over time, however, it gave in to pressure from the north to join the moral crusade. The current penalty for these two crimes in South Carolina is up to one year in prison.[40]

The history of the United States has been one of variable interest in using the criminal law to maintain "morality." The Victorian era in England and the United States brought renewed interest in stamping out adultery, sodomy, and fornication along with the consumption of alcoholic beverages. Interest in such things subsided at the beginning of the twentieth century and peaked again during the 1920s with the effort to end alcoholic consumption once and for all. The 1980s saw renewed interest in both enforcing morality with the criminal law and ending drug use. Throughout this evolution the laws placed on the books have generally remained there, in some cases exactly as written centuries ago. For example, the Massachusetts Penal Code does not use the word sodomy; it prohibits performing the "abominable and detestable crime against nature either with mankind or with beast."

CONCLUSION

During most of the history of Indo-European society, laws have been used to guarantee legitimate heirs inherited their proper position in society. Thus, legal codes have generally outlawed adultery and incest.

Beyond that it is difficult to generalize. It seems the issue of what moral offenses should be punished has depended more on what religion was in power and what kind of religious practices needed to be suppressed. The Hittites were troubled with people inside the empire who committed sodomy with cows, sheep, pigs, and dogs, so this became a criminal offense. Sodomy with horses was specifically allowed suggesting that this may have been part of the most ancient Indo-European religious practices. The ancient Greeks and Romans were unconcerned with sexual activity as long as the proper rules of inheritance were followed. Europe in the Middle Ages became more concerned with issues of sex and morality as the powerful Catholic church (and the Anglican church in England) tried to enforce one religion and morality on everyone. This reached its peak with the Puritans in England and New England in the seventeenth century. The general trend during the last three centuries has been to reduce the penalties for violating "moral crimes" or to leave them on the books but not enforce them. The practical problems with trying to enforce "morality" with the legal system have been a major deterrent. The Model Penal Code of 1955 encouraged states to drop from their penal codes "all sexual practices not involving force, adult corruption of minors, or public offense." That has not happened in most states.

In a very real sense America and Europe are still living through the breakup of the feudal system. This system was already disintegrating in the seventeenth century when Thomas Hobbes, the English philosopher, wrote his great work, *Leviathan*. His concern was the justification of the absolute power of the king, and he argued that without that power society would disintegrate into the chaos that feudal society had been trying to avoid since the death of Charlemagne. His argument was not that kings ruled by divine right, but that kings with absolute power were the only realistic alternative if society hoped to maintain some level of civilization. The book was published in 1651. By that time Charles I of England had lost his head and Europe had seen over a century of religious wars between Protestants and Catholics. The old society was breaking up and the sight was terrifying. How could society avoid the chaos that seemed to be engulfing it? Some, like Hobbes, argued for a return to the safety of the feudal system and absolute monarchy. Others hoped society would move forward, but, forward to what? The philosophers discussed in the next chapter tried to provide an answer to that question.

NOTES

1. E. Benveniste, INDO-EUROPEAN LANGUAGE AND SOCIETY (1969); G. Cardona, H. Hoenigswald, A. Senn (eds.), INDO-EUROPEAN AND INDO-EUROPEANS (1970); J. P. Mallory, IN SEARCH OF THE INDO-EUROPEANS (1989).

2. M. Gimbutas, THE GODDESSES AND GODS OF OLD EUROPE (1982); E. Gadon, THE ONCE & FUTURE GODDESS (1989).

3. For an overview of the history of this region see: M. Roaf, CULTURAL ATLAS OF MESOPOTAMIA AND THE ANCIENT NEAR EAST (1990).

4. For a copy of the Code of Hammurabi see: J. Pritchard (ed.), ANCIENT NEAR EASTERN TEXTS (1969), 163. The following notes refer to the Code of Hammurabi.

5. Laws 1, 3.

6. Law 2.

7. Laws 6–11, 14, 15, 19, 22.

8. Laws 196, 197, 200.

9. Laws 27–29.

10. Laws 42–107.

11. Law 129.

12. Laws 154, 155.

13. Law 157.

14. Laws 228–252.

15. Laws 253–277.

16. Laws 137–143.

17. Laws 209–214.

18. For a copy of the Hittite law code see: J. Pritchard (ed.), ANCIENT NEAR EASTERN TEXTS (1969), 188. The following notes refer to the Hittite law code.

19. Laws 1–5, 7–16.

20. Laws 17, 18.

21. Laws 26.

22. Laws 57–73, 94–97, 101–133.

23. Laws 150–161.

24. Law 170.

25. Laws 176, 177.

26. Laws 178–186.

27. Laws 187–200.

28. Law 193.

29. Laws 126, 173.

30. Laws 1, 174.

31. D. MacDowell, THE LAW IN CLASSICAL ATHENS (1978).

32. K. J. Dover, GREEK HOMOSEXUALITY (1989).

33. For a discussion of the Twelve Tables of Rome see: E. H. Warmington, REMAINS OF OLD LATIN, Vol. 3 (1967).

34. B. Montesquieu, THE SPIRIT OF LAWS (translation by T. Nugent, 1899), Book 30, Sections 19, 20.

35. For an overview of the history of English law see: R. C. Van Caenegem,

THE BIRTH OF THE ENGLISH COMMON LAW (1973); F. Pollock & F. Maitland, HISTORY OF ENGLISH LAW (2d Ed.) (1968).

36. For an overview of American legal history see: L. Friedman, A HISTORY OF AMERICAN LAW (2d Ed.) (1985).

37. Id. at 70-1.

38. Mass. Statutes, Chapter 272, Sections 14, 17, 18, 34.

39. Penn. Statutes, Title 18, Sections 3124, 4302.

40. South Carolina Statutes, Title 16, Section 16-15-60.

3

The Philosophical Foundation: From Natural Law to Natural Rights

The topic of this book is the right to privacy. This right to be free from government interference grows out of the general concept that there are freedoms beyond the power of the state to control, even if that state is a democracy. At the same time there is a belief that the majority should rule on most issues. The question of which issues may be left to majority will and which are beyond the power of government is the fundamental dilemma of a democratic liberal state.

The basic political ideology of the United States is democratic liberalism. This philosophy stands on four basic principles: democracy, liberty, education, and free enterprise. The fundamental problem for this ideology is that natural conflicts occur among these principles. Democracy assumes political equality, but that is difficult when there is economic inequality, a necessary consequence of the free enterprise system. Democracy assumes rule by the majority, but what if the majority wants to interfere with the liberty of a minority? This in turn raises the question: What areas should be left to the conscience of the individual citizen and what areas are legitimately subjects of legislation? Put another way: Where does democracy end and liberty begin?

Four political philosophers have provided the most influential commentaries on these questions: John Locke, Baron de Montesquieu, Jean-Jacques Rousseau, and John Stuart Mill. Over the last three centuries their voices have had the most impact on how democratic liberals think and how democratic liberal societies function. Throughout this book the concern will be the interpretation of the first fifteen amendments to the U.S. Constitution (for a copy of these Amendments see the Appendix). What did the people think who voted to place those amendments into the Constitution? The founding fathers frequently acknowledged their intellectual debt to Locke and Montesquieu. Rousseau's ideas were very much in the air during the American Revolution, while John Stuart Mill was the most influential political thinker of the nineteenth century.

The basic concept of philosophy during the seventeenth and eighteenth centuries was that of natural law. During the confirmation hearings for Justice Clarence Thomas in September 1991, there was much discussion of what natural law is and how it should affect U.S. Supreme Court decisions. While there are many opinions about what natural law means today, centuries ago it was a fairly simple concept. The law of nature meant a law discoverable by the use of observation and reason, such as the law of gravity. The main question for the time involved the extent to which natural law could be used to determine which political system was best or which morality was more "natural."

The idea of natural law is often counterpoised with the ideas of utilitarianism and relativism. Utilitarians argue that the "best" political system or morality is one that brings the greatest happiness to the greatest number of people. Relativists argue that there is no such thing as a "natural" political system or morality since observation of social systems around the world demonstrates that every conceivable type of political system has existed along with almost every conceivable type of morality.

Centuries ago, believers in natural law thought it possible to "discover" through reason and observation what the best political system would be. They also believed there were certain natural rights that could be discovered by reason and the observation of nature. There is no better statement of these tenets than the opening lines of the Declaration of Independence:

When in the Course of human events it becomes necessary for one people to dissolve the political bands which have connected them with another, and to assume among the powers of the earth, the separate and equal station to which the Laws of Nature and of Nature's God entitle them, a decent respect to the opinions of mankind requires that they should declare the causes which impel them to the separation.—We hold these truths to be self-evident, that all men are created equal, that they are endowed by their Creator with certain unalienable Rights, that among these are Life, Liberty and the pursuit of Happiness.— That to secure these rights, Governments are instituted among Men, deriving their just powers from the consent of the governed,—That whenever any Form of Government becomes destructive of these ends, it is the Right of the People to alter or to abolish it, and to institute new Government, laying its foundation on such principles and organizing its powers in such form, as to them shall seem most likely to effect their Safety and Happiness.

With these words Thomas Jefferson and his fellow delegates expressed the basic philosophy of a new nation. It would be one founded on the principles of natural law and unalienable rights. The Ninth Amendment to the U.S. Constitution stated: "the enumeration in the Constitution, of certain rights, shall not be construed to deny or disparage others retained by the people." These "unenumerated" rights would be the natural rights, the "unalienable" rights mentioned in the Declaration of Independence. But what are they? Who should decide what falls into this category? It has been argued that the right to privacy is such a natural right, one not enumerated in the Bill of Rights but none the less a right that should be protected by the Supreme Court and the Constitution.

Another belief became fundamental to the new nation and set it apart from every other nation then or previously existing: the belief in religious tolerance. Thomas Jefferson fought for six years to get through the Virginia legislature a bill guaranteeing religious freedom. This concept of religious toleration came directly from the writings of Locke and Montesquieu. But how much religious difference should or can be tolerated? Some said the Bill of Rights guaranteed to everyone the right to be any kind of Protestant they desired, within limits of course. Others disagreed. It must be remembered that for the Puritans of Massachusetts in the seventeenth century the greatest crime someone could commit was that of being a Quaker.

THE RISE OF PROTESTANTISM

It is impossible to discuss the origins of democratic liberalism and natural law without first examining Protestantism. In any discussion of the rise of Protestantism one man must come first, John Wycliffe (1320–1384). John Wycliffe became master of Balliol College, Oxford, some time after 1356. He was the great philosopher of his time at Oxford University. During the 1370s many in the English Parliament tried to limit the power of the Catholic church in England because of what were viewed as ecclesiastical abuses. Wycliffe argued in his treatise *De Civili Dominio* that an unrighteous clergy had no right to hold title to church land and that the ultimate question of who should own religious property should rest with the civil authority (king and Parliament). His theology was that God created the universe, set down the universal laws of nature; and does not intervene in the daily workings of the universe. This belief had a profound effect on the political and legal system. For example, trial by combat or ordeal had no place in such a world view. There would be no God to pick a winner or to save the innocent.

The medieval Catholic church against which the Protestants rebelled was a far cry from the Catholic church of today. The supposedly celibate clergy had concubines and the church did everything it could to make money, including selling forgiveness of crimes and passports to heaven (immunities and indulgences). The difference between what the Catholic clergy preached and how they lived was viewed by many as a threat to the very existence of Christianity.

Wycliffe argued that Christ and his apostles had no property and the clergy should follow their example. With the election of the "unrighteous" Pope Clement VII, Wycliffe began his revolution. He ordained "simple" priests and translated the Bible into English so that Christians could read it and decide for themselves what God and Christ intended for them. The Peasant's Revolt of 1381 was inspired by Wycliffe's ideas of individual worth and simple Christian communal ownership of property. This revolt cooled the enthusiasm of many of Wycliffe's supporters who saw for the first time where the concept of individual dignity and religious equality might lead. Wycliffe died of a stroke in 1384, but his lay preachers went on. His followers, called Lollards, probably accounted for half the Christians in England a century after his death. The scholars who came to England with Richard II's queen, Anne of Bohemia, took many of Wycliffe's ideas back to Bohemia where John Huss turned them into a national religion until he was burned at the stake in 1415.

The sale of indulgences increased during the 1400s to pay for the construction of St. Peter's in Rome. These indulgences guaranteeing absolution from sin were bought, sold, and used for wagers. Martin Luther posted his ninety-five theses against this system in 1517. In 1520 he wrote his three treatises calling for national churches free from papal interference, a limitation of holy days, and a married clergy. The fundamental question was: Were issues of faith to be entrusted to the reason of the common people, or the holy councils called by the Pope? Luther, arguing the former position, was condemned to death and forced to work in hiding on his own translation of the Bible. In 1524 the peasants of northern Germany revolted and Luther was ultimately forced to side against them. The Protestant German princes could see where this idea of everyone developing their own theology might lead, and they convinced Luther to come up with a standard theology for his new religion that would discourage revolutions. In 1525, the 300 German states formed into Catholic and Protestant leagues determined to settle questions of theology with the sword.

From Luther's time to today there has remained a fundamental tension between the Protestant ideal of every person reading the Bible and deciding religious and moral questions for themselves and the need of each sect to express its unique dogma. During the summer of 1991 a holy war was fought in Wichita, Kansas, over the issue of abortion. It forced many local Protestant ministers to face this dilemma for the first time. Many came out publicly in favor of the right of Protestants to make a free choice after consulting their conscience and the Bible.

In 1499 Switzerland broke away from the Holy Roman Empire. Ulrich Zwingli (1484–1531) was ordained a priest in 1506 and in 1518 expelled the indulgence sellers from the canton of Schwyz. In 1523 the magistrates of Zurich held a public debate between Catholics and the new Protestants led by Zwingli and declared Zwingli the winner. The city of Geneva joined Switzerland in 1534 and declared itself Protestant. In 1536 Calvin settled there and French-speaking Geneva became the font of Protestant literature for France. This ultimately led to civil war between the Catholics and the Huguenots. In 1534 Henry VIII created the Protestant Church of England over the question of his divorce, while Protestantism spread rapidly in Denmark, Sweden, and the Netherlands with the help of the printing press.

In England matters came to a head with the ascension of Charles I, who reigned from 1625 to 1649. Because Parliament would not vote him the taxes he needed, he imposed forced loans on the population to help pay for unsuccessful attempts to aid the Huguenots in France. He billeted soldiers in people's homes because he could not afford quarters for them and imposed martial law. The Parliament in 1628 passed the Petition of Right, condemning royal taxation without Parliamentary approval, imprisonment without charge or trial, martial law, and the billeting of soldiers. Puritan colonies were established in New England, while Lord Baltimore established Maryland as a Catholic refuge. Charles tried to force Episcopacy on the Scottish, who had learned their Protestantism from John Knox and refused to give up their Presbyterian church. Instead they rebelled and invaded England.

LOCKE

It was into this England of Puritans, Episcopalians, and Presbyterians that John Locke was born (1632–1704). His father was a small landowner and attorney as well as a Puritan. When Charles I was executed on January 30, 1649, Locke was seventeen and in a classroom a short distance away. His father fought on the Parliamentary side in the Civil War that ultimately brought Oliver Cromwell to power as the Lord Protector of the Commonwealth. In 1652 Locke entered Christ Church, Oxford, then under the control of a Puritan dean. From then until 1660 and the restoration of the Stuart king, Charles II, Locke witnessed the inability of those favoring a republic to agree on what shape it would take. Each Protestant sect was unwilling to tolerate the others.

In 1667 Locke went to London as the secretary and personal physician of Lord Shaftesbury. The earl of Shaftesbury was rich, powerful, and sufficiently astute politically to be a minister for Cromwell and part of the Restoration of the monarchy. It was through his long association with the earl that Locke gained first-hand knowledge of politics and government. During his first months with the earl he composed his *Essay on Toleration* defending the right of religious and political dissent. He worked for the earl for the next fifteen years, during a time of plots and counterplots in England. The earl of Shaftsbury fled to Holland and died in 1683. Locke spent the next five years in Holland hiding from the English.

With the death of Charles II and the ascension to the throne of his brother James II, fear spread that James II (reigned 1685–1688) meant to impose Catholicism on the country. He put Catholic officers in the army and Catholic advisors on the privy council. William of Orange landed from Holland with a small force. King James found his own generals would not support him and was forced to flee to France. In 1689 a Parliament met, passed a bill of rights, and offered the crown to William on consideration that he accept the Bill of Rights. The Bill of Rights forbade a Catholic king and declared a standing army illegal in time of peace. It also required frequent Parliaments and free elections.

Locke returned to England and spent his last fourteen years in peace. This gave him time to prepare his many writings for publication. He published his *Essay Concerning Human Understanding* in 1690, the *Third Letter for Toleration* in 1692, and *Some Thoughts Concerning Education* in 1693. His *Reasonableness of Christianity as Delivered in the Scriptures*, published in 1695, sought to separate the teachings of Jesus from all the later theology that had been added. He also wrote on questions of psychology and economics.

His *Two Treatises of Government*, published in 1690, is the most important. The *First Treatise* is subtitled an essay in which "the False Principles and Foundation of Sir Robert Filmer and His Followers are Detected and Overthrown." The *Second Treatise* is subtitled an "Essay Concerning the True Original, Extent, and End of Civil Government." The two treatises were not published until King William ascended to the throne of England but were written some time earlier.

The *First Treatise* is a response to Sir Robert Filmer's *Patriarcha*. Sir Robert was knighted at the beginning of the reign of Charles I and was a loyal royalist throughout the civil wars. Though he died in 1653 his great work was not published until 1680. Its publication near the end of the reign of Charles II caused a sensation. It is ironic that the kind of public debate over the meaning of Scripture that Wycliffe had dreamed of finally took place not over the issue of the infallibility of popes but over the legitimacy of kings.

Filmer argued that kings ruled by divine right as the legitimate descendants of Adam, whom God had given dominion over the world. Locke, however, using logic, reason, and the same Scriptures that Filmer cited, took his argument apart piece by piece. In doing so he not only annihilated the idea of the divine right of kings but he also set the stage for a new world view.

Filmer said that Adam was given power over all the world and that princes ruled as his descendants; he also said that God gave fathers absolute and arbitrary power over their children, so the same must be true of kings. Locke argued that although the Scriptures say God gave Adam dominion over the "fish" and the "fowl," it says nothing about "people," and that if God had intended to grant power over people he would have mentioned them. When God later granted power to Noah, he gave him power over the fish, birds, and animals with no mention of people. Filmer also said that God gave Adam power over "every living thing," to which Locke responded that God also gave him power to eat "every living thing," proving again that this did not include people. Locke also pointed out that God granted dominion not to Noah alone, but to "Noah and his Sons," and that ultimately Noah divided the world among his three sons, not giving total power to the eldest son as would be the case if the rule of primogeniture was laid down by God.[1]

Locke next took on Filmer's statement that because everyone is born subject to the absolute power of a father, everyone is born a slave, noting that Filmer provided no "reason" why this should be so. Locke then turned to other authors who had made similar arguments. They had argued, for example, that since the father gives life he must logically have the power to take it away, to which Locke responded: (1) giving someone something does not necessarily imply the right to take it back, quite the contrary, it would generally be considered theft to do so; (2) it is God who gives life, not man, not even fathers; (3) if fathers do give life then what about mothers, do they not have a life-giving role at least as great as that of the father?[2] To the argument that it was once accepted practice to expose infants to certain death, Locke responded that this was clearly against the law of God and Nature. Killing anyone violates the Ten Commandments (there is no exception for children in "thou shalt not kill"). Also, Locke argued that people need only watch wild animals and see how they treat their offspring to see that it is unnatural to kill one's children.

Filmer's next argument that kings rule by divine right was based on the biblical command to "Honor thy Father," to which Locke responded that the command goes on to say "and Mother."[3] Locke pointed out that this simply meant that children should obey their parents, both parents, and there was no logical way to get from this to the divine right of kings to absolute power. Filmer also argued that this power of the father could be seen in cannibalistic tribes who raised children in order to eat them. Locke responded that tribes can be found that do all manner of strange things, some even allowing "Adultery, Incest and Sodomy" even though these acts clearly violate the laws of the Scriptures and the Laws of Nature, which wants to see the "increase of Mankind and the continuation of the Species in the highest perfection."[4]

Locke asked: If Adam was the first king and ruled by divine right, and God intended this power to flow from Adam, which descendant of Adam is the rightful heir to the throne?[5] The Bible says all people are the children of Adam, so how can one person have any better claim to the throne than another? In fact, should not everyone have the right to be king? Locke pointed out that if the right to be king is limited to Adam's posterity this was a significant limitation, a "limitation to all mankind."

At the beginning of the *Second Treatise* Locke summarized the arguments of the *First Treatise*. He believed he had demonstrated that (1) Adam had no kingly power over the people of the world; (2) if he did his heirs had no right to inherit that power; and (3) if they did, there is no way to determine who the rightful heir is today.

Having proven that kings have no divine right to rule, the question then became who, if anyone, has that right? To answer, Locke posited a state of nature where all men were free and equal. In that state people had only to consult their reason to discover a natural law which said that everyone should refrain from harming the "life, health, liberty or possessions" of others. Locke argued that the only legitimate justification of power over others was a power freely given; in other words, only by consent of the governed did any government gain the "right" to rule. The "liberty of Man, in Society, is to be under no other Legislative Power, but that established by consent, in the Commonwealth."[6]

Even though God gave the earth to everyone in common, Locke argued that individuals could make it theirs by mixing their labor with it.[7] But one could only have what one could use. "As much Land as a Man Tills, Plants, Improves, Cultivates, and can use the Product of, so much is his Property."[8] Locke went on to explain that larger holdings became justifiable only with the invention of money, which allowed people to sell their excess and turn it into coins which did not waste away.

As for liberty, Locke argued it could exist only where there was law to protect everyone from the violence of others. Liberty consisted of the right of an individual to control his "Person, Actions, Possessions, and his whole Property."[9] For Locke, liberty meant the freedom to become part of whatever commonwealth one chooses.[10] Is there a limit in the *Second Treatise* to the power of the majority in a democracy? Power is granted to the government to do whatever is necessary to achieve the purposes of the community; to determine the limits of government power, one needs to know why the government was set up.[11] The main reason people unite into a commonwealth, Locke believed, is to protect their "Lives, Liberties and Estates."[12] The power given to the government "can never be supposed to extend farther than the common good."[13] Locke also argued that conquerors and usurpers never have a right to rule.[14]

Locke seemed to be saying that there is a natural law of society, just as there is a natural law of chemistry, and that it provides a set of objective moral principles that are cross-culturally and trans-historically valid and discoverable by reason. In this he was arguing against both the relativists, who claimed morals are culturally or historically relative (suggesting that man or society is the creator of morals rather than God), and the utilitarians who contended that morals are only good to the extent that they have utility. This can be seen in the *First Treatise* when he suggested that the moral rules against adultery, incest and sodomy were good because they fit in with Nature's plan to "increase Mankind" and Nature's desire to see the "continuation of the Species in the highest perfection."[15]

But there is something very different in his *Essay Concerning Human Understanding* written several years later. There he suggested that there are no innate or self-evident moral rules. Natural law philosophers such as Thomas Aquinas and Richard Hooker had maintained that the natural law of morality could be discovered by looking to the conscience, which is mankind's innate sense of right and wrong. Locke, however, said that there is nothing in the conscience but "our own Opinion." That there are so many different societies with so many different moral rules proves there is no such thing as an innate morality discoverable by examining the conscience of mankind. All the search for a fundamental foundation of morality reveals is that everyone seems to be driven toward pleasure and away from pain; in other words, people are in a constant "pursuit of happiness." Thus different moral rules seem to have developed, depending on the type of happiness the people involved valued most. Locke noted that what seemed to be the highest pleasure for one individual or society was not for another; for example, while some found the greatest pleasure in riches, others found it in "bodily Delights, or Virtue, or Contemplation."[16] Indeed, this even seemed to apply to individuals: "what they themselves have enjoyed with great pleasure and delight at one time, has proved insipid or nauseous at another."[17]

Locke had finally concluded that there was only one principle sufficiently universal to provide a foundation for morality, government, and even religion: that of self-preservation. The innate desire to preserve "life, liberty and property" was the only natural law Locke could find. Governments are set up to increase the probability of this self-preservation and to protect the freedom to pursue happiness as defined by each individual within the society; when they no longer do that they should be changed. People do not seem to agree on what brings them pleasure, but they do on what brings them pain. This avoidance of pain is the only universal principle. In this way Locke could claim to be both a natural law philosopher, a relativist, and a utilitarian. There is a natural law, but it is limited to this "self-preservation" principle which looks a lot like the "utility" of the utilitarians. Otherwise, morality, politics, and religion are relative and different for different societies.

Locke's *Letter Concerning Toleration, Two Treatises of Government, Essay Concerning Human Understanding,* and other writings establish that he believed the purpose of government was basically to preserve people and their property, and that government lacks the power to enforce religious belief or morality. Of course, most of his contemporaries disagreed. When the Puritans were in power they imposed their views on everything from entertainment—there was no dancing or theater—to religious practice, and this hastened the restoration of the Stuart monarchy. The tyranny of the democratically elected had helped to bring about the demise of democracy itself. Anyone who lived through that period would be quick to acknowledge that to protect the existence of democracy, the power of the democratically elected government had to be limited and the liberty of the individual protected. The more one group felt oppressed the more likely they were to rebel, even against the democratically elected government. It was, after all, the oppressive ways and religious beliefs of James II, not his being a monarch, that brought his downfall.

At the same time Locke believed in the power of education and reason. He assumed that most educated people would discover a "right" morality through either reading Scripture or reasoning about natural law. The idea that anyone other than a few ignorant savages in the uncivilized world would not see the correctness of the moral prohibitions against "Adultery, Incest and Sodomy," for example, probably never occurred to him.

It did occur to him that in attacking Filmer's arguments in *Patriarcha* he was challenging the view of women that had prevailed in his society since the beginning of recorded history. He pointed out that Eve was placed under Adam as a personal punishment for her transgressions in the Garden of Eden, not as a condemnation of all women. He also pointed out that in the Bible, when fathers are mentioned, mothers are usually also mentioned in the same sentence and to the same result. The Bible, for example, says "Honor thy Father and Mother." The ultimate rejection of the principle of patriarchy, begun by Locke, would have a profound effect on the legal, political, and moral foundations of late twentieth-century America.

MONTESQUIEU

In the same year in which William ascended the throne of England, Charles Louis Secondat was born in France (1689–1755). He became first the Baron de La Brede upon the death of his mother and the Baron de Montesquieu upon the death of his uncle. His Protestant wife brought a dowry of 100,000 livres and that, together with his estates, provided him lifetime security. He inherited from his uncle the office of deputy president of the Parliament of Bordeaux and studied the natural sciences, history, and law at the newly formed Academy of Bordeaux.

In 1721 Montesquieu shocked the world with the publication of his first book *Persian Letters*. While he published it anonymously in Holland he could not stay anonymous; the book was too popular, selling out ten editions in the first year. His fame brought him both social and amorous success in a France that was ready to move on from the reign of Louis XIV (1643–1715). He abandoned his legal career in 1726, sold his seat in the Bordeaux Parliament, and became a member of the French Academy in Paris. He published his *Considerations on the Causes of Roman Greatness and Decadence* in 1734 and his masterpiece *The Spirit of Laws*, in 1748. So many people attacked his great work of history, law, and philosophy that he felt obliged to defend it with his *Defense of the Spirit of Laws* in 1750. The Pope condemned *The Spirit of Laws* in 1751 and Montesquieu died in 1755.

What amazes the modern reader about the *Persian Letters* is that a Catholic member of the French nobility could write such a satire of French society. Every aspect of Montesquieu's time was fair game. The book was a fictional set of letters by two travelers from Persia. In Letter 24 they observed that the king of France raised a vast sum of money simply by selling "honorific titles" which by a "miracle of human vanity" resulted in his fortresses being supplied and his fleets being equipped. In Letter 29 the travelers observed that Christianity was so complex that the only way to get by was to purchase dispensations from the bishops. In this way people could "break their vows" and "marry when the Christian law forbids it." Presumably Montesquieu had done this himself when he married a wealthy Protestant.

In Letter 76 the Persian travelers noted the strange custom of dragging suicide victims through the streets and then confiscating their property. They found this very unjust and wondered why someone overcome by anguish, poverty, or humiliation should be prevented from ending their troubles. Letter 85 was a plea for religious tolerance as elegant as any, made more so by its brevity. It pointed out that having competing sects put everyone on their guard so as not to dishonor their sect in the eyes of the other sects. Montesquieu had his traveler say that anyone who thinks they can force others to believe a particular religion must be mad. As the Persian says: "Someone who tries to make me change my religion does so only, I presume, because he would not change his own, even if attempts were made to compel him; so that he finds it strange that I will not do something that he would not do himself, perhaps not even to be ruler of the world."

Letter 116 was an eloquent plea for divorce. There was much discussion at the time concerning why the population had declined since Roman times. Everyone accepted that this was indeed the case, but disagreed on the extent of the depopulation and the cause. Montesquieu had the Persian say that forbidding divorce had not only taken "all the pleasure out of marriage, but it also discouraged its purpose." The Persian said that among Christians after the first three years the main purpose of marriage was neglected, and "thirty years are then spent frigidly together." The Persian went on to say that this forced men to resort to prostitutes, "a shameful and anti-social kind of union which cannot fulfill the purpose of marriage." Because of this population declined. The Persian noted that everywhere in the world marriage is a kind of contract except among Christians, who do not define marriage as "consisting in sensual pleasure, which they seem, on the contrary, to want to banish from it as far as possible, . . . instead it is an image, a symbol, and something mysterious which I cannot understand." Montesquieu was already several years into an arranged marriage and obviously viewed his future in this regard with dismay.

Letter 119 criticized the rule of primogeniture because it forced a father to provide for only one child and it destroyed "equality between citizens, on which their prosperity entirely depends." Letter 122 stated that "equality between citizens, which usually produces an equal distribution of wealth, itself conveys life and prosperity throughout the nation, diffusing them everywhere."

Letter 124 was such a funny and direct attack on the way monarchy had been practiced in France for a century that it still causes laughter today. It has the Persian imagine a royal decree which begins by recognizing all the nobles who were ever present when the king got up in the morning. It then calls on everyone engaged in "low menial employment" and "who have never been present while our Majesty gets up" to "cease to buy clothes for themselves, their wives, and their children, more than once in every four years" so that taxes could be

raised to pay pensions to the noble persons who have witnessed the
King rise in the morning. A more direct attack on a system that rewarded ridiculous behavior and punished honest work cannot be found.
Finally, Letter 131 has the Persian marvel at the democracy that had
reigned in Greece, in the Greek colonies in Italy, Spain and Gaul, and
among the German tribes that took over the Roman Empire in the west.

The *Persian Letters* was a radical attack on French society, made all
the more effective because it was not a sermon but a satire. It attacked
the Catholic church with its celibate clergy and a social system that
rewarded those who wasted their lives witnessing the king rise in the
morning and punished those who put in an honest day's work. It mar-
veled at the waste caused by religious intolerance, particularly that of
one Christian sect for all other Christian sects, and the strange practices that had risen in Catholicism such as buying indulgences, punishing suicide, and holding inquisitions. If someone wanted to find the
beginnings of a radical attack on the ancient regime that would culmi-
nate in the storming of the Bastille in 1789, they would have to look
no further than the *Persian Letters*.

But Montesquieu was not a radical calling for equal property and an
end of religion; rather, he was a democratic liberal asking for a system
of checks and balances and laws that recognized the limitations of the
power of law. He worked out these ideas in *The Spirit of Laws*.

The Spirit of Laws was his masterpiece, consisting of two volumes,
thirty-one books, and as originally published 1,086 pages. If democratic
liberalism has two fathers, the first is Locke in England and the second
is Montesquieu in France. Locke had demolished Filmer's arguments
that a reading of the Scriptures proves that kings ruled by divine right.
The Abbé du Bos in France then wrote a book entitled *The Establishment
of the French Monarchy in Gaul* in which he argued that the people of
Gaul had asked the king of the Franks to come and rule them. Where
Filmer argued Scripture, du Bos argued history; where Filmer argued
divine right, du Bos argued consent. In Books 30 and 31 of *The Spirit of
Laws* Montesquieu refuted du Bos' claims by going to all the historical
sources then available. What he found was overwhelming evidence that
the people of Gaul did not ask the Frankish kings to rule them and
that in fact the Franks came as conquerors to what later became France.

But his main purpose in writing was to find the basis of law, morality, and government. Accordingly he made suggestions and tried to
draw conclusions based on his observations of the world and the application of reason. He argued that democracy needs equality and fru-
gality and that in a republic, land holding should be small and as equal
as possible. He also argued that the rule of primogeniture should not
apply to republics, in which an equal division of the estate among the
children would be better. In Book 9 he said that small republics will be

destroyed by foreign force and large ones will be susceptible to destruction by internal imperfections. The answer is a confederate republic (a federal system).

Book 11 suggested that the best way to protect liberty is to arrange things so that "power should be a check to power." It discussed the separation of powers between the legislative, executive, and judicial branches of government and held up England as a model. In Book 12 Montesquieu argued that there are four types of crimes: religious, moral, crimes against public tranquillity, and crimes against property. He felt that God should punish crimes against religion, that shame and public infamy should be used to punish crimes against morality, while imprisonment should be used only for crimes against tranquillity and property. He also argued that law should not punish thoughts and beliefs, but only "overt acts."

Montesquieu could not find much "natural law." What he did find were three basic types of governments: republican, monarchical, and despotic. By monarchical he meant rule by a single person under "fixed and established laws," while the despot ruled by his "own will and caprice." Montesquieu, as a good historian and social scientist, could not say that any one of these forms of government was more "natural" than another, but did argue that different factors tended to produce one or the other form. He suggested that differences in climate, national character, culture, religion, and so on tended to bring about one of the three types, with the climate of northern Europe and the Protestant religion likely to bring about republics. He also suggested that societies tended to develop a system in which the government, religion, culture, and morality fit together.

He searched for a natural law of morality, but suggested in the end only that mothers should not marry their sons because that would reduce the number of new citizens born to the society. If this is the only argument against incest, then fathers should be allowed to marry their daughters and brothers their sisters, because in both cases there is a good chance of many children. While Montesquieu found this distasteful, he could find no "natural law" against it.

As to the question of liberty versus democracy, Montesquieu suggested two solutions: a system of checks and balances among the three branches of government, and a limitation of government-made law to the areas of protecting property and ensuring domestic tranquillity. Questions of religion and morality should be left to God and society to enforce with the weapons of excommunication and social ostracism.

Montesquieu found himself born into a social, governmental, and legal system that did not make sense to him. His world was moving from the feudal to the modern and he was astute enough to notice the problems and sensitive enough to feel the inconveniences. Montesquieu published his last work, a defense of his masterpiece, in 1750, which also saw the publication of Rousseau's first work, the *Discourse on the Sciences and the Arts*.

ROUSSEAU

If Montesquieu was born into the ancient world of aristocrats, arranged marriages and absolute monarchs, Jean-Jacques Rousseau (1712–1778) was very much a modern man. His ancestor, a Calvinist, had taken refuge in Geneva five generations before, and Rousseau was born into a Protestant city, which had a large middle class and a sort of democracy. At thirteen he was apprenticed to an engraver but he hated his master and ran away. He met Madam de Warens, who had left her husband and her Protestant religion to become a Catholic (one way to acquire a divorce) and spent the rest of her life working to convert others to Catholicism. She was so good at this that the King of Sardinia gave her a pension. She sent Rousseau to Turin, where he became a Catholic at the age of fifteen. Rousseau decided that he did not want to be a priest so he declared himself a music teacher. He taught music for a while, although he had no real qualifications, and ultimately returned to Madam de Warens who offered herself to him when he turned 21. He was part of a ménàge à trois that included her steward, Claude Anet, for several years.

In 1742 he went to Paris seeking fame and fortune with a new system of musical notation, an opera, a comedy, and a collection of poems. He was not successful. His one real friend was Diderot, who was working on a compilation of all the world's knowledge called the *Encyclopedia*. In 1745 Rousseau began to live with Thérèse, who shared the rest of his life. She bore him five children, with each being sent to the foundling hospital at birth, a common fate for poor children of the time.

In 1749 Diderot was imprisoned for writing his *Letters on the Blind*, an attack on the argument that God must exist because the world is so beautiful. One day, on his way to visit Diderot, Rousseau read an advertisement for an essay contest sponsored by the Academy of Dijon. The question was: Has the reestablishment of the sciences and the arts helped to purify morals? At that moment Rousseau's life changed forever. He tells us that he sat for half an hour under a tree thinking over the ideas that would become his life's work. Diderot encouraged him to enter the contest and he won by arguing that the advance of arts and sciences had caused a decay in morals.

His essay was published the next year as the *Discourse on the Sciences and Arts*. His friends, who believed in progress, thought he was kidding but he was very serious. Rousseau argued that arts and sciences bring a love of luxury, which is the enemy of virtue. Montesquieu had said that the fundamental principle of democracy is virtue. Rousseau found virtue and love of country in decay everywhere; in view of this, he wondered how there could be any hope for democracy and freedom. To have a democracy, virtue would have to be increased, and social institutions would have to be changed along with the people themselves. His solutions would be new social institutions that encouraged virtue and new people formed by education to be virtuous.

The 1753 essay contest asked: What is the origin of inequality among men, and is it authorized by natural law? Rousseau's answer did not win the prize but it was published in 1755 as the *Discourse on the Origin and the Foundation of Inequality Among Mankind*. It traced the origins of inequality to the invention of metallurgy and agriculture, which brought war and the need to submit to kings for protection. Ultimately social institutions were created that resulted in the sorry state of society Rousseau found in France. He said at the end that inequality "derives its force and its growth from the development of our faculties and the progress of the human mind, and at last becomes permanent and lawful by the establishment of property and of laws." This leads, moreover, to what is called civilization, which must surely be against the law of nature because it had resulted in "fools leading the wise" and a handful of people gorging themselves "while the starving masses lack the barest necessities of life." [18]

Rousseau could not imagine a more "unnatural" society than eighteenth-century France. He did not say that society should try to return to the ways of the savage; instead, he asserted that it had taken a wrong turn and that great inequality of wealth and privilege were a fundamental cause of many of its ills. But if mankind took a wrong turn, what next? Rousseau tried to answer that in his three other great works, his two novels *The New Héloïse* and *Emile*, and his treatise *The Social Contract*.

The New Héloïse touched many readers and reaffirmed Rousseau's reputation. The novel explored religion and love. Rousseau said that in making the heroine a devout Christian and the hero an atheist, he hoped to show his former friends such as Diderot that people can believe in God and not be hypocritical and to show the religious that people can be atheistic without being dishonest. Ultimately the novel was about the search for happiness. Rousseau had come to reject the idea that the blueprint of the good society could be found in natural law; it would have to be invented, not discovered like the law of gravity.

In *Emile* Rousseau presented both a treatise and a work of fiction about education. Emile, the student, is taught to achieve freedom from obsessive private appetites and to become a good citizen concerned with the common welfare.

Rousseau believed *The Social Contract* was his masterpiece. Where John Locke had argued (in his mind proven) that man is born free, Rousseau began his treatise with the famous line "Man was born free, and everywhere he is in chains." Rousseau argued that the social contract was the act of forming society itself, not an historical agreement between the people and some government. In agreeing to form society people agreed to give up natural liberty and equality in exchange for political liberty and civil equality. Private property came into existence only because the society allowed it; therefore, the society also had the right to limit or control it. He proposed that society came before government and thus had a right to control and change it.

Rousseau argued that the purpose of government was to determine the "general will" (the best interest of the whole society). Democracy is one way to do this, perhaps the best way, but Rousseau recognized that it was an imperfect way. The interests of small groups would interfere with the public good. Rousseau wanted a society where people could be happy, as opposed to that of France at the time where the great majority lived in poverty. He recognized that this would require great changes in both institutions and in people, but he believed these were possible. People are born free and good; it is society that corrupts them and thus society can remake them, leaving them free to do what is virtuous, not to waste their lives in search of luxury. He imagined a democracy of "new men" who would have been taught virtue and who then could be trusted to rule for the good of all. In such a society there would be no need for a Bill of Rights. Rousseau was willing to tolerate religions that promoted the common good and were not themselves intolerant. He did not seem to think that it would be possible to separate moral law from civil law; on the contrary, he had learned from Montesquieu that religion, morality, politics, law, and culture all fit together.

Every modern ideology has found something to like and something to fear in Rousseau's writings. Some readers find the origins of twentieth-century totalitarianism, while others see the roots of existentialism. The fact remains that basically Rousseau was a democratic liberal trying to figure out how a democratic liberal system could be created in light of what Montesquieu said about the relationship between society and political-legal institutions. Ultimately, if the new system was to survive and prosper, society and people would have to be remade. While his friends argued that the best way to establish this new system was through revolution, Rousseau was not certain; at the same time, he wrote the best justification for revolution ever composed. Others argued that social divisions would be useful to a democracy, but Rousseau did not agree; he did, however, agree with Montesquieu that the "principle of democracy" is virtue. But where do virtuous people come from? Rousseau recognized that this was the real problem and that no amount of violence could produce the necessary change. Education would do so, but that would take time and few social systems would watch while new citizens who would bring about its destruction were created.

Rousseau wanted people to be happy but he recognized the difficulty in that goal as well. Was happiness simply to be found in being a slave to "mere appetite"? If not then what? His observations of society showed him that people find pleasure in doing what their "opinions" tell them is pleasurable, but these opinions are simply creations of society. It was a kind of "chicken and egg" question for which Rousseau had no answer.

When Rousseau and Montesquieu used the term "democracy" they meant what people today would call "direct democracy." After reading what Rousseau says direct democracy requires, most people would despair of ever achieving it. But Montesquieu had the answer. He suggested a third way between direct democracy and despotism and called it monarchy, by which he meant a monarch checked by laws made by an independent legislature and interpreted by an independent judiciary. He looked to this new system of representative democracy, then taking shape in England, to solve the dilemma. It would allow much more freedom than was believed to be compatible with direct democracy. The spirit of commercialism and faction could be used to balance power, not destroy the system. But how would this system work out the contradictions between political and economic equality, and between liberty and democracy?

MILL

John Stuart Mill (1806–1873) lived and wrote in the midst of the new social-political experiment that was England in the nineteenth century. He was taught by his father to be the kind of "new" man of whom Rousseau might have been proud. He began to learn Greek when he was three and Latin at the age of eight. His *Autobiography* tells not of a happy childhood but of an amazing education. He read history and biographies while he studied math and science. He studied oration along with law and political economy. At the age of fourteen, having already had a more complete education than men twice his age, he left for a year of travel in France. He spent that year in the company of Samuel

Bentham, brother of Jeremy Bentham, and came back to England a convinced utilitarian.

Jeremy Bentham (1748–1832) was the recognized father of what became Utilitarianism. Bentham studied law at Queen's College, Oxford. He heard Blackstone's lectures on the common law and immediately saw the fallacies in Blackstone's adoration of the ancient English common law. In his great work, *An Introduction to the Principles of Morals and Legislation* published in 1789, Bentham said that the test of moral and legal systems was the extent to which they furthered utility, which he defined as anything tending to produce "pleasure, good or happiness" and to prevent "mischief, pain, evil or unhappiness." The object of legislation must be "the greatest happiness of the greatest number."

Bentham had very definite ideas how one decides on the greatest good for the greatest number. First, there would be a real representative democracy with annual elections, equal electoral districts, wide suffrage, and a secret ballot. There would also be a guarantee of civic rights, rights necessary for a democracy to function, such as freedom of speech, press, and association. Then the one-house legislature would decide what is best. In other words, the majority would decide what is best for everyone, which should at least be what is best for the majority (greatest good for the greatest number). If Montesquieu wrote the blueprint for modern American government with its checks and balances, Bentham wrote the blueprint for modern English government with its dictatorship of the House of Commons. Bentham did not see any need for a bill of rights or any other impediment to the will of the majority.

John Stuart Mill tried to work out the fundamental problems of democratic liberalism in light of the principle of utility. He lived the ultimate life of a liberal, questioning every institution of the old society in view of the demands of democracy, liberty, and utility. He founded debating societies, periodicals, and a breakfast study group. He earned his living as a bureaucrat with the East India Company, as his father had done, which he said gave him time to rest his mind between the morning study group and the evening debating society. Society was to be remade and he was going to figure out the best way to remake it by debate, discussion, and the application of reason.

Mill argued for democracy (only a very few citizens owned enough property to qualify to vote for the House of Commons at the time), free speech, public education, and women's liberation. When Malthus published his treatise purporting to prove that as the wages of the working class increased that class simply produced more children, driving the wages back down, most people found this depressing; for Mill it simply meant that the working class had to be taught to use birth control. He began to see value in the socialism of St. Simon, and he recognized that democracy would be the main impetus for change because as the working class acquired political power, the higher classes would realize they had more to fear from an uneducated than an educated citizenry.

In 1840 he fell in love with Mrs. Taylor. Theirs was a platonic love affair for many years until her husband died and they married. She was to be his companion, advisor, and trusted critic from their meeting until her death. All of what are considered to be his greatest works were written with her help. He read Tocqueville's *Democracy in America* and saw clearly the potential danger of the tyranny of the majority. While he still believed in democracy, he realized the need to try to "neutralize" its less beneficial tendencies. He also read with revulsion Comte's *Système de Politique Positive.* Here was Rousseau's proposal for a new state spelled out in terrifying detail: a system of "spiritual and temporal despotism" where a group of "spiritual teachers" would reign supreme over every "thought" and "action" in the name of "general opinion." This book frightened him and reminded him of what can happen when "thinkers on society and politics" lose sight of the values of liberty and individuality.

In the end Mill resolved the conflict between political and economic equality by becoming a Socialist. He called not for the nationalization of the economy, but rather for a willingness to tax the rich and otherwise interfere with the distribution of society's goods for the benefit of everyone. His *Autobiography* stated that the fundamental social problem of the future would be figuring out how to "unite the greatest individual liberty of action, with a common ownership in the raw material of the globe, and an equal participation of all in the benefits of combined labor."[19]

Mill believed *On Liberty* was his greatest work. In it he argued that historically there have been two basic methods of protecting liberty from governmental encroachment: constitutional checks and the recognition of rights. While some believed that with the advent of real democracy there would be no need for these limits on state authority, Mill believed otherwise. Too often the "will" of the people turned out to mean the will of the most numerous or the most active "part" of the people and resulted in "the tyranny of the majority." But where is the line between the legitimate power of government and individual liberty to be drawn? He found the same answer that Locke and Montesquieu had found. The only reason for interfering with anyone's liberty is "self-protection." Power can be used against an individual to prevent harm to others, but not to prevent him from harming himself. Power cannot be used because it might make someone "happier" or because in the opinion of the wise it would be "right" to use it. This liberty included the freedom of conscience, speech, and association but also the "liberty of tastes and pursuits."

This was a break with Bentham, who found the greatest good for the greatest number in acts of the freely elected legislature. For Mill, in contrast, the greatest number should find the greatest good by being left free to do so for themselves. Section Two of the book is an eloquent defense of free thought and speech. Section Three is concerned with freedom of action. Society is evolving, Mill noted, and people free to "experiment" with living are needed. Only by allowing these experiments can society find out what works. Mill argued that there may have been a time when allowing people to be free endangered society, but now the greater danger was in the opposite. People's "impulses and preferences" were so controlled by conformity that human progress was threatened. Individuals must be free to develop themselves and they in turn would help society to develop. Society needs people of genius and only in an "atmosphere of freedom" can they develop. Mill also argued that everything deemed wise and noble usually springs originally from one person. He found in England a "despotism of custom" that hampered human advancement. He spoke to a people that believed in progress and pointed out that progress comes not from conformity with the present, but only from experimentation with the future.

Section Four of the book outlines the "rightful limit" to the "sovereignty of the individual over himself." Mill said that everyone must refrain from hurting others and must also bear their fair share to support the society (pay taxes). Beyond that they should be left free to control their own life and "stand the consequences." If others found someone distasteful they had a right to stay away. He acknowledged the argument that those who allow their faculties to deteriorate bring harm to those who depend on them but he felt that the shame was society's, not the individual's. If society, with public education and the power of public opinion, could not keep its members from doing such things it was society's fault, not the individual's. Besides, if society was worried about the harmful example such behavior gives to others, Mill argued that allowing observers to see the "painful and degrading consequences" of that conduct would have a strong educational effect. Mill cited laws in the United States against buying "fermented drinks" and doing business on Sunday as examples of laws that did not serve to prevent harm to others.

In the final section Mill suggested some practical ways to apply his principle. He first took up business regulation, maintaining that because business is a "social act" government may control it. He pointed out the advantages of free competition, suggesting that it is usually a mistake for governments to interfere with prices or markets or the "processes of manufacture," but he said the "principle of individual liberty" was not involved in such regulation. Questions of consumer protection and workplace safety would also be open to government control. What did involve the "principle of individual liberty" were laws against the sale of alcohol or drugs in an effort to "protect" the buyer from his own impulses. Government may validly "warn" people of the danger, he argued, by labeling drugs for example, but it may not prohibit the use of drugs. While public "offenses against decency" may be prohibited, this should not include private conduct. He spoke in favor of the freedom of divorce and of compulsory education, but also argued that the state should "require" everyone to receive an education rather than "provide" one and help pay the costs for poor children. He argued for a system of national examinations that would certify that people had attained a level of competence in particular subjects.

He ended his discussion with the comment that even if what he calls the "principle of liberty" is not involved, government should try, wherever possible, to leave things to individuals or voluntary associations, and to function as a depository of information so each new group could benefit from the mistakes and successes of the past. He warned of the dangers of having government bureaucracy do everything and he pointed to the "melancholy condition of the Russian empire" as an example of the dangers of bureaucracy gone mad.

He ended *On Liberty* with a plea for both individuals and society. He said the worth of a society, in the long run, is really nothing more than the worth of the individuals that compose it. Any state content to "dwarf" its people will find that with small people "no great thing can really be accomplished." With these comments Mill made it clear that he was arguing for liberty not as some "natural right," but because the future and "utility" of society depended on it.

Mill provided the best set of arguments ever written for the principle that people should be left to experiment with life and develop themselves as they wish. Rousseau could not imagine where the new people that the new society needed would come from, except from a kind of forced education that might be called "brainwashing." Mill read Comte's book and found this idea repugnant; for him the only hope was to leave people free to create themselves. Those who were successful would be an example to others, and this would be more likely to lead to the next stage of human progress than any efforts at thought control. As a political economist he wanted to alter the distribution of wealth and mobilize public opinion in favor of birth control; at the same time he wanted to protect private property and the free market, and he found the idea of the bureaucratic state repulsive. He believed that allowing people to have more control over their own lives would help them to develop into the kind of people a democratic liberal society needs most.

He was so afraid of the consequences of unlimited birth, both on the society in general, and on the unwanted children it would produce in particular, that he was willing to accept government control of this very personal area. People who could not afford children could be kept from having any. It is ironic that the first battle over the constitutional right to privacy in the United States would be fought over the right of individuals to receive information that would help them to exercise birth control.

NATURAL LAW

During the confirmation hearings for Justice Clarence Thomas in September 1991 the nation was treated to a discussion of natural law and its proper place in modern American jurisprudence. All four of these philosophers worked in an atmosphere of natural law. What did they mean by natural law? Basically, a law written by nature for all time in all circumstances. The classic example is the law of gravity.

John Locke searched for a natural law of society, but found only that people tend to seek pleasure and avoid pain. While nature defines pleasure and pain to some extent, they are also defined by society, which makes it very difficult to speak of a natural law of society. Montesquieu sought a natural law of politics and law, particularly as regards morality, but could not find one. He suggested that civil law should not be used to enforce any particular morality as none was any more natural than any other. Rousseau was asked to write on the relationship between natural law and inequality. He felt that the extreme inequality of his time was clearly unnatural but he could not prove it to be so. His inability to find a natural way out of society's sorry state led him to despair. Finally, John Stuart Mill and his teacher Jeremy Bentham completely rejected the idea of a natural law for society. For them, natural law was simply a cover for the particular prejudices of one group as against another. The question was one of utility, not nature.

NATURAL RIGHTS

The concept of natural rights follows from the concept of natural law. The idea is that there are certain basic rights that everyone has because they are human. John Locke went in search of natural rights and could only come up with the right of "self-preservation." Governments are created to serve specific purposes and when they no longer do so they should be reformed or abolished.

Montesquieu suggested that rights are only natural given the social and geographical setting of a nation. It was natural, for example, for people to seek individual rights in a Protestant, cold country that believed in free enterprise, but it might not be natural for people in other societies living under other conditions. His search for natural rights led to social relativism. Rousseau rejected the idea of natural rights. Society had to be transformed, even if that meant bending individuals to the will of the majority. Jeremy Bentham rejected the idea of natural rights as completely as anyone could. Utility was the question, not natural rights. For John Stuart Mill rights were not natural, but they were called for if the greatest good for the greatest number was to be achieved. He believed he had found a "natural" place to draw the line between the state power and individual rights, at the point where someone else might be hurt by the individual's actions.

The United States was founded, however, on the idea that there are "laws of nature," "self-evident truths," and "unalienable rights." But who would decide what was in the law of nature and what rights are unalienable? Only the Supreme Court of the United States was in a position to make these kinds of decisions. As will be seen in the next chapter, the members of the Court have debated for two centuries the extent to which they should play the role of guardian of the natural law and protector of the unalienable rights.

NOTES

1. J. Locke, Two TREATISES OF GOVERNMENT (Cambridge University Press, 1960 ed.) Book One, Section 27.
   2. *Id.* at Book One, Sections 52–56.
   3. *Id.* at Book One, Sections 60–65.
   4. *Id.* at Book One, Section 59.
   5. *Id.* at Book One, Chapter 7.
   6. *Id.* at Book Two, Section 22.
   7. *Id.* at Book Two, Chapter 5.
   8. *Id.* at Book Two, Section 32.
   9. *Id.* at Book Two, Section 57.
   10. *Id.* at Book Two, Section 73.
   11. *Id.* at Book Two, Section 99.
   12. *Id.* at Book Two, Section 123.
   13. *Id.* at Book Two, Section 131.
   14. *Id.* at Book Two, Chapters 16–17.
   15. *Id.* at Book Two, Section 59.
   16. J. Locke, AN ESSAY CONCERNING HUMAN UNDERSTANDING (Clarendon Press, 1979 ed.) Book Two, Chapter 21, Section 55.

17. *Id.* at Book Two, Chapter 21, Section 65.

18. J. Rousseau, Discourse on the Origin of Inequality (Washington Square Press, 1967 ed.) 246.

19. J. Mill, Autobiography, in The Essential Works of John Stuart Mill (Bantam Matrix, 1961 ed.) 137.

4

The Constitutional Foundation: From Natural Rights to Substantive Due Process

The right to privacy is not mentioned in the U.S. Constitution. It was "discovered" by the U.S. Supreme Court in 1965 in a case involving people who wished to obtain birth control information. How can the Supreme Court discover a constitutional right? Is this a legitimate exercise of the Court's power? Before that question can be answered the history of the Court's interpretation of the U.S. Constitution must be explored.

The founding fathers had the benefit of the ideas of Locke, Montesquieu, and Rousseau, along with other contemporary philosophers. The Declaration of Independence provides a good summary of what they accepted. They believed in "self-evident truths" and "unalienable Rights," including the rights of "Life, Liberty and the pursuit of Happiness." They also believed that governments derived "their just powers from the consent of the governed" and had a right to exist only as long as they worked to "secure these rights."

With these words the United States began a revolution for independence from England, for democracy, and for individual liberty. After the Revolution the thirteen states adopted their own constitutions, many containing a bill of rights. In 1781 the states ratified the Articles of Confederation, but by the summer of 1787 it was clear to everyone that some other arrangement would be necessary. The Articles of Confederation had failed because they left the national government weak and unable to raise revenue, which threatened to bring about chaos in both foreign policy and internal economic affairs. The result was the drafting of a constitution that gave more power to the national government to deal with what many considered to be national problems.

THE FEDERALIST PAPERS

Ratification of the Constitution by New York was considered crucial because of its large population and its already powerful economic structure. Beginning in October 1787 Alexander Hamilton, James Madison, and John Jay published a total of eighty-five letters in New York newspapers signed "Publius." These letters are commonly called the Federalist Papers. While Locke may be the grandfather of the Declaration of Independence, Montesquieu is the major thinker behind the Federalist Papers. The first Federalist paper by Hamilton expressed his conviction that there can be no liberty without "the vigour of government." The papers by Hamilton spoke to the needs of what would become a great industrial and commercial power.

The papers by James Madison, in contrast, tended to be more a discussion of liberty. In Federalist No. 10, Madison spoke of the problem of factions, which he defined as a number of citizens, whether a majority or a minority, "who are united and actuated by some common impulse of passion, or of interest, adverse to the rights of other citizens, or to the permanent and aggregate interests of the community." He believed factions work only to serve their selfish goals rather than societal interests and would threaten the existence of democracy itself.

Madison said factions could be prevented from forming either by destroying liberty or by giving to every citizen the same opinions. He rejected both methods, the first because it would be fatal to democracy, and the second because it was both impractical and undesirable. In his view, the effort instead should be to control the effects of factions rather than to eliminate the causes. The issue was how to create a government that secured both the "public good" and "private rights" against the danger of factions and at the same time have a functioning democracy. Direct democracy was not the answer because history taught that direct democracies were the victims of factions. The only hope was representative democracy. Madison argued that the large size of the United States, and the variety of interest groups, would act as a check on the power of any one faction.

In later installments of the Federalist Papers, Hamilton and Madison (following Montesquieu) wrote that the checks and balances set up by the constitution would help to protect liberty. In Federalist No. 14 Madison argued that the fact that the constitution limits the jurisdiction of the new federal government to "certain enumerated objects" would also help to protect liberty. In No. 47 he pointed out that the separation of the government into separate legislative, executive and judicial branches would provide an "essential precaution in favor of liberty." Hamilton argued in many of the papers that a bill of rights was not needed because of the structures already built into the new federalist system. In No. 78 he claimed that an independent judiciary would also help to protect liberty.

In No. 51 James Madison submitted that, although the three branches would be divided, the legislature would become dominant. He saw this as a potential problem because a dominant legislature controlled by factions might threaten the liberties of individual citizens. The answer, as he saw it, was to divide the legislature into two houses. The protection of liberty would also come from the sheer number of different interest groups. As he said, the "security for civil rights" would come from the "multiplicity of interests," just as the protection of religious rights would come from the "multiplicity of sects."

Despite these arguments, several states indicated that they would ratify the constitution only if a bill of rights were added soon after. Patrick Henry and Thomas Jefferson were particularly adamant about this. Thomas Jefferson wrote to James Madison from Paris on December 20, 1787, that the first thing he did not like about the proposed constitution was:

the omission of a bill of rights, providing clearly, and without the aid of sophism, for freedom of religion, freedom of the press, protection against standing armies, restriction of monopolies, the eternal and unremitting force of the habeas corpus laws, and trials by jury in all matters of fact triable by the laws of the land, and not by the laws of nations.[1]

His letters of July 31, 1788, and March 15, 1789, make similar arguments. In the latter, for example, Jefferson says that a bill of rights might "cramp government" but this evil will be "short-lived, moderate and reparable." The problems caused by not having a bill of rights would be "permanent, afflicting and irreparable."

Hamilton felt it was not necessary to have a bill of rights because the powers of the new government were limited to specific tasks that would not infringe on the rights of the people. Others, however, remembered the problems they had under former royal governors: billeting soldiers in private homes without asking permission or paying rent, searching homes without reason or warrant, limits on freedom of speech and assembly, and so on. They felt that even a democracy should be kept from performing such crimes against the natural rights of the citizens.

While the constitution had been ratified by eleven states by 1788, six states sent Congress proposed amendments to constitute the bill of rights. In 1789 James Madison turned these suggestions into twelve proposed amendments, ten of which were passed and became the Bill of Rights that was ultimately ratified by December 1791. There were, however, those who feared that stating specific rights in the Bill of Rights would allow those who interpreted them in the future to think that these were the only "rights" of the people. James Madison, in the debate about the ratification of the Bill of Rights, said:

It has been objected also against a bill of rights, that, by enumerating particular exceptions to the grant of power, it would disparage those rights which were not placed in that enumeration; and it might follow by implication, that those rights which were not singled out, were intended to be assigned into the hands of the General Government, and were consequently insecure. This is one of the most plausible arguments I have ever heard urged against the admission of a bill of rights into this system; but, I conceive, that it may be guarded against. I have attempted it, as gentlemen may see by turning to the last clause of the fourth resolution.[2]

That last clause of the fourth resolution became the Ninth Amendment to the Constitution. It said: "The enumeration in the Constitution, of certain rights, shall not be construed to deny or disparage others retained by the people." It was hoped that, with that statement, the unalienable rights of the people would be protected even if they had been left out of the first ten amendments.

THE SUPREME COURT

To understand the origins of this problem of deciding what rights other than those specifically mentioned are protected by the Constitution, requires turning next to the history of the U.S. Supreme Court's interpretation of the Constitution. That history can be divided into three periods: pre-Civil War, Civil War to the end of the Great Depression, and the modern era.

The fear of those who argued so strongly for a Bill of Rights because the federal government would pose a threat to liberty seemed unfounded between the signing of the Constitution and the Civil War. Far more problems were caused by Congressional inaction than by Congressional action, such as the failure to regulate interstate commerce in a comprehensive way. It was the Civil War and the passage of the Thirteenth, Fourteenth, and Fifteenth Amendments that would ultimately bring the Supreme Court to bear on the question of which rights were protected by the Constitution besides those spelled out in the document itself and in the Bill of Rights. The Fourteenth Amendment (ratified in 1868) states in part that:

No State shall make or enforce any law which shall abridge the privileges or immunities of citizens of the United States; nor shall any State deprive any person of life, liberty or property, without due process of law; nor deny to any person within its jurisdiction the equal protection of the laws.

The reason for passage of the Fourteenth Amendment was to give the federal government power to control the states, particularly those states that had been part of the Confederacy. It was believed that they would never willingly grant full civil rights to the former slaves without federal intervention.

The power of the Fourteenth Amendment was limited by the Court's early interpretation of the "privileges or immunities" clause, however. In 1873 the Supreme Court ruled that the "privileges or immunities" clause only protects rights that people have in their relations with the federal government. For example, a state could not interfere with the right of citizens to petition Congress, vote in federal elections or travel to Washington, D.C.[3] It would be in the due process clause that the Court would find the power to strike down laws passed by the states. The doctrine on which the Court relied to achieve this result would come to be called substantive due process.

SUBSTANTIVE DUE PROCESS

The American legal and political system is based on a belief in procedure. If free elections bring representatives to the legislature, where free debate produces a bill which is signed by the duly elected governor or president, the bill is assumed to be a good law. If an impartial judge and jury hear a case in which both sides are represented by competent counsel, the jury's verdict is assumed to be correct. In other words, if the proper "procedures" have been followed when a particular result is accomplished, that result should be accepted.

But this reliance on procedure has its price. What if the procedure was subverted in some way not known to the judge, but obvious by the result? Judges in the United States decided early in the nineteenth century that they had the power to overturn jury decisions if these decisions were clearly unreasonable. If a judge could honestly say "no reasonable jury" could have come to that conclusion, the judge could issue a verdict "notwithstanding" the jury's verdict.

This power is generally used conservatively. If the jury, for example, has found someone guilty of a crime, but the judge concludes that no reasonable jury could so find, the judge can declare the accused not guilty. The right of trial by jury has been interpreted to prevent a judge from using this power to declare people guilty when the jury has found them not guilty. In civil cases, this power can also protect the defendant from a jury verdict. The explanation for the existence of this power is usually that juries are subject to prejudice and judges must protect defendants from irrational juries.

An argument could certainly be made that this kind of doctrine has no place when judges review legislative acts; during the post-Civil War era, however, supreme courts at both the state and federal level decided they did have this power. The U.S. Supreme Court held that this power to declare a state law "irrational" and therefore unconstitutional came from the due process clause of the Fourteenth Amendment. A similar power to declare Congressional acts unconstitutional was found in the due process clause of the Fifth Amendment, which applies to the federal government. The Court reasoned that by enforcing an "irrational" law the state or federal government was depriving citizens of "life, liberty or property without due process of law."

The Supreme Court also felt justified in examining legislation because the United States was founded on the idea that there are certain "unalienable" or "natural" rights on which government should not infringe. This question came up as early as 1798 in the case of *Calder v. Bull.*[4] Although the decision in that case was to uphold an act of the Connecticut legislature, Justice Chase argued that the authors of both the state and federal constitutions intended to create governments of limited powers and that the U.S. Supreme Court could declare an act of either Congress or a state legislature to be in violation of "natural law" as well as of specific provisions of the constitution. He said "there are certain vital principles in our free republican governments which will determine and overrule an apparent and flagrant abuse of legislative power," and that some "abuses" that would justify overruling the legislature are "to authorize manifest injustice by positive law; or to take away that security for personal liberty, or private property, for the protection whereof the government was established." In words reminiscent of John Locke, he went on to say that "an act of the Legislature (for I cannot call it a law), contrary to the great first principles of the social compact, cannot be considered a rightful exercise of legislative authority."[5]

When the philosophers of the seventeenth and eighteenth centuries discussed natural law and natural rights these were abstract concepts in an abstract debate. In this 1798 Supreme Court decision, however, the very concrete question became the extent to which these abstract concepts could be used by the Court to strike down acts of democratically elected legislatures. In addition, there was the question whether the Constitution gave the U.S. Supreme Court any power to void state legislation. Even in 1798, the prevailing legal theory, known as "dual federalism," was that the states are separate and equal governments along with the national government. While the Constitution did state that it was the "supreme law" of the land, it was not clear in 1798 what would happen if something conflicted with that supreme law. There had never been a court in the history of the world with the power to strike down legislation because it conflicted with a constitution. Of course, there had never been a written constitution before either. Justice Iradell argued for judicial restraint. He said:

if then, a government, composed of legislative, executive and judicial departments, were established, by a constitution which imposed no limits on the legislative power, the consequences would inevitably be, that whatever the legislative power chose to enact would be lawfully enacted, and the judicial power could never interpose to pronounce it void.[6]

He went on to say that this is why state and the federal constitutions should contain limits on governmental power. Absent specific limits, the judicial branch should not intervene. He said: "the ideas of natural justice are regulated by no fixed standard; the ablest and the purest men have differed upon the subject."[7] Justice Iradell could find no legal doctrine that gave the courts the power to overrule the acts of the people's elected representatives unless some specific provision of a constitution or bill of rights had been violated.

This debate between Justices Chase and Iradell in 1798 was very much a continuation of a debate that had raged when a bill of rights was first proposed. Would the passage of a bill of rights stating that "particular" rights are protected mean that any rights not listed would be forever lost to the people? Justice Chase argued that this should not be allowed to happen; Justice Iradell claimed, on the contrary, that to overturn an act of the democratically elected legislature without some firm basis in law was to usurp the democracy. This debate has continued on much the same basis for the last two hundred years.

During the period from the founding of the federal government to the Civil War the Supreme Court only declared unconstitutional two acts of the federal government. The first was the section of the Judiciary Act overturned in *Marbury v. Madison* in 1803.[8] The second was the Missouri Compromise, voided in 1857 in *Dred Scott v. Sandford*.[9] In *Marbury* the Court established that it had the power to declare acts passed by Congress and signed by the president to be unconstitutional and therefore without legal force, even though the U.S. Constitution did not specifically authorize this.

In 1833 the Court decided in *Barron v. Mayor and City Council of Baltimore* that the Bill of Rights applied only to acts of the federal government, not state governments.[10] This limited the Court's power to invalidate acts of state legislatures. That would be left up to state supreme courts interpreting state constitutions.

Throughout the nineteenth century, courts across the country developed the notion that any interference by state legislatures with "property rights" was unreasonable and therefore a denial of due process of law. At the same time another doctrine also developed: the concept of "police power." This doctrine held that state governments have the power by the fact of their existence to protect the "health, safety and morals" of their citizens. State supreme courts developed this idea of the "police power" because, while the federal constitution provides a specific list of the "powers" of the federal government, most state constitutions do not. Did that mean the people had given state governments absolute power, limited only by their bill of rights if one existed? Many state supreme courts rejected this idea of unlimited power, ruling instead that state constitutions granted "police powers" to further, in a reasonable way, the legitimate goals of government.

In 1857, the Supreme Court decided *Dred Scott v. Sandford*.[11] Dred Scott was a slave who had been taken through the "free" state of Illinois and the part of the Louisiana Purchase territory that had been declared to be "free" by the Missouri Compromise. A number of courts around the world had concluded that the moment slaves entered a "free" state they became forever free. Dred Scott sued his owner arguing that he was now free by virtue of having passed through "free" territory. He lost. There were eight different opinions in the case, which makes it difficult to say precisely what the "Court" decided and why. The main point was that the Missouri Compromise was held to be beyond the power of Congress to enact.

Chief Justice Taney reasoned essentially as follows: slaves are "property," not people, and the Constitution did not give Congress any power to interfere with people's property, human or otherwise. The Missouri Compromise was therefore invalid because it deprived slave owners of their property without due process of law. He argued that the Constitution granted citizenship to citizens who were free at the time of the Revolution and their descendants, and it also gave Congress the power to provide for immigration and naturalization. But the chief justice believed that this power to grant citizenship applied only to people who were born in foreign countries and came to America to become citizens; it did not give Congress the power "to raise to the rank of a citizen anyone born in the United States, who, from birth or parentage, by the Laws of the country, belongs to an inferior and subordinate class."[12] In other words, the only way Congress could ever turn former slaves into citizens would be through a constitutional amendment, but the possibility of getting one proposed or approved was nonexistent, short of civil war. Two justices dissented, pointing out that in most civilized countries slavery was no longer recognized, and that anyone arriving within the borders of those civilized countries as slaves became, by their laws, instantly free. They argued that Congress should have the same power these other countries enjoyed and should be able to declare particular territory either slave or free.

After the Civil War the Thirteenth, Fourteenth, and Fifteenth

Amendments were added to the Constitution. In 1873 the Supreme Court interpreted the Fourteenth Amendment for the first time. The *Slaughter-House Cases* involved a Louisiana law that gave a monopoly to a particular slaughter-house company in the city of New Orleans.[13] Those who wanted to compete sued, arguing that their rights under the Fourteenth Amendment had been violated in that they had been denied the "privileges and immunities" of full United States citizenship. It is important to realize that this was a new and unique argument in the history of western law. From the Hittites through the Greeks and Romans to the English and the American colonies, the government had always had the power to control business enterprises any way it chose. The English kings commonly granted monopolies to particular companies. Thomas Jefferson had argued for a provision in the Bill of Rights preventing the federal government from granting monopolies but this was not part of the Bill of Rights adopted in December 1791.

The Court ruled that the "privileges and immunities" clause simply protected the right of citizens to travel to Washington, D.C., petition the federal government, use the navigable waterways and so on, in other words, the rights due citizens because they are citizens of the federal government. The Court said the "due process" clause had not been violated because it only protected the right to "procedural" due process, and this Louisiana law had been passed following accepted legislative procedure. The "equal protection" clause had not been violated because the people involved were not being discriminated against because of their race. A majority of the Court felt at that time that the only purpose for the equal protection clause was to protect against racial discrimination, particularly against the former slaves who were now free.

The three main clauses of the Fourteenth Amendment are the "privileges and immunities" clause, the "due process" clause, and the "equal protection" clause. In 1873, on the heels of both the Civil War and Reconstruction, a majority of the Supreme Court felt these clauses should be interpreted narrowly. Words like "privileges and immunities" could obviously have an expansive meaning but a majority of the Court apparently worried that they would become a license to overturn any legislation with which a majority of a future Court disagreed. The concept of "due process" seemed straightforward enough to the majority. Process meant procedure and might allow a future court to strike down a criminal conviction if proper trial procedures had not been used, or to order the return of property if it had been taken without correct procedures and proper payment. As for "equal protection," this clearly referred to the requirement that the new black citizens be treated as equals with white citizens by the states, particularly the states that had been part of the Confederacy.

Four justices dissented. Justice Field argued that this interpretation of the "privileges and immunities" clause made it all but useless (the Supreme Court's interpretation of this clause has never changed). The dissenters also argued that the Fourteenth Amendment protected the natural and unalienable rights of all citizens. They felt the Amendment should be used to strike down unreasonable and arbitrary laws that limited the rights of people, particularly their right to own and use private property.

These views of the dissenters were rejected in 1873, but they soon were accepted by a majority of the Court. The industrial revolution was beginning and states were moving to regulate industry within their borders in ways that had never before been seen. At first the Court invalidated these regulatory schemes only if it felt they interfered with the power of Congress to regulate interstate commerce. But it was the general consensus of the American legal community, a majority of which depended on this ever expanding industrial machine for their livelihood, that the Court should take a more active stand to protect business from unreasonable regulation. The dominant economic theory among lawyers and businessmen at the time was that the best government policy was to allow business as much freedom as possible from government interference (laissez-faire).

In 1876 the Court had not yet subscribed to the laissez-faire theory, and it was still willing to tolerate state regulation of business activities. In *Munn v. Illinois*, for example, the operators of grain elevators in Illinois argued that state laws which regulated the rates they could charge violated the due process clause of the Fourteenth Amendment.[14] The Court disagreed, upholding this use of state power on the ground that grain elevators are "affected with a public interest."[15] Foreshadowing its future approach, however, the Court went on to say that it would be unreasonable for the legislature to regulate "mere private contracts" in a similar way.[16] In 1886 and 1887 the Court upheld the power of states to regulate the rates charged by railroads and to control the sale of alcoholic beverages, but it also said there was a limit beyond which states could not go in regulating business.[17] A statute would have to bear a substantial relationship to the desire to protect health, safety or morals before the Court would allow it to interfere with the use of property. Also, in 1886, the Court held that the word "persons" in the Fourteenth Amendment included business corporations.[18]

Finally, in 1897, laissez-faire became the operative principle, as the Court used the concept of substantive due process to invalidate a state statute. *Allgeyer v. Louisiana* involved a Louisiana law that made it a crime to further marine insurance unless the company involved had fully complied with Louisiana law.[19] Allgeyer mailed a letter to a New York insurance company concerned with the shipment of some insured goods. The Supreme Court overturned the conviction, holding that the statute interfered with the "liberty to contract" that was protected by the due process clause of the Fourteenth Amendment. Although he had gotten a fair trial and the legislature had followed accepted *procedures*, the *substance* of the statute was held to be unreasonable, as the law interfered with a "liberty" that was protected by the Fourteenth Amendment. With this decision the Court announced that it was ready to strike down statutes that unreasonably interfered with the liberty of businesses to form contracts.

The substantive due process engine rapidly picked up speed during the first third of the twentieth century, as the Court with increasing frequency used this doctrine to hold that legislation which interfered with this liberty had to bear a reasonable relationship to the goal of protecting health, safety and morality, or had to involve a business that was "affected with the public interest." As a general rule, the Court could not see how labor regulations or price controls had any relationship to these legitimate goals. In 1898, however, the Court did uphold a Utah law that limited the number of hours employees could work in mines and smelters as a legitimate use of the police power to protect public health.[20]

In 1905, in *Lochner v. New York*, the Court reviewed a New York statute that limited the hours bakers could work to sixty a week and ten a day.[21] A majority felt this was unconstitutional because it was an arbitrary and unnecessary interference with the "liberty to contract" of both employers and employees. Justices Holmes and Harlan dissented. Harlan argued that the statute was a valid health measure and therefore should be upheld.

Justice Oliver Wendell Holmes was the only justice to dissent from the idea that *substantive* due process existed and gave the Court the power to overturn laws duly passed by legislatures. Holmes was a philosophical and ideological skeptic. As a student at Harvard Law School he had doubted what he was taught, that the English common law system was the perfect legal system. He was wounded three times fighting for the Union during the Civil War, and he returned from the war to become a member of the Massachusetts bar. In 1881 he published his treatise, *The Common Law*, which begins with a famous line that the "life of law has not been logic: it has been experience." He became a Harvard law professor, a Supreme Court justice in Massachusetts, and in 1902 a U.S. Supreme Court justice by appointment of President Theodore Roosevelt. Holmes fathered the idea of judicial restraint. During 1903 he wrote: "While the courts must exercise judgment of their own, it by no means is true that every law is void which may seem to the judges who pass upon it excessive, unsuited to its ostensible end, or based upon conceptions of morality with which they disagree. Considerable latitude must be allowed for differences of view." He went on to say that the Court should not become "the partisan of a particular set of ethical or economical opinions."[22]

His dissenting opinion in *Lochner* became one of the most famous dissents ever written. He said:

This case is decided upon an economic theory which a large part of this country does not entertain. If it were a question whether I agreed with that theory, I should desire to study it further and long before making up my mind. But I do not conceive that to be my duty, because I strongly believe that my agreement or disagreement has nothing to do with the right of a majority to embody their opinions in law. It is settled by various decisions of this court that state constitutions and state laws may regulate life in many ways which we as legislators might think as injudicious or if you like as tyrannical as this, and which equally with this interfere with the liberty to contract. Sunday laws and usury laws are ancient examples. A more modern one is the prohibition of lotteries. The liberty of the citizen to do as he likes so long as he does not interfere with the liberty of others to do the same, which has been a shibboleth for some well-known writers, is interfered with by school laws, by the Post Office, by every state or municipal institution which takes his money for purposes thought desirable, whether he likes it or not.[23]

A majority of the Court was not concerned with protecting the general freedom of citizens to decide for themselves what was in the best interest of their "health, safety, or morals." They were concerned with protecting the freedom of business to engage in what were considered "normal" business practices of the day. Holmes went on to say that:

a constitution is not intended to embody a particular economic theory, whether of paternalism and the organic relation of the citizen to the State or of *laissez faire*. It is made for people of fundamentally differing views, and the accident of our finding certain opinions natural and familiar or novel and even shocking ought not to conclude our judgment upon the question whether statutes embodying them conflict with the Constitution of the United States.[24]

The majority of the Court, however, believed that freedom of contract had to be protected and were willing to use substantive due process, the equal protection clause, and the fact that the power to regulate interstate commerce belonged to the federal, not the state, governments to protect this freedom.

In 1908 in *Adair v. United States,* the Court overturned a federal law that made it illegal for railroads to discriminate against employees because they belonged to a labor union.[25] In his dissent Holmes said:

I quite agree that the question what and how much good labor unions do, is one on which intelligent people may differ,—I think that laboring men sometimes attribute to them advantages, as many attribute to combinations of capital disadvantages, that really are due to economic conditions of a far wider and deeper kind—but I could not pronounce it unwarranted if Congress should decide that to foster a strong union was for the best interest, not only of the men, but of the railroads and the country at large.[26]

However, in 1908 the Court upheld the power of the state of Oregon to limit the number of hours women could work in *Muller v. Oregon*.[27] Attorney Louis D. Brandeis, who later served on the Supreme Court, authored what has become the most famous brief ever submitted to the Court. It is famous because it did not cite one judicial decision; instead it contained reams of documentation to prove that the health of women was indeed at stake. The Court was willing to protect the weaker sex. In the same vein, the Court in 1917 upheld state laws that regulated the hours men could work in some occupations because similar evidence was provided to support the need for the legislation.[28]

The Court had decided that the federal power to regulate interstate commerce included the power to prohibit the interstate transportation of certain things such as lottery tickets, tainted food and women who were transported for "immoral purposes."[29] However, there was a limit to this power, which the Court made clear in the 1918 case of *Hammer v. Dagenhart*.[30] Congress had passed a law outlawing the interstate transportation of products produced with child labor. The Court said this was not within the power of the federal government because it was really an attempt to control business within state lines, which was exclusively the power of the states (supervised by the Supreme Court, of course). Justice Holmes again dissented, arguing for a broad reading of the power to control interstate commerce. That the goal was not to stop the transportation of things that were inherently bad, such as lottery tickets, tainted food, and immoral women, but instead was to achieve some other worthy goal, such as stopping child labor, was irrelevant in his eyes. As he said, if there is something "civilized countries have agreed far more unanimously than they have with regard to intoxicants and some other matters over which this country is now emotionally aroused—it is the evil of premature and excessive child labor."[31] He was joined in dissent by three other justices, including the recently appointed Justice Louis D. Brandeis.

In the 1930s the doctrines of substantive due process and a limited power to regulate interstate commerce for the federal government ran into the Great Depression and the presidency of Franklin D. Roosevelt. To get the country out of the depression, Congress passed a number of statutes which came up for review by the Court between 1934 and 1936. The Court struck down much of this legislation as unconstitutional. In 1936 the Court also struck down New York's minimum wage law for women.[32] Justice Holmes had by this time retired and it fell to Justice Stone to state the case for the four dissenters. He said: "there is a grim irony in speaking of the freedom of contract of those who, because of their economic necessities give their services for less than is needful to keep body and soul together."[33] He went on to say that the Court had learned that:

a wage is not always the resultant of free bargaining between employers and employees; that it may be one forced upon employees by their economic necessities and upon employers by the most ruthless of their competitors. We have had opportunity to perceive more clearly that a wage insufficient to support the worker does not visit its consequences upon him alone; that it may affect profoundly the entire economic structure of society, and, in any case, that it casts on every taxpayer, and on government itself, the burden of solving the problems of poverty, subsistence, health and morals of large numbers in the community. Because of their nature and extent these are public problems. A generation ago they were for the individual to solve; today they are the burden of the nation."[34]

In November 1936 the people voted overwhelming to send Roosevelt back to the White House. That election could be seen as a referendum in favor of Roosevelt's activist policies and against the idea of laissez-faire economics. Roosevelt responded by proposing a scheme whereby a president could appoint an additional Supreme Court justice for every justice over the age of seventy. Congress debated this plan for six months and ultimately rejected it. At the same time the Supreme Court reversed its stand and began to validate the new social and economic statutes passed by Congress and the states. Decisions which had been five to four against, were now five to four in favor of the New Deal. There had been a "switch in time that saved nine."[35]

It is important to stress that not all the substantive due process decisions favored big business. In 1917 the Court struck down a Louisville ordinance that kept blacks from moving into areas that were primarily white because this was an unreasonable interference with the liberty to sell property.[36] In 1923 the Court struck down a Nebraska statute that forbade the teaching of foreign languages because it interfered with the freedom to get an education.[37]

In 1931 the Court began a new approach to Fourteenth Amendment interpretation by concluding that the Amendment made at least some provisions of the Bill of Rights applicable to the states. The state statutes involved were struck down because they interfered with the freedom of speech and freedom of the press.[38] Between 1937 and 1965 this became the main basis for declaring state statutes to be unconstitutional violations of the due process clause of the Fourteenth Amendment.

This change became clear in 1949 when Justice Black stated for the majority that a state statute would be upheld unless it ran "afoul of some specific federal constitutional prohibition, or some valid federal law."[39] In 1963 Justice Black said that the court refused to sit as a "superlegislature to weigh the wisdom of legislation" and that whether the legislature took "its textbook from Adam Smith, Herbert Spencer, Lord Keynes, or some other is no concern" of the courts.[40]

For a generation the U.S. Supreme Court had used the doctrine of substantive due process to strike down legislation that it felt was "unreasonable." This experiment with unbounded judicial discretion failed, and in response the Court turned to the Bill of Rights to provide some basis for its decisions. This was the case until 1965, when the right to privacy emerged as a new license for more expansive Court action. By then the concept of a "right to privacy" already had a long history in the civil law of the United States.

NOTES

1. L. S. Kramer, PAINE AND JEFFERSON ON LIBERTY (1968), 89–97.
2. Quoted by Justice Goldberg in Griswold v. Connecticut, 381 U.S. 479, 489–90 (1965).
3. Slaughter-House Cases, 83 U.S. 36 (1873).
4. 3 U.S. 386 (1798).
5. Id. at 388.
6. Id. at 398.
7. Id. at 399.
8. 5 U.S. 137 (1803).
9. 60 U.S. 393 (1857).
10. 32 U.S. 243 (1833).
11. 60 U.S. 393 (1857).
12. Id. at 417.
13. 83 U.S. 36 (1873).
14. 94 U.S. 113 (1876).
15. Id. at 126.
16. Id. at 134.
17. Railroad Commission Cases, 116 U.S. 307 (1886); Mugler v. Kansas, 123 U.S. 623 (1887).
18. Santa Clara County v. Southern Pacific R.R., 118 U.S. 394 (1886).
19. 165 U.S. 578 (1897).
20. Holden v. Hardy, 169 U.S. 366 (1898).
21. 198 U.S. 45 (1905).
22. Otis v. Parker, 187 U.S. 606, 608–9 (1903).
23. 198 U.S. 45, 75 (1905).
24. Id. at 75–76.
25. 208 U.S. 161 (1908).

26. *Id.* at 191–2.

27. 208 U.S. 412 (1908).

28. Bunting v. Oregon, 243 U.S. 426 (1917).

29. Lottery Case, 188 U.S. 321 (1903); Hipolite Egg Co. v. United States, 220 U.S. 45 (1911); Hoke v. United States, 227 U.S. 308 (1913).

30. 247 U.S. 251 (1918).

31. *Id.* at 280.

32. Morehead v. New York ex rel. Tipaldo, 298 U.S. 587 (1936).

33. *Id.* at 632.

34. *Id.* at 635.

35. West Coast Hotel v. Parrish, 300 U.S. 379 (1937).

36. Buchanan v. Warley, 245 U.S. 60 (1917).

37. Meyer v. Nebraska, 262 U.S. 390 (1923).

38. Stromberg v. California, 283 U.S. 359 (1931); Near v. Minnesota, 283 U.S. 697 (1931).

39. Lincoln Federal Labor Union v. Northwestern Iron & Metal Co., 335 U.S. 525, 536 (1949).

40. Ferguson v. Skrupa, 372 U.S. 726, 731–2 (1963).

5

The Common Law Foundation: Creating the Right to Privacy

While the historical, philosophical, and legal foundations of constitutional privacy have been discussed, the immediate stimulus to its creation was the existence of a privacy right in civil law. Long before the U.S. Supreme Court decided that the Constitution includes a right to privacy, state court judges had decided that privacy had roots in the common law of their states. The evolution of that common law can be traced over the course of a century.

THE FIRST QUARTER CENTURY: THE RIGHT OF PUBLICITY

In 1890 the *Harvard Law Review* published an article called "The Right to Privacy."[1] In it, Boston attorneys Samuel Warren and Louis D. Brandeis (later a Supreme Court justice), argued that the law should recognize a right to an "inviolate personality" that would protect "thoughts, emotions, and sensations . . . whether expressed in writing, or in conduct, in conversation, in attitudes, or in facial expression." Noting that the common law responded well to societal needs, they also argued that courts should create this new right rather than wait for legislators to act. "The intensity and complexity of life" and "modern enterprise and invention," they said, made the time ripe for judges to redefine the nature of personal rights to protect "appearance, sayings, acts, and . . . personal relation[s], domestic or otherwise."[2]

This redefinition, they argued, would not require much rewriting of the law, for recent court cases had already come close to recognizing a legally enforceable privacy right. In the 1880s, for example, professional photographers who sold their customers' pictures without their consent were held liable for breaching an implied agreement that the prints would be "appropriated to the use of the customer only."[3] Courts were using nuisance and defamation law to shield people from, respectively, "offensive noises and odors . . . dust and smoke, and excessive vibration" and harm to reputation.[4] And the concept of "intangible property" guarded "the products and processes of the mind, such as works of literature and art, goodwill, trade secrets, and trademarks."[5] Believing that what these cases really protected was privacy, the authors argued that courts should simply recognize this right rather than try to force new cases into old legal categories. This would further the common law trend toward acknowledging both "nonphysical" injuries, such as harm to reputation, and "intangible property," such as goodwill and copyright, by recognizing the nonphysical injury of emotional distress and the intangible property rights inherent in one's private life. It would also fill the void left by the "implied contract" theory, which logically could not apply when the parties involved were strangers.

The crux of the authors' argument was that everyone should own the "facts relating to his private life." While they argued for a general privacy right, however, Warren and Brandeis had a specific problem in mind: The press was "overstepping in every direction the obvious bounds of propriety and of decency," and "idle gossip" was crowding out real news. This caused great "mental pain and distress" to innocent people who found the "sacred precincts of [their] private and domestic life" invaded as intimate personal facts were splashed across the pages of newspapers. The right sought by the authors would combat this problem by giving people a legal remedy for unwanted and unjustified public exposure.

In exchange for the recognition of two principles, Warren and Brandeis said they would accept four limitations on the right of privacy. The principles were that truth should not be a defense in an action for privacy invasion, as it is in defamation law, and that what motivates someone who publishes intimate personal facts should be irrelevant. Only what is printed, the justification for printing it, and the impact of publication on the plaintiff should matter. The limits were: (1) one can consent expressly or impliedly to a privacy invasion; (2) oral publications should not be actionable unless special damages are proven; (3) some communications should be privileged, as in defamation cases, such as those made in court or before legislatures; and (4) the press can publish what is of "general interest," with this right applying expansively to "public figures," such as politicians, who in putting themselves in the public eye automatically renounce some of their privacy.

As an example of proper versus improper publication, the authors offered a man with a lisp: if he seeks public office people have a right to know about his impediment, but not otherwise.[6]

Four years after "The Right to Privacy" appeared, Herbert S. Hadley published an article by the same title.[7] He argued that the limitations on privacy that Warren and Brandeis were willing to accept would mean that "the small class who would thus be entitled to enjoy the privilege of privacy and seclusion would probably find that their habits of life and appearance would be of as little importance to the general public as would the right to privacy itself." He also insisted that the common law should not recognize mental anguish as a basis for damages "except where a physical condition results [from] the act producing the anguish," and that, "when an individual goes among people, when he walks along the streets in the sight of all who care to look upon him, he has waived his right to the privacy of his personality."

To illustrate how courts were handling privacy claims, Hadley discussed cases which had arisen before and after the publication of the Warren and Brandeis article. One was *Pollard v. Photographic Co.*, noted above,[8] where a British Court enjoined the unauthorized commercial use of pictures taken for a woman by a photographer. But in 1893 the heirs of a Mr. Corliss failed to persuade a court to halt the publication of an unauthorized biography of him with his picture on the cover.[9] There was no claim of libel, only that publication would harm the heirs' feelings. Saying that people should be free to publish what they wish if there is no "offense against public morals or private reputation," the court held that whether Corliss was a public figure, or for that matter was dead or alive, was irrelevant. The picture had been obtained legitimately, and the judge did not feel that its use on a biography cover, authorized or not, warranted damages or an injunction against publication.

Both ends of the spectrum of judicial attitudes toward privacy can be seen in these cases. On the one hand, while it stopped short of recognizing a "right to privacy," the *Pollard* court was plainly concerned about the effect on the plaintiff's sensibilities of the unauthorized use of her picture, and it ruled in her favor. It held that in accepting employment the photographer had formed a confidential relationship with the plaintiff, and that his use of her picture without her consent violated both an implied part of their contract and her "faith" in him, as such use was not within the parties' contemplation when they bargained. In so doing, the court rejected the claim that "a person has no property in his own features" and that "short of doing what is libellous or otherwise illegal, there is no restriction on the photographer's using his negative." On the other hand, the *Corliss* court did not speak of property rights in one's likeness, implied agreements or confidences, and it seemed unconcerned with sensibilities. In its view the issues were clearcut: The photo had been legitimately bought, its use involved "free speech" and would not harm "public morals" or anyone's reputation, and no law shielded the heirs' "feelings" from the effects of publication.

With the publication of these articles, the points of contention regarding the "right of privacy" became explicit. Warren, Brandeis, and Hadley agreed that the law should recognize this right but differed over who should create it and what shape it should take. Noting that the common law adapted well to the needs of a changing society, Warren and Brandeis argued that judges should develop the right case-by-case, whereas Hadley felt that this task was better left to lawmakers. Warren and Brandeis thought that mental anguish should be compensated in invasion of privacy cases, while Hadley would require a physical manifestation of harm. Finally, responding to Warren and Brandeis' claim that privacy should be a broad right protecting against unwanted exposure and intrusions, Hadley asserted that much of what they would put under the privacy umbrella should be left to the realm of ethics and morals and not be made part of the legal system.

A few years later, a Ms. Roberson sought relief in the New York courts when she found her picture used to advertise flour without her consent. In a 4–3 vote, the Court of Appeals turned her down.[10] Outraged at the court's refusal to recognize her "right of privacy," the press vilified the court, prompting one judge to defend the ruling in an article.[11] The decision and the article appeared in 1902; a year later, the New York legislature barred the "unauthorized use of the name or picture of any person for the purposes of trade" and permitted injured parties to recover damages and to stop further unsanctioned use.[12] In so doing, they plainly responded to commentators who had condemned the court for refusing to endorse the emerging common law notion of "intangible property" rights inherent in one's private life. These writers argued that the commercial use of one's name or picture should be protected and that this would not raise the free speech issues that might arise in other applications of the privacy theory.

In 1912 Wilbur Larremore reviewed the privacy cases reported since 1890—all twelve of them.[13] Like Warren, Brandeis, and Hadley, he sought the recognition of a right to control the commercial use of one's name and image, and he surveyed the cases which found this right in the common law. The Georgia Supreme Court did this in 1905, when Mr. Pavesich found his picture being used without his consent to advertise an insurance company.[14] Missouri soon followed suit, with its high court saying: "Property is not necessarily a taxable thing any more than it is always a tangible thing. It may consist of things incorporeal, and things incorporeal may consist of rights common in every man."[15]

Larremore noted that some courts refused to recognize this right absent a statute expressly creating it, but argued that the trend was toward acceptance of the concept and that other courts should follow Georgia and Missouri and adjust their common law accordingly.

Two cases reviewed by Larremore dealt with another concept discussed by Warren and Brandeis: the right to protect intimate facts. One was the case involving Mr. Corliss' heirs. The other involved a Ms. Hillman, who sued a newspaper after finding her picture in an article about her father's arrest for fraud.[16] There, the court refused to recognize a privacy right absent legislation creating it and ruled against Hillman. Larremore disagreed with the outcome of the case but conceded the need to distinguish between the "right to keep private facts private" at stake in that case and the "right of publicity," which he felt was more deserving of recognition. He also endorsed Warren and Brandeis' view that damages should be awarded for mental anguish even if there is no physical manifestation of injury; specifically, he backed a 1904 court ruling which let a railroad passenger sue for mental distress because a conductor had used "abusive language" toward her, even though she had suffered no physical harm as a result.[17]

In sum, twenty-five years after the appearance of the Warren and Brandeis article, the "right of publicity" was well on its way to becoming rooted in the common law. While courts still used the "breach of faith" and "breach of contract" theories seen in cases like *Pollard*, they had begun to accept the idea that people have rights in their name and image and that recognizing a theory which protects these rights is preferable to forcing cases into old legal pigeonholes. As the idea of a "right to publicity" gained ground, the issues became: (1) how does one decide if the use of a name or image is legitimate? and (2) does the right of publicity survive death? On the other hand, it was also clear that the "right to keep private facts private" was not faring well. With just one case involving a live person decided, and with it lost, it seemed that Herbert Hadley may have been right when he speculated that the class of people actually covered by this right was too small to worry about.

THE SECOND QUARTER CENTURY: THE RIGHT OF SECLUSION

Through the 1930s scholars continued to debate whether legislatures or courts should create a right of privacy and what its contours should be. While the academicians argued, however, the courts went about fine-tuning this right. By 1936 things had evolved to the point that Gerald Dickler could say that the "privacy" concept really embraced three distinct rights: a "right of publicity," which barred the unauthorized appropriation of one's name or image; a "right of seclusion," which shielded people from unwanted intrusions; and a "right to keep private facts private."[18]

The "right of publicity" was the most widely accepted. While courts and commentators still found it hard to delineate between proper and improper use, they agreed that the commercial use of one's name or image should be controlled by the individual as other property is. Dickler also felt that a second set of cases stood for the principle that people have a right to avoid unwanted intrusions on their lives. In perhaps the first case involving this theory, a woman won damages in 1881 for the distress she suffered when she found that a man brought to her childbirth by a doctor was not a medical assistant.[19] In 1929 courts refused to let a "crusading law enforcer" examine the bank accounts of city police to "assist him in some investigation" he was making."[20] And in 1931, a man recovered for anguish caused by the tapping of his phone.[21] None of these cases involved proof of physical harm.

The "private facts" right, on the other hand, continued to lag far behind. When it was asserted against newspapers that published personal facts, courts often conceded that the publication implicated privacy interests but ruled for the defendants under the Warren and Brandeis "public figure" and "news of general interest" exceptions. The Kentucky Supreme Court, for example, refused to let a plaintiff recover for the publication of his picture in a paper even though the story falsely attributed statements to him. The Court said that at times one "whether willingly or not, becomes an actor in an occurrence of public or general interest. When this takes place, he emerges from seclusion, and it is not an invasion of his right of privacy to publish his photograph with an account of such occurrence."[22] Dickler disagreed with the case, not because it recognized a press privilege, which he favored, but because it extended the privilege to the "false recording of news."

Only if the outrageousness of a publication was extreme could plaintiffs expect to win. In 1930, for example, a family recovered damages when a paper printed a picture of their "abnormal deceased child" without their consent.[23] The child was born with its heart outside its body and died soon after birth. And in Kentucky, a doctor successfully sued a creditor who posted a five-by-eight foot sign proclaiming that the doctor owed him $49.67. Interestingly, the defendant was not permitted to claim truth as a defense, although truth was then an absolute defense to defamation actions in Kentucky.[24]

The close of the second quarter century after the Warren and Brandeis article saw the "right of publicity" become even more firmly entrenched and a "right of seclusion" gaining a foothold in the law. At best, however, judges remained lukewarm towards the "right to keep private facts private."

THE SECOND HALF CENTURY: THE RIGHT OF FREE SPEECH

In 1941, Louis Nizer argued that in focusing so much on privacy, courts had paid too little attention to the right of free speech.[25] This right, he claimed, is implicated in privacy suits against the media. After citing with approval cases recognizing a privilege to report whatever might remotely be deemed news, Nizer examined cases involving the depiction of newsworthy events. For example, in *Binns v. Vitagraph Corp. of America*,[26] which involved a film dramatization of a rescue at sea, the court distinguished between "news" and "commercialization" so that dramatizations fell on the commercial side of the line and allowed the real hero to win damages for invasion of privacy. Nizer objected, saying this line should be moved so that dramatizations would be included with news reports. In his view, press freedom should be broad enough for the media to be able to truthfully dramatize newsworthy events without fearing lawsuits.

Two other dramatization cases had been decided by 1941, both for the plaintiffs. One writer summarized the facts of *Melvin v. Reid* as follows:

The fact situation rivals the English problem play of the nineties: Gabrielle Darley, erstwhile prostitute and defendant in a murder trial in which she was acquitted, marries into respectable society. She reforms, gaining many friends who are unaware of her early transgressions. Then appears, on the local screens, and in the moving picture cathedrals of the country, a film entitled "The Red Kimono," based on the true history of her past life, and employing her maiden name as that of the principal character; and billboards and fences are plastered with smug announcements that the production was plotted around the true story of her life.[27]

The California courts let Darley sue for invasion of privacy because her married name had been used in advertising the film. This use, said the court, violated a state constitutional provision guaranteeing citizens the right to pursue happiness. That Darley's new name was a matter of public record for anyone to look up seemed to make no difference to this court.

Mau v. Rio Grande Oil Co.[28] involved the radio show "Calling All Cars," which dramatized real crime stories. The plaintiff claimed that he suffered anguish when he heard a broadcast of a reinactment of an incident in which he was robbed and shot. His distress, he said, was so acute that he could not work the next day, which caused him to be fired. Relying on state statutes and on the *Melvin* case, the court ruled for the plaintiff, thus joining the *Melvin* court in finding that dramatizations are not "news" shielded by a broad publication privilege.

In 1960 Dean William Prosser published a seminal article on privacy.[29] Prosser agreed with Dickler that privacy involves three rights, but he went further and said that the "private facts" right had two parts. In one line of disclosure cases, he observed, the facts were private but the plaintiff's reputation was unharmed; in the other, the information revealed was misleading and put the plaintiff in a "false light," but its disclosure did not rise to the level of defamation. Plaintiffs usually won false light cases, he said, but not the others. Unlike other commentators such as Larremore and Dickler, Prosser did not single out this category of cases with an eye toward stimulating their growth; on the contrary, he worried that false light privacy might swallow up defamation law. He asked, "What of the numerous restrictions and limitations which have hedged defamation about for many years, in the interest of freedom of the press and the discouragement of trivial and extortionate claims? Are they of so little consequence that they may be circumvented in so casual and cavalier a fashion?"[30]

Prosser's article spawned debates over whether privacy rights should be recognized at all and whether privacy is one right or several smaller ones. His four-part analysis has been accepted by nearly all courts, however, and was incorporated in the 1977 *Restatement (Second) of Torts*. Several states have adopted his description of privacy, summarized below.

In 1963 Marc Franklin revived concern over the free speech/privacy conflict on which Louis Nizer had focused in 1941.[31] He began with *Hubbard v. Journal Pub. Co.*,[32] where a newspaper was sued for revealing that a girl had been sexually assaulted by her brother. The newspaper had gotten the facts from court records. The New Mexico Supreme Court held for the paper on three grounds: it was privileged to publish information in public records; the information was newsworthy; and the plaintiff was, albeit involuntarily, a public figure.

Rather than base its ruling on the common law concepts of "privilege," "public figure," and "newsworthiness," Franklin thought the court should have found the publication protected by the First Amendment. He was appalled that in most privacy cases against the media the defendants did not even invoke the amendment, and he especially feared a case then on appeal to the Supreme Court. In that case, *New York Times v. Sullivan*,[33] Alabama courts had awarded $500,000 in libel damages against the paper. Franklin thought this was government censorship of the press.

At issue was a *Times* advertisement which was critical of the behavior of Birmingham, Alabama's police during civil rights protests. Sullivan, a city commissioner, sued for libel, arguing that while the ad did not mention him by name, its criticism reflected adversely on him in his capacity as police commissioner. But the U.S. Supreme Court said that the press must have "breathing room" if free speech is to survive, and that a rule requiring a "critic of official conduct to guarantee the truth of all his factual assertions" would lead to self-censorship which would inhibit the free exchange of ideas. It held that "public figures" suing the media for defamation must prove not only that a publication was false and had hurt their reputation, but also that the media acted with "malice," that is, knew what they were saying was false or acted with reckless disregard of its truth.

In *Time Inc. v. Hill*,[34] escaped convicts held the Hill family hostage for nineteen hours. The incident attracted widespread publicity and led to a novel, play, and movie. When the play opened, *Life Magazine* published an article entitled "True Crime Inspires Tense Play," which noted similarities between the fictional work and the real event and indicated incorrectly that the play depicted the true facts. The Hills sued in New York under the 1903 law that had overturned the *Roberson* case. The jury awarded $30,000 in damages, and the New York Court of Appeals affirmed based on the inaccuracies in the story. The Supreme Court reversed, however, holding that these plaintiffs had to prove malice just as public figures must do in defamation actions.

In 1974, the Court held that private figures who prove damages and fault need not prove malice in libel suits against the media.[35] Law review commentators argued that the test should be the same in privacy suits—if private parties need not prove malice to win libel cases, in other words, they should not have to do so in false light privacy cases. In 1890 Warren and Brandeis had said that neither truth nor malice should be issues in privacy cases, but in the 1960s the U.S. Supreme Court found that in view of the constitutional right of free speech they were major issues. Thus, in false light privacy suits, truth would be a defense, absent a showing of malice.

By the 1980s "false light" privacy law was in disarray, and scholars were calling for its abandonment. One writer claimed that cases in this area were really trying both to protect reputation and to punish people who cause emotional distress, and he observed that other branches of tort law already did this.[36] The law of defamation protects reputations, and the "intentional infliction of mental distress" tort, which affords relief to those who suffer mental distress at the hands of people who should have known that their acts might cause such distress, protects peace of mind. In 1984 the North Carolina Supreme Court heeded the advice of these commentators, refusing to recognize a false light privacy tort in that state.[37]

How would courts react to "infliction of mental distress" suits against the media? In 1988, the Supreme Court gave a partial answer in *Falwell v. Flynt*,[38] the facts of which were summarized by the Court as follows:

> The inside front cover of the November 1983 issue of Hustler Magazine featured a "parody" of an advertisement for Campari Liquer that contained the name and picture of respondent and was entitled "Jerry Falwell talks about his first time." This parody was modeled after actual Campari ads that included interviews with various celebrities about their "first times." Although it was apparent by the end of each interview that this meant the first time they sampled Campari, the ads clearly played on the sexual double entendre of the general subject of "first times." Copying the form and layout of these Campari ads, Hustler's editors chose respondent as the featured celebrity and drafted an alleged "interview" with him in which he states that his "first time" was during a drunken incestuous rendezvous with his mother in an outhouse. The Hustler parody portrays respondent and his mother as drunk and immoral, and suggests that respondent is a hypocrite who preaches only when he is drunk. In small print at the bottom of the page, the ad contains the disclaimer, "ad parody—not to be taken seriously." The magazine's table of contents also lists the ad as "Fiction: Ad and Personality Parody."[39]

Falwell sued for false light invasion of privacy, libel, and infliction of mental distress. The district court directed a verdict for *Hustler* on the libel claim, ruling that no one could have reasonably thought that the ad described true facts about Falwell. But the jury accepted the mental distress claim and awarded Falwell $150,000 in damages.

The Supreme Court reversed. Although the case involved intentional infliction of mental distress and not libel, Chief Justice Rehnquist said for a unanimous Court, Falwell was a "public figure" who must meet the "malice" test set out in *Sullivan* and *Hill*. That test requires public figures to prove that a publication contains a false statement of fact and that the authors knew the statement was false or acted with reckless disregard of its truth. Because Falwell had not claimed that *Hustler* had printed a "statement of fact," false or not, the test had not been met. As a result of *Flynt*, public figures in both libel and emotional distress suits against the media now face quite imposing obstacles to recovery.

So do private figures. In *Florida Star v. B.J.F.*,[40] the Supreme Court overturned a damage award against a newspaper which printed the name of a rape victim which it had obtained from police records. Although state law made it unlawful to "print . . . in any instrument of mass communication" the name of the victim of a sexual offense, the Court found that under the facts of this case, prosecuting the newspaper violated the First Amendment. The Court conceded that there were important privacy interests at stake, but it also stressed that the newspaper had simply published truthful information contained in records which the police department had placed in a press room accessible to the public. If fault lay anywhere, it was with the department, which itself violated the statute noted above in including the victim's name in records made available to the public, or with the state, which could have taken several stringent protective measures to guard against the release of this information to the media. The newspaper, the Court held, should not be blamed for printing newsworthy information that was essentially handed to it on a platter, especially in view of the vital free speech interests involved.

Florida Star was not a libel case, because what the paper printed was true; instead, the plaintiff claimed, as Falwell had in *Flynt*, that the release of the information at issue caused her severe emotional distress and violated her privacy rights. Before trial, the plaintiff settled with the police department, leaving only the newspaper as a defendant, and in view of the Court's ruling that proved to be a poor choice—if the plaintiff had a valid complaint against anyone, it was the department. The upshot of this case is that in a conflict between privacy and First Amendment rights, the latter will generally prevail. Put another way, *Florida Star* should make it as hard for private plaintiffs to prevail in privacy and infliction of emotional distress suits against the news media as *Flynt* makes it for public figures.

The one hundredth birthday of privacy law thus finds all states having incorporated in their constitutional, statutory, or common law some variation of the privacy rights identified by Dean Prosser in 1960. Federal law also embraces some of these rights, which are summarized below:

Appropriation of Name or Likeness

This right prohibits the appropriation for commercial use of one's name or likenesses without his consent. Often called the "right of publicity," it has, for example, been cited by people when companies have used their photographs to advertise products without their consent. It is the most firmly established and the least controversial of the four privacy rights.

Intrusion in Intimate Areas

This theory imposes liability for intrusions on one's seclusion or private affairs if the intrusion would be highly offensive to a reasonable person and no valid reason for it exists. The intrusion may be physical, such as breaking into a home or examining a wallet or purse, or nonphysical, such as wiretapping a conversation. To be protected, the area invaded must truly be "private"; no privacy right, for example, prevents someone from watching a person on a street.

The tort is based on the psychological distress caused by the intrusion; whether the defendant learned anything private or embarrassing about the plaintiff, or disclosed such data is irrelevant.

Public Disclosure of Private Facts

This tort prohibits the public disclosure of private facts if the publicity would be highly offensive to a reasonable person and the facts are not of valid public concern. Liability may result whether or not the information is true or the plaintiff could sue for defamation. For information to be protected it must be truly private, such as facts about sexual relations, personal illnesses with negative connotations, and other intimate details of one's private life.

False Light Privacy

This tort involves publicity which puts the plaintiff in a false light in the public eye. The portrayal must be highly offensive to a reasonable person, but the plaintiff need not be defamed.

As noted, the status of false light privacy is unclear. Recent cases raise doubts about how much is left of this tort where "public figures" sue the media, since "public figure" is now defined broadly and these plaintiffs must prove falsity, harm to reputation, and malice. As for private parties, it can be argued that they should have to prove the same things, for otherwise the media would always have to worry about how to classify those about whom they report, and this could chill free speech. But it can also be said that by now the definition of "public figure" is fairly clear and the media need only refrain from putting purely private individuals in a false light, and that this is not too onerous a burden given our common interest in privacy.

CONCLUSION

Since the publication of "The Right to Privacy," courts have struggled to define the scope of the civil law privacy right. Most have agreed that it encompasses the right to benefit from the commercial exploitation of one's name or likeness and to be left alone in seclusion. The difficult question has been the extent to which individuals have a right to keep "private facts" out of the media and unknown to the general public. This will be discussed in detail in Chapter 10. Because this right conflicts with the rights of free speech and free press, it is particularly troubling for the courts.

While the right to privacy was developing as a civil law concept it also began to appear in cases involving the U.S. Constitution. Over time the U.S. Supreme Court decided that common law privacy had a counterpart in the Constitution. How that constitutional right to privacy was created is the subject of the next chapter.

NOTES

1. 4 HARV. L. REV. 193 (1890).
2. *Id.* at 196, 206 and 213.
3. Pollard v. Photographic Co., 40 Ch. Div. 345, 350 (1888); Tuck v. Priester, 19 Q.B.D. 639 (1887).
4. Warren and Brandeis, *supra* note 1, at 194.
5. *Id.* at 194–95.
6. *Id.* at 213–220.
7. Hadley, *The Right to Privacy*, 3 Nw. U.L. REV. 1 (1894).
8. See *supra* text accompanying note 3.
9. Corliss v. Walker Co., 57 Fed. Rep. 434 (Cir. Mass. 1893).
10. Roberson v. Rochester Folding Box Co., 171 N.Y. 538 (1902).
11. O'Brien, *The Right of Privacy*, 2 COLUM. L. REV. 437 (1902).
12. New York Cons. Laws, Civil Rights Law, Art. 5.
13. Larremore, *The Law of Privacy*, 12 COLUM. L. REV. 693 (1912).
14. Pavesich v. New England Life Ins. Co., 122 Ga. 190 (1905).
15. Larremore, *supra* note 13, at 695.
16. Hillman v. Star Pub. Co., 64 Wash. 691 (1911).
17. Gillespie v. Brooklyn Heights R.R. Co., 178 N.Y. 347 (1904). This right to sue common carriers for abusive language is alive and well today. *See* Ricci v. American Airlines, 544 A.2d 428 (N.J. App. 1988), where a man recovered damages for the unkind treatment he received from a flight attendant.
18. Dickler, *The Right of Privacy: A Proposed Redefinition*, 70 ST. LOUIS U.L.J. 435 (1936).
19. DeMay v. Roberts, 46 Mich. 160, 9 N.W. 146 (1881).
20. Brex v. Smith, 104 N.J. Eq. 386 (1929).

21. Rhodes v. Graham, 238 Ky. 225 (1931).

22. Jones v. Herald Post Co., 230 Ky. 227, 229 (1929).

23. Bazemore v. Savannah Hospital, 171 Ga. 257 (1930).

24. Brents v. Morgan, 221 Ky. 765 (1927).

25. Nizer, *The Right of Privacy, A Half Century's Development*, 39 MICH. L. REV. 526 (1941).

26. 210 N.Y. 51, 103 N.E. 1108 (1915).

27. 112 Cal. App. 285 (1931). The facts are summarized in Dickler, *supra* note 18, at 446.

28. 28 F. Supp. 845 (D.C. Cal. 1939).

29. Prosser, *Privacy*, 48 CALIF. L. REV. 383 (1960).

30. *Id.* at 401.

31. Franklin, *A Constitutional Problem in Privacy Protection: Legal Inhibition on Reporting of Fact*, 16 STAN. L. REV. 107 (1963).

32. 69 N.M. 473, 368 P.2d 147 (1962).

33. 376 U.S. 254 (1964).

34. 385 U.S. 374 (1967).

35. Gertz v. Robert Welch, Inc., 418 U.S. 323 (1974).

36. Note, *False Light Invasion of Privacy: False Tort?*, 17 SW. L.J. 135 (1987).

37. Renwick v. News & Observer Pub. Co., 310 N.C. 312, 312 S.E.2d 405 (1984).

38. 108 S. Ct. 876 (1988).

39. *Id.* at 878.

40. 109 S. Ct. 2603 (1989).

PART II

Constitutional Privacy

6

Creating Constitutional Privacy

Louis D. Brandeis grew up in Louisville, Kentucky. His family, German Jews, immigrated to the United States after the failure of the 1848 revolution. He graduated from Harvard Law School in 1877 and turned down an offer to teach there in 1882. For over three decades he practiced law in Boston, often representing those who wanted to see the country "move forward" with new kinds of social legislation. He was appointed by President Wilson to the U.S. Supreme Court in January 1916 and took his seat in June after an "epic battle" over his confirmation in the Senate. He served until his retirement in 1939 and was replaced by William O. Douglas, who served until his retirement in 1975. Douglas, who grew up in Yakima, Washington, worked his way through college and went on to become a law professor, the first chairman of the Securities and Exchange Commission (at the age of thirty-eight) and a Supreme Court justice.

Although a justice's replacement usually does not hold a philosophy similar to that of the justice he replaces, this was the case with these two men. In a very real sense they occupied the "privacy" seat on the Court for over half a century. At the same time they both supported legislative efforts to deal with the social problems of the twentieth century. Brandeis wrote many famous dissents during the Lochner era. Douglas was part of the New Deal Court.

It is often necessary when speaking about the development of a legal concept to talk about the idea being "in the air" and ultimately finding its way into court decisions by intellectual osmosis. This was not the case with constitutional privacy. The concept was brought to the Court by Justice Brandeis and developed by Justice Douglas. However, Brandeis did not get his chance to present the case for constitutional privacy until 1928 when he was already seventy-one years of age. His vehicle for doing so was *Olmstead v. United States,* a case which dealt with the Fourth Amendment ban on "unreasonable searches and seizures."[1]

THE FOURTH AMENDMENT

Before discussing *Olmstead*, it is important to outline three possible interpretations of the Fourth Amendment. The amendment says people have a right to be "secure in their persons, houses, papers and effects against unreasonable searches and seizures," but it does not define "unreasonable." That has been left to the U.S. Supreme Court. One approach to the interpretation of this amendment is to argue that it means exactly what is says: It does not protect fields, or phone lines, or anything other than "persons, houses, papers and effects." Under this view, it is not reasonable to search "persons, houses, papers and effects" unless the government has "probable cause" to think it will find what it is looking for and in most situations a search warrant. A second interpretation is that the Fourth Amendment was intended to generally protect the right of private property against government trespass. Before police can trespass on private property, in other words, they need a license in the form of a search warrant. During the first half of the twentieth century a majority of the U.S. Supreme Court held a combination of these two views.

OLMSTEAD

Olmstead involved an FBI wiretap of Olmstead and over seventy others who were engaged in a conspiracy of "amazing magnitude" to transport and sell intoxicating liquors in violation of the National Prohibition Act. Evidence of the conspiracy was obtained mainly through the use of several wiretaps. The Court ruled that the wiretaps were made without having to "trespass" on private property because the phone wires were not part of Olmstead's "house or office." Because there had been no trespass in the sense of a physical invasion and "persons, houses, papers and effects" had not been searched, the Court found that the Fourth Amendment had not been violated.

Justice Brandeis, in his famous dissent, argued that even though "persons, houses, papers and effects" had not, strictly speaking, been searched and there was technically no trespass, Olmstead's rights had still been violated. Brandeis argued that the question should be whether a person's right to privacy had been violated, not whether their property had been trespassed upon. Olmstead clearly thought he was having a private conversation, so the government should have had to obtain a search warrant before invading that privacy. Brandeis said in his dissent:

The makers of our Constitution undertook to secure conditions favorable to the pursuit of happiness. They recognized the significance of man's spiritual nature, of his feelings and his intellect. They knew that only a part of the pain, pleasure and satisfactions of life are to be found in material things. They sought to protect Americans in their beliefs, their thoughts, their emotions and their sensations. They conferred, as against government, the right to be let alone— the most comprehensive of rights and the right most valued by civilized men. To protect that right, every unjustifiable intrusion by the government upon the privacy of the individual, whatever the means employed, must be deemed a violation of the Fourth Amendment.[2]

To some this sounded familiar. Brandeis had used similar language in his *Harvard Law Review* article almost forty years before, when he spoke of the "spiritual nature" of mankind and of the need to protect the "right to be let alone."[3]

In tracing the origins of constitutional privacy, it must be remembered that Justice Brandeis was often one of the dissenters during the Lochner era, but not for the same reason Justice Holmes dissented. As Chapter Four noted, Justice Holmes argued for the general principle of judicial restraint. Justice Brandeis, on the other hand, was willing to give state legislatures more room than the majority of justices before deciding something was "arbitrary and capricious" or "transcended the bounds of reason," but he was not totally against the idea of using the Fourteenth Amendment to strike down state laws.

NEW STATE ICE CO.

This is perhaps best illustrated by the 1932 case of *New State Ice Co. v. Liebmann.*[4] While the court had allowed states to require certain "natural monopolies" (railroads being the classic example) to obtain a license to operate a business, the question in this case was whether Oklahoma could treat ice companies the same way. Put another way: Could the state limit competition in the business of making and delivering ice? A majority of the Court answered in the negative. Although in the *Slaughter-House Cases* of 1873 the Court had refused to hold that the Fourteenth Amendment protected the "right to compete," by 1932 the Court had clearly come to the opposite conclusion.[5] Dissenting,

Justice Brandeis argued not that the Court should never use the Four-teenth Amendment to strike down legislation, but that it should not do so lightly. Brandeis said:

To stay experimentation in things social and economic is a grave responsibility. Denial of the right to experiment may be fraught with serious consequences to the Nation. It is one of the happy incidents of the federal system that a single courageous State may, if its citizens choose, serve as a laboratory; and try novel social and economic experiments without risk to the rest of the country. This Court has the power to prevent an experiment. We may strike down the stat-ute which embodies it on the ground that, in our opinion, the measure is arbitrary, capricious or unreasonable. We have power to do this, because the due process clause has been held by the Court applicable to matters of sub-stantive law as well as to matters of procedure. But in the exercise of this high power, we must be ever on our guard, lest we erect our prejudices into legal principles. If we would guide by the light of reason, we must let our minds be bold.[6]

At the same time he did not disagree that there was a point beyond which legislatures could not go and that the Court should protect in-dividual liberty from infringement by the majority. While Holmes was arguing that the Court should bow to the will of the majority, Brandeis was willing to bend, but not bow. This is illustrated by two cases de-cided in the 1920s where Brandeis voted with the majority to declare laws unconstitutional.

MEYER AND PIERCE

In *Meyer v. Nebraska* the court struck down a Nebraska law that made it illegal to teach "any modern language other than English" to elemen-tary school children whether they were in public or private school.[7] Meyer was convicted of teaching German in Zion Parochial School to a child of ten. This law struck close to home for Brandeis, since his ele-mentary school education had been in German and he had learned English as a second language (as did Justice Clarence Thomas).

It was argued that the purpose of this legislation was to inhibit edu-cation in "foreign tongues and ideals" before the children had learned English and acquired "American ideals." Justice McReynolds, writing for a majority of the Court, pointed out that although the State may do a great deal to "improve the quality of its citizens, physically, mentally and morally . . . the individual has certain fundamental rights that must be respected."[8] He went on to point out that in Plato's ideal commonwealth wives and children were to be held in common and in Sparta when male children reached seven years of age they were placed in barracks and educated from then on by guardians. Justice Mc-Reynolds, faced with these clearly impermissible situations, recognized that a line had to be drawn somewhere, and he and a majority of the Court were prepared to draw it at the point of prohibiting education in foreign languages. In his opinion Justice McReynolds made a famous statement of what kinds of "liberty" the Fourteenth Amendment protects. He said liberty:

denotes not merely freedom from bodily restraint but also the right of the individual to contract, to engage in any of the common occupations of life, to acquire useful knowledge, to marry, establish a home and bring up children, to worship God according to the dictates of his own conscience, and generally to enjoy those privileges long recognized at common law as essential to the orderly pursuit of happiness by free men.[9]

Justices Holmes and Sutherland dissented, arguing that this statute was not beyond "the bounds of reason." Justice Brandeis voted with the majority.

Brandeis also voted with the majority in *Pierce v. Society of Sisters*.[10] A provision requiring all children to attend public school had been added to the Oregon Constitution by the initiative process through a direct vote of the citizens. Its constitutionality was challenged by a Catholic school and a private military academy; both would have been put out of business by the new law. Again, while arguments could be made that the law was necessary to assure a basic education free from religious indoctrination, the Court felt this was beyond the power of the state and interfered with the rights of parents and children to control their own education. There were no dissenting opinions in this case. Apparently this provision was beyond the limit for every justice, even Holmes.

It should also be noted that in 1935 Justice Brandeis voted with the majority to strike down much of the New Deal legislation including the National Recovery Act.[11]

Justice Brandeis was replaced by Justice Douglas in 1939. Thereafter the Court continued to debate the issue of what a state legislature could legitimately do, eventually deciding that what the Fourteenth Amendment "really did" was to make the Bill of Rights applicable to the states. By the end of the 1930s a majority of the Court had been appointed by President Roosevelt with the express purpose of putting an end to *Lochner* and its progeny. In 1937 the Court renounced the idea that substantive due process protects some kind of general right to contract.[12] In 1938 it said that state economic regulations are entitled to a presumption of constitutionality.[13] By 1949 a majority of the Court agreed that states are free to regulate "their internal commercial and business affairs, so long as their laws do not run afoul of some specific constitutional prohibition, or of some valid federal law," and in 1963 the majority said it would "emphatically refuse to go back to the time when courts used the Due Process Clause to strike down state laws . . . because they may be unwise, improvident, or out of harmony with a particular school of thought."[14]

By the early 1960s it was clear that some of the things listed by Justice McReynolds in his opinion in *Meyer v. Nebraska* were no longer protected by the Fourteenth Amendment. The right "to contract" and the right to "engage in the common occupations of life" had been used to strike down too much social legislation. The "right to worship God" was now protected because most of the Bill of Rights were applicable to the states and freedom of religion was protected by the First Amendment. But what about the right to "acquire useful knowledge, to marry, establish a home and bring up children?" *Meyer* had never been overruled; did this area of substantive due process still exist?

GRISWOLD

The answer came in 1965 with the decision in *Griswold v. Connecticut.*[15] Connecticut law made it illegal to use or distribute contraceptive devices. This law, along with one prohibiting abortions, basically said that people who engaged in heterosexual conduct had to leave to God (and the state) the question of whether children would be the result of that conduct. Dr. Buston examined a married woman and prescribed a contraceptive device. Mr. Griswold was the director of the Planned Parenthood Clinic where Dr. Buston worked. Both were convicted of violating a statute that made even counseling about contraception a crime.

Justice Douglas wrote the Court's opinion. This must have been very difficult for him. On the one hand he recognized that he occupied the "privacy" chair on the Court, and this law interfered with what must be considered the most private sphere of life. At the same time he was a member of a Court dedicated to the proposition that states should be allowed to regulate commerce, and in one sense all the Connecticut law did was regulate (in the extreme) the sale and distribution of a commercial product, contraceptive devices.

Justice Douglas (whose opinion was joined by Justice Clark) began by declining the invitation to let *Lochner* be his guide. Referring to *Meyer* and *Pierce* as examples of cases where the Court had been guided by the spirit of the First Amendment even though it had not been mentioned in those decisions, he argued that the ideal of a right of free speech included the right to receive knowledge. Because of this he "reaffirmed" those decisions. He concluded that the "First Amendment has a penumbra where privacy is protected from governmental intrusion," and, more generally, that "the Bill of Rights have penumbras, formed by emanations from those guarantees that help give them life and substance."[16] The First Amendment (free speech), the Third Amendment (no quartering of soldiers in homes), the Fourth Amendment (no unreasonable searches and seizures), the Fifth Amendment (no forced self-incrimination), and the Ninth Amendment (declaring that rights not specifically listed in the Bill of Rights are still protected by the Bill of Rights), he argued, all speak to the existence of a general right of privacy. He ended the opinion by saying:

Would we allow the police to search the sacred precincts of marital bedrooms for telltale signs of the use of contraceptives? The very idea is repulsive to the notions of privacy surrounding the marriage relationship.

We deal with a right older than the Bill of Rights—older than our political parties, older than our school system. Marriage is a coming together for better or for worse, hopefully enduring, and intimate to the degree of being sacred. It is an association that promotes a way of life, not causes; a harmony of living, not political faiths; a bilateral loyalty, not commercial or social projects. Yet it is an association for as noble a purpose as any involved in our prior decisions.[17]

Justice Goldberg wrote his own opinion (joined by Chief Justice Warren and Justice Brennan) concurring in the result, but stating his own reasons. He wrote because he did not think the Fourteenth Amendment made all the Bill of Rights applicable to the states but he did think its "concept of liberty protects those personal rights that are fundamental, and is not confined to the specific terms of the Bill of Rights."[18] He then proceeded to speak of the Ninth Amendment as protecting rights to privacy. He quoted James Madison who, upon introducing the Ninth Amendment in Congress, said:

It has been objected also against a bill of rights, that, by enumerating particular exceptions to the grant of power, it would disparage those rights which were not placed in that enumeration; and it might follow by implication, that those rights which were not singled out, were intended to be assigned into the hands of the General Government, and were consequently insecure. This is one of the most plausible arguments I have ever heard urged against the admission of a bill of rights into this system; but, I conceive, that it may be guarded against. I have attempted it, as gentlemen may see by turning to the last clause of the fourth resolution (the Ninth Amendment).[19]

Justice Goldberg went on to say:

to hold that a right so basic and fundamental and so deep-rooted in our society as the right of privacy in marriage may be infringed because that right is not guaranteed in so many words by the first eight amendments to the Constitution is to ignore the Ninth Amendment and to give it no effect whatsoever.[20]

Justice Goldberg then turned to the opinions of the two dissenting justices, Black and Stewart, to ask if they would be willing to allow a state to sterilize everyone who has given birth to two children. He argued that if a law outlawing voluntary birth control by married persons is valid then, by the same reasoning, a law requiring compulsory birth control would also be valid.

Justice Goldberg admitted that states do have a right to be concerned with limiting "extra-marital relations" but this law went far beyond what was needed to achieve that goal. He also stated that his opinion in no way interfered with the state's "proper regulation of sexual promiscuity or misconduct" such as "adultery or homosexuality."[21]

Justice Harlan wrote his own concurring opinion to agree with the result but for a different reason. He felt the process of trying to limit the reach of the Fourteenth Amendment by using the Bill of Rights and its "penumbras" was misguided. He said the Fourteenth Amendment "stands . . . on its own bottom."[22] At the same time he felt it could be used to strike down this statute.

Justice White also wrote his own concurring opinion arguing that the statute deprived people of "liberty." He quoted the decisions in *Meyer* and *Pierce* for the proposition that the Fourteenth Amendment protects the "right to marry, to establish a home and bring up children" and to "direct the upbringing and education of children." Justices Harlan and White based their opinions on substantive due process, not on a "right to privacy."

Justices Black and Stewart dissented. They saw in these other opinions the specter of *Lochner* and the bad old days of substantive due process when justices used the Fourteenth Amendment to enforce their personal prejudices against badly needed social legislation. Justice Black said "I like my privacy as well as the next one, but I am nevertheless compelled to admit that government has a right to invade it unless prohibited by some specific constitutional provision."[23] He felt that Justices Harlan and White would grant to the Court the power to strike down any laws it considers "arbitrary, capricious, unreasonable or oppressive," a power he did not believe the Court had been given by the Fourteenth Amendment.

Justice Stewart agreed with Justice Black. While he found this Connecticut law to be "uncommonly silly" he could not find it to be unconstitutional. Justice Stewart could not find a right to privacy in the Bill of Rights or "any other part of the Constitution."[24]

In *Griswold* five justices were willing to find a constitutional right to privacy, two in the "penumbras" of the Bill of Rights, three in the

Ninth Amendment. Two justices were willing to use traditional substantive due process reasoning to strike down the statute, while two justices did not believe the Court had the power to declare this law unconstitutional. With this decision the right to privacy had finally found its way into the constitution. Justice Brandeis' dissenting opinion in *Olmstead* had come to be a guiding light for the Court.

BEYOND GRISWOLD

In 1967, in *Katz v. United States*, the Supreme Court finally overturned *Olmstead*.[25] The case involved an FBI wiretap on a telephone booth used to intercept conversations about illegal gambling. Justice Stewart (one of the dissenters in *Griswold*) wrote the majority opinion, finding that "privacy" had been violated and an unreasonable search and seizure had resulted.

Justice Harlan wrote a concurring opinion in *Katz* which has since been cited as explaining the basic principle of the decision. He said his "understanding of the rule that has emerged from prior decisions is that there is a twofold requirement, first that a person have exhibited an actual (subjective) expectation of privacy and, second, that the expectation be one that society is prepared to recognize as reasonable."[26] What bothered some people then, and continues to bother them, is that this new "right to privacy" principle used to interpret the Fourth Amendment replaced a fairly objective standard with one that is subjective in two ways. First, does the person claiming privacy protection have a "subjective" expectation of privacy? Second, does the judge in the case feel (subjective) that this expectation is reasonable? Justice Black dissented arguing that the express words of the Fourth Amendment would not uphold this result. He felt it was not the Court's job "to bring the Amendment into harmony with the times."[27]

In 1969 the Court decided *Stanley v. Georgia* where the police, armed with a search warrant, searched Stanley's home looking for evidence of his alleged bookmaking activities.[28] They found obscene films in his bedroom and charged him with violating Georgia's obscenity statute. Justice Marshall wrote for the Court, holding that a statute which outlawed the "mere possession of obscene matter" violated the First Amendment, made applicable to the states by the Fourteenth Amendment. Justice Marshall then cited Justice Brandeis' opinion in *Olmstead* and the opinions in *Griswold* for the proposition that the Constitution protects citizens from unwanted governmental intrusions into their privacy. All nine justices agreed with the result that Stanley would be set free, but not necessarily for the reason stated by Justice Marshall.

After *Griswold*, *Katz*, and *Stanley*, two types of constitutional privacy developed; one tied to the Fourth Amendment and the other tied to the "penumbras" of the First, Third, Fourth, Fifth, and Ninth amendments; with the second looking a great deal like substantive due process except that it protected personal rather than commercial liberty. While the Fourth Amendment will be discussed in more detail in Chapter Nine, it is important to mention a few landmark decisions that followed *Katz* to suggest what happens when one moves from a "trespass" to a "privacy" principle in deciding when searches are unreasonable. It has been a surprise to many legal scholars that not much happens.

This is illustrated by two decisions from the late 1980s. In *Florida v. Riley* the police used a helicopter to fly over Riley's greenhouse, which was located behind his privacy fence in his backyard.[29] The police thought, accurately it turned out, that he might be growing marijuana in the greenhouse. The police could see the marijuana because some of the glass was missing from the greenhouse roof. The Supreme Court felt this helicopter search did not violate the Fourth Amendment, observing that although people might expect to have privacy in their backyards and greenhouses, they must realize that at any moment a helicopter or plane might fly over. It was not "reasonable" to think this would not happen. In *California v. Greenwood* the police searched garbage bags left on the sidewalk for the garbage collectors.[30] They were looking for evidence of drug use. Justice White, writing for the majority, said "It is common knowledge that plastic garbage bags left on or at the side of a public street are readily accessible to animals, children, scavengers, snoops, and other members of the public."[31] In other words, no one has a legitimate expectation of privacy in their garbage once it is placed on the sidewalk.

Both decisions have been criticized extensively in the legal literature. At the same time, would the former principle of "trespass" have prevented either search? Probably not. No one can sue passing helicopters for trespass in this day and time, nor can they sue someone walking down the sidewalk in front of their home. Also, did either case really involve "persons, houses, papers or effects?" While moving to a "privacy" concept in Fourth Amendment cases does protect against wiretaps and electronic eavesdropping, it seems little else has been gained by this change.

To return to the other branch of constitutional privacy law, *Griswold* inspired a great deal of criticism from law professors who could not find any "penumbras" in the Bill of Rights and who feared a return to the days of substantive due process. But Justice Douglas had been a member of the New Deal Court appointed to end those days and he did not want to return to them either. Accordingly, he did not frame his opinion in terms of "substantive due process," but instead tried to put it in the same category with decisions relying on the Bill of Rights as a basis for overturning state statutes. While Douglas could not find "privacy" specifically mentioned in the Bill of Rights, he believed that the Bill of Rights, taken as a whole, clearly justified providing protection for some kinds of privacy beyond those specifically listed therein.

Two years after *Griswold,* in *Loving v. Virginia,* the Court struck down a Virginia law which made interracial marriage illegal.[32] The Court said this law interfered with the right of people to decide whom they would marry. Some might have thought that the Equal Protection Clause alone afforded the basis for voiding this law since it obviously was intended to prevent marriages between blacks and whites, but it was not that simple. The law applied equally in a strange way to both races; it interfered with whites as much as it did blacks. The Court decided the law violated both the Equal Protection Clause and the right to privacy. The Court also used the right to privacy and the Equal Protection Clause to strike down laws which made it difficult for poor people to obtain either a marriage or a divorce in *Zablocki v. Redhail* and *Boddie v. Connecticut.*[33]

In 1972 the Court extended the holding in *Griswold* to unmarried people by ruling in *Eisenstadt v. Baird* that unmarried people were also entitled to receive contraceptives. "If the right to privacy means anything," the Court said, "it is the right of the individual, married or single, to be free from unwarranted governmental intrusion into matters so fundamentally affecting a person as the decision whether to bear or beget a child."[34]

In 1977, in *Carey,* the Court struck down a New York statute that made it a crime to distribute contraceptive devices to anyone under sixteen years of age; for anyone other than a licensed pharmacist to distribute contraceptives; and for anyone, even a licensed pharmacist, to advertise or display contraceptives.[35] The Supreme Court found this statute to be an unconstitutional violation of the right to privacy as established in *Griswold.* In his majority opinion, Justice Brennan spoke of this branch of privacy as a right to make decisions that are fundamentally private. He said:

While the outer limits of this aspect of privacy have not been marked by the Court, it is clear that among the decisions that an individual may make without unjustified government interference are personal decisions "relating to marriage . . . procreation . . . contraception . . . family relationships . . . and child rearing and education."

The decision whether or not to beget or bear a child is at the very heart of this cluster of constitutionally protected choices. That decision holds a particularly important place in the history of the right of privacy, a right first explicitly recognized in an opinion holding unconstitutional a statute prohibiting the use of contraceptives, *Griswold v. Connecticut* . . . and most prominently vindicated in recent years in the contexts of contraception . . . and abortion.[36]

Justice Brennan went on to find that restrictions on the distribution and sale of contraceptives violated this right to privacy.

Chief Justice Burger and Justice Rehnquist dissented. In his dissenting opinion Justice Rehnquist argued that the men who fought and died in the Revolutionary War and the Civil War would be horrified to learn that their efforts went to protect the right of vendors to place contraceptive vending machines in the men's rooms of truck stops. He argued that New York should have the power to deal with the "problem of promiscuous sex and intercourse among unmarried teenagers" by denying to them the use of contraceptives.

It is important to remember that before *Griswold* the Court had often stated its desire to let states "regulate commerce" within their own borders. This was still the case with one exception: contraceptives could not be regulated in a restrictive way.

Did this right to make decisions concerning childbirth also include the right to have an abortion? The Court answered that question in the affirmative with the 1973 decision of *Roe v. Wade*.[37] There, seven justices agreed that constitutional privacy protects to some extent the right of a woman to have an abortion. The difficult question involved the extent to which a state could regulate abortions, an issue with which the Court has struggled ever since. In most cases the decision has been either six to three or five to four overturning the regulations. Finally, in 1989, five justices found a set of abortion regulations they could uphold and several states took that as a sign that the Court was ready to overturn *Roe v. Wade* in its entirety. These states passed very restrictive abortion laws which the Court will ultimately be called upon to review.

Before 1977 the "right to privacy" seemed limited to the right to make decisions concerning childbirth, children and marriage. In 1977 this right was expanded to include decisions related to who people could live with in *Moore v. City of East Cleveland*.[38] This case figured prominently in Justice Thomas's confirmation hearings because he had signed a report that was critical of the decision. However, at the hearings in September 1991, he said he agreed with the decision. The case involved a zoning ordinance that limited occupancy of dwelling units to members of a nuclear family: the "nominal head of a household," his or her spouse, and their parents and children. Justice Powell wrote an opinion joined by Justices Brennan, Marshall and Blackmun. Justice Stevens agreed that the ordinance was unconstitutional and filed his own opinion. Chief Justice Burger dissented along with Justices Stewart, Rehnquist and White.

The case involved Mrs. Inez Moore and her household, which included her son, Dale, his son, Dale Jr., and another of Mrs. Moore's grandsons, John Jr. The city said the presence of John Jr. violated the ordinance. Justice Powell said the city had tried to "regulate the occupancy of its housing by slicing deeply into the family itself," and believed this was a violation of the rights protected by *Meyer, Griswold,* and *Loving.* He did not speak of a "right to privacy," however, but instead spoke of a "respect for the teachings of history" and "the basic values that underlie our society."[39]

Justice Stevens, the fifth vote needed to declare the ordinance unconstitutional, filed his own opinion. To him the issue was not one of "privacy" but of "property," specifically: was the ordinance a reasonable restriction on the way Mrs. Moore could use her private property? He concluded that it was not. He could find no "precedent" or "justification" for an ordinance that excluded "any of an owner's relatives from the group of persons who may occupy his residence on a permanent basis."[40]

Chief Justice Burger dissented, along with Justices Stewart, Rehnquist and White. Justice Stewart's dissent spoke to the right to privacy issue raised in this case and argued that the interest Mrs. Moore "may have in permanently sharing a single kitchen and a suite of contiguous rooms with some of her relatives simply does not rise" to the level of constitutional privacy.[41]

In 1986 the Court rejected the use of the right to privacy in a case involving private consensual sex. The decision in *Bowers v. Hardwick,* simply put, was that the right to privacy does not protect homosexuals from prosecution for violating state sodomy laws.[42] This decision raised a number of questions that as yet have not been answered. Does the right to privacy protect the right of heterosexuals to engage in sodomy? Does it protect the right of heterosexuals to have normal heterosexual sex outside of marriage (fornicate)?

In 1989 the Court handed down its first drug testing decisions in the cases of *Skinner v. Railway Labor Executives' Ass'n.* and *National Treasury Employees Union v. Von Raab.*[43] *Skinner* involved federal rules requiring railroads to test their workers' blood and urine after an accident. In a seven to two decision the Court ruled that the tests were a search required by government and were therefore covered by the Fourth Amendment; at the same time, it decided that neither "probable cause" nor a search warrant was required in these cases. The Court "balanced" the privacy interests of the railroad employees, which it felt were minimal, against the government interest in railroad safety, which it felt was very great, and concluded that not only was probable cause not required, but the company and the government did not even need "individual suspicion" of drug impairment to conduct the tests. In *Von*

Raab, by a vote of five to four, the Court also upheld the drug testing of Customs Service employees who were likely to come into contact with drugs in the course of their employment. What is unique about these decisions is that for the first time the Court allowed government searches of "persons" without any reason to suspect that the particular individual had done anything wrong. Thus, in a very real sense, the balancing test led to the abandonment of what had been considered the fundamental principle of the Fourth Amendment for almost two centuries: the principle that people had a right to be free in their "persons, houses, papers, and effects" unless the government or its agents had some "reason" to believe a search would turn up evidence of wrongdoing.

The right to privacy can be divided into three major areas: the right to engage in sex and marriage, the right to have an abortion and the right to be free from searches that invade privacy. The next three chapters will discuss each area of constitutional privacy in more detail.

NOTES

1. 277 U.S. 438 (1928).
2. *Id.* at 478.
3. Warren and Brandeis, *The Right to Privacy,* 4 Harv. L. Rev. 193, 220 (1890).
4. 285 U.S. 262 (1932).
5. 83 U.S. 36 (1873).
6. 285 U.S. 262, 311 (1932).
7. 262 U.S. 390 (1923).
8. *Id.* at 401.
9. *Id.* at 399.
10. 268 U.S. 510 (1925).
11. Panama Refining Co. v. Ryan, 193 U.S. 430 (1935); Humphrey's Executor v. United States, 295 U.S. 602 (1935); Louisville Bank v. Radford, 1295 U.S. 555 (1935); Schechter Poultry Co. v. United States, 295 U.S. 528 (1935).
12. West Coast Hotel Co. v. Parrish, 300 U.S. 379 (1937).
13. United States v. Carolene Products Co., 304 U.S. 144 (1938).
14. Lincoln Fed. Labor Union v. Northwestern Iron & Metal Co., 335 U.S. 525, 536 (1949); Ferguson v. Skrupa, 372 U.S. 726, 731–2 (1963) quoting Williamson v. Lee Optical Co., 348 U.S. 483, 488 (1955).
15. 381 U.S. 479 (1965).
16. *Id.* at 483–4.
17. *Id.* at 485–6.
18. *Id.* at 486.
19. *Id.* at 489–90.
20. *Id.* at 491.
21. *Id.* at 498–9.
22. *Id.* at 500.

23. *Id.* at 510.
24. *Id.* at 530.
25. 389 U.S. 347 (1967).
26. *Id.* at 361.
27. *Id.* at 364.
28. 394 U.S. 557 (1969).
29. 109 S. Ct. 693 (1989).
30. 108 S. Ct. 1625 (1988).
31. *Id.* at 1628–9.
32. 388 U.S. 1 (1967).
33. 434 U.S. 374 (1978); 401 U.S. 371 (1971).
34. 405 U.S. 438 (1972).
35. Carey v. Population Servs. Int'l, 431 U.S. 678 (1977).
36. *Id.* at 684–5.
37. 410 U.S. 113 (1973).
38. 431 U.S. 494 (1977).
39. *Id.* at 502–3.
40. *Id.* at 520.
41. *Id.* at 537.
42. 106 S. Ct. 2841 (1986).
43. 109 S. Ct. 1402 (1989); 109 S. Ct. 1384 (1989).

7

Sex and Marriage

One major theme of the constitutional right to privacy is the right to make fundamental decisions involving sex, childbirth and marriage without governmental interference. However, these decisions invoke more than the right to privacy; they bear on the question of the separation of church and state in the United States. Before turning to the right to privacy, the general issue of freedom of religion must be discussed.

SEPARATION OF CHURCH AND STATE

The First Amendment to the U.S. Constitution prohibits the "establishment" of religion and interference with the "free exercise thereof." Similar provisions appear in many of the state constitutions. These provisions have proved to be among the most difficult for the U.S. and state supreme courts to interpret. Many of the U.S. Supreme Court decisions in this area have been five to four and at least two justices have changed their minds about their past opinions in this area while still on the Court (Douglas and Brennan).

The U.S. Supreme Court's first "free exercise" of religion case was not difficult: it was a unanimous decision in the 1878 case of *Reynolds v. United States* that involved the appeal of a conviction for bigamy from the Utah territory.[1] The defendant argued that his Mormon religion required him to have more than one wife. No justice felt this justified breaking the criminal law. They ruled that the "free exercise" clause protected "beliefs," not "overt acts." They pointed out that polygamy had always been "odious" to European society; therefore, it could not have been the intent of the authors of the First Amendment to prevent the outlawing of such behavior. Besides, if the Court held that people could violate some criminal laws simply because their religion allowed it, an entirely "new element" would be introduced into the criminal law. There would be one law for the religious and another for the nonreligious. The justices' imaginations told them that such a concept could only lead to disaster for the legal system at some point in the future.

A decade later the Court decided (six to three) that the federal government's confiscation of most of the Mormon church's property also did not violate the First Amendment.[2] The federal government had withdrawn the church's charter and therefore the land, which could not be owned by a nonexistent entity, reverted to the federal government. This confiscation did not apply to the church buildings. While this was a technically correct interpretation of ancient property law, the Court did not stop there. It called the Mormon church a "blot on our civilization" and said polygamy was "a return to barbarism."

There was another aspect to the case, however. The Mormon church had attempted to set up what might be called a theocratic state in Utah where the land and businesses would be owned by the church and the church and state would be united. If the Supreme Court's role is one of balancing diversity against the need for some kind of basic social unity, then this clearly was beyond the pale. Polygamy was in one sense the "excuse" for breaking up this attempt at extreme "social experimentation."

In 1890 the Court again upheld a conviction for polygamy pointing out that polygamy was "pernicious to the best interest of society."[3] The Court ruled that the "free exercise" clause protected belief, not "form of worship." To rule otherwise would be to license both "free love" and "human sacrifice." Since there were religious communes in the United States at the time that advocated free love this was not just a question of imagination. In 1891 the Court upheld a law passed by the Utah territorial legislature that allowed illegitimate children to inherit property from their fathers. The Court felt this was not merely a law in support of polygamy.[4]

In 1896 the Court took up the question of statutes that made Sunday a special day under the law. The case involved a Georgia law that made it illegal for freight trains to travel through the state on Sunday. The Court said this was a "proper use of the police power" that did not interfere with interstate commerce.[5] In 1961 the Court upheld laws that required most businesses to close on Sunday, finding them to be simply laws controlling commercial enterprise.[6] The three dissenters argued that this put a special burden on people whose religion did not allow them to work on Saturday and that the "religious" nature of Sunday closing laws could not be denied.

In the 1940s the Court faced a series of cases involving Jehovah's Witnesses that moved it down the road toward allowing the right of "free exercise" to include "action" as well as "belief." In 1943 the Court held (eight to one) that a public school could not force the children of Jehovah's Witnesses to say the pledge of allegiance to the flag. The Court felt this was a kind of "forced communication" and "forced belief" that the state should not be allowed to require. What is particularly interesting is that the Court had come to the opposite conclusion in 1940 and had to overturn that decision to allow these children the privilege of refusing to salute the flag.[7] The Court came to a similar conclusion in 1961 when it overturned a state law that required public officials to take an oath declaring their belief in God. The Court found this to be a government-enforced profession of belief and beyond the power of the state.[8]

In the 1940 case of *Cantwell v. Connecticut*, a Jehovah's Witness was convicted of violating a law prohibiting the solicitation of money for religious purposes, except from members of one's own religion, without a license. The Court ruled the state could not single out religious solicitation in this way.[9] In 1942 a Jehovah's Witness had been convicted of using offensive words when he called someone "a God damned racketeer;" the Court upheld the conviction.[10] In 1943 the Court overturned the conviction of Jehovah's Witnesses charged with "ringing door bells to pass out leaflets" and selling door to door without paying the license fee.[11] The Court said the state could impose a normal sales tax or income tax on the religious door to door sellers, but not a flat tax. In 1946 a Jehovah's Witness was convicted of trespass when he refused to stop passing out religious literature on the sidewalk of a company-owned town. The Court said the town was not the equivalent of a private home and the state could not prevent this kind of activity.[12]

With these Jehovah's Witnesses decisions the Court had moved away from the bright line of not allowing any "religious based" exceptions to criminal prosecution. The question then became one of finding a new place to "draw the line." That proved to be very difficult.

In 1946 the Court divided five to four over a case involving a Mormon who practiced polygamy.[13] He transported his wives across a state line for the purpose of cohabitation and was convicted of violating the Mann Act, which makes it a federal crime to "transport a woman or girl across state lines for an immoral purpose." Justice Douglas, writing for the majority, cited the *Reynolds* decision for the proposition that "polygamy has always been odious" to Europeans and is therefore clearly "immoral." The conviction stood. Justice Murphy in his dissent pointed out that polygamy was historically the most common form of marriage and that it is a religious institution that should not be considered "immoral." It is important to remember that this was not a constitutional case; the question was only what the word "immoral purpose" meant in the Mann Act. The four dissenters felt that it could not mean the transportation of "wives," even though having more than one wife was illegal.

During the post-World War II decades the Court tried to find the proper line between church and state, but many decisions were five to four with little agreement on where the line should be drawn. In 1947 in *Everson v. Bd. of Ed.* five justices, including Justice Douglas, felt it was permissible for the state to pay the cost of transporting students to Catholic school.[14] Later Justice Douglas regretted this decision and wished he had "defended the bright line" in this area of support for religious education.[15] In 1971 the Court ruled, five to four, that federal funds could be used to build buildings on the campus of a religious college.[16]

In 1972 the Court decided *Wisconsin v. Yoder.*[17] In that case Amish parents had been found guilty of violating Wisconsin's compulsory education law. The Amish parents did not want their children to attend school after the eighth grade because attendance at high school would expose the children to "worldly influence." This was a very different case from *Pierce v. Society of Sisters*, which upheld the right of all parents to send their children to private school (religious or secular) if the school met minimum state requirements.[18]

The *Yoder* case, put in the harshest terms, involved the right of religious parents to keep their children ignorant in a society where education is the main passport to economic advancement and full participation in the larger political and social community. While the right to privacy can logically be extended to include the parental right to send children to private school, it cannot embrace the right to keep children out of school altogether. *Yoder*, therefore, had to be decided on the basis of religious freedom. In writing the majority opinion, Chief Justice Burger employed a classic Burger-era balancing test. He said the extent to which this law burdened the "free exercise" of religion must be balanced against the interests of the state. He found that the Amish religion required a particular way of life different from modern society, one mandated by an organized religion of long standing. He said this was not an area where the Court was prepared to allow "every person to make his own standards on matters of conduct in which society as a whole has important interests."[19] In other words, only the members of organized religious sects would be protected by this decision. This was a significant departure from past Supreme Court decisions which had carefully avoided tying religious freedom to membership in an "organized" religious sect. He found that in this case the burden on religious freedom was great, and the interest of the state in seeing children educated beyond the eighth grade was small. All seven justices agreed with this decision. Justices Powell and Rehnquist did not participate in the decision.

In 1990 the Rehnquist Court decided the case of *Employment Division v. Smith*.[20] The case involved employees discharged for using peyote. They argued their peyote use was required by their religion and that peyote use could not, therefore, be found to be misconduct under the unemployment statute. The Oregon Supreme Court determined that peyote use did violate the state criminal drug statute, but that this statute, as applied to the religious use of drugs, was an unconstitutional violation of the "free exercise" clause of the First Amendment. The U.S. Supreme Court overturned this decision, ruling that the free exercise clause does not protect the use of drugs for religious purposes if such use is otherwise illegal. Justice Scalia wrote for the majority. He pointed out that most Supreme Court decisions in this area protected the right to hold a belief and tell others about it, not the right to engage in conduct that is otherwise illegal. Of course that was clearly not the case in *Yoder*, but Justice Scalia argued that *Yoder* was really protecting "the interests of parenthood," not the right to freely exercise religion.[21] *Yoder* had done no such thing, but it was being reinterpreted by a majority of the Court.

The peyote smokers argued that the Court should engage in the kind of balancing test used in *Yoder*. The Court refused to do that for obvious reasons. How many "victim-less crimes" would survive such a test? If no one is harmed outside those engaging in the behavior, why should people not be allowed to engage in it if their religion requires? Justice Scalia said:

to make an individual's obligation to obey such a law contingent upon the law's coincidence with his religious beliefs, except where the State's interest is "compelling"—permitting him, by virtue of his beliefs, "to become a law unto himself," . . . contradicts both constitutional tradition and common sense.[22]

The peyote smokers argued that only "conduct central to the individual's religion" would be protected but Justice Scalia could just imagine the problems that would bring to the Courts. He asked:

What principle of law or logic can be brought to bear to contradict a believer's assertion that a particular act is "central" to his personal faith? . . . Repeatedly and in many different contexts, we have warned that courts must not presume to determine the place of a particular belief in a religion or the plausibility of a religious claim.[23]

In a very real sense, although his name was never mentioned, Justice Scalia imagined that the world of John Stuart Mill would be introduced through the back door of protecting religious freedom. He could have quoted Justice Holmes' dissent in *Lochner* for the proposition that the Fourteenth Amendment did not enact the philosophy of John Stuart Mill any more than it enacted the philosophy of Herbert Spencer.[24]

Employment Division v. Smith was correctly decided. A contrary result would indeed have opened a Pandora's box for the courts. At the same time, there are behaviors and personal decisions that most Americans feel should be beyond the power of government to control. That is why the Court needs the concept of the "right to privacy." To save the result in *Yoder* Justice Scalia had to reinterpret it as a right to privacy case protecting the "interests of parenthood." If there are behaviors and decisions that should be beyond the power of the state to control, they should be available to everyone, not just to members of particular religious sects.

In *Employment Division v. Smith,* Justice Scalia pointed out that several states, including Arizona, Colorado, and New Mexico, have an exception in their drug laws for the religious use of peyote. He referred to those laws by way of noting that the state may grant religious exemptions if it so desires. But are these exemptions not a kind of "establishment of religion" prohibited by the First Amendment? Would people not be encouraged to join religious sects that were given these exemptions? May a state outlaw sodomy "except for religious purposes?" Thousands of years ago in the Middle East men went to the Temple prostitutes to make a special offering to the Gods. Could states permit prostitution if done for religious purposes? Could Utah make polygamy legal if engaged in because of the command of a religion? Would every victimless crime be open to this kind of exemption, and would this not run afoul of the equal protection clause of the Fourteenth Amendment?

Some have argued that the religious rights protected by the First Amendment amount to the right to behave and worship the way a mainstream Protestant behaves and worships. If the same is true of the right of privacy then it does not protect much. On the other hand, it could be argued that the right of privacy is a genuine attempt on the part of the Court to protect intimate decisions and behaviors from governmental control in a way that does not require venturing into the thicket of religious freedom.

Another area of ancient legal practice that bears on this discussion and has been the subject of several Supreme Court decisions concerns what a state may do to illegitimate children.

ILLEGITIMATE CHILDREN

During the twentieth century, laws that punished wives who committed adultery but not husbands were criticized. If one examines the ancient law codes, however, this arrangement seems more understandable. The legally sanctioned "deal" between a husband and wife from the beginning of written Indo-European history through the nineteenth century was that the wife would be faithful and bear only the husband's children and the husband would in turn leave all his property to her children alone. It has been common in many Indo-European societies over the millennia for men to cohabit with more than one woman, but it has never been "legal" to have more than one wife. At the end of the nineteenth century it was made clear to the Mormons that they would have to give up their belief in polygamy if Utah was to become a state. The Mormons complied.

The U.S. Supreme Court became involved in this issue of "legitimacy" in 1968 with *Levy v. Louisiana*.[25] Louise Levy gave birth to five illegitimate children, who all lived with her as she worked as a domestic servant to support them. She took them to church on Sunday and paid to have them attend parochial school. When she died, the administrator of her estate tried to bring suit in Louisiana on behalf of the five children against the people he believed had caused her death. A Louisiana statute allowed children to sue for the wrongful death of a parent. The Louisiana courts ruled that the word "child" in the statute did not include an illegitimate child and said their decision was based on "morals" and the "general welfare" because it would discourage bringing illegitimate children into the world.

Justice Douglas, in the majority opinion, said he could not see how the legitimacy of the children had any bearing on the wrong that had been done to them. He ruled that the law discriminated against the children in violation of the Equal Protection Clause of the Fourteenth Amendment.

Justice Harlan dissented, joined by Justices Black and Stewart. He argued that a state has the right to require people to go through the formalities of marriage or legal legitimation before certain rights dependent on family relations are accorded to them. He pointed out that wives have many rights which "paramours" do not, and concluded that the line drawn by Louisiana was reasonable in this case.

Three years later, in *Labine v. Vincent*, the Court upheld Louisiana's law concerning intestate succession.[26] Louisiana, like most states, had a statute which spelled out which relatives would inherit property if someone died without a will. On March 15, 1962, a baby girl, Rita Vincent, was born to Lou Bertha Patterson. On May 10, 1962, Lou Bertha Patterson and Ezra Vincent executed before a notary a state form which acknowledged that Ezra was the "natural father" of Rita Vincent. Under Louisiana law this entitled Rita to claim child support but not to inherit his property unless he wrote a will.

Ezra Vincent died without a will in 1968. The Louisiana statute provided that an illegitimate child could inherit in this situation only if there were no other relatives, and Ezra did have other relatives. Justice Black, writing for the majority of the Court, declined to extend the holding in *Levy* to this case. He argued that in *Levy* the state had created an "insurmountable barrier" over which illegitimate children could not climb.[27] In this case, in contrast, all Ezra Vincent had to do was write a will.

Labine was five to four against illegitimate children, whereas *Levy* had been six to three in their favor. In the three intervening years Chief Justice Warren had been replaced by Chief Justice Burger and Justice Fortas had been replaced by Justice Blackmun. Justice Brennan wrote a scathing dissent joined by Justices Douglas, White, and Marshall. He argued that this could not "even pretend to be a principled decision."[28] He traced the evolution of Louisiana's law from Roman and French law and pointed out how extensively it regulated family relations. Under Louisiana law Ezra Vincent could not have disinherited a legitimate child in a will, for example, even if he had wanted to. Justice Brennan then pointed out that the "insurmountable barrier" argument did not hold up. Mrs. Levy could have formally acknowledged her children in the *Levy* case just as Ezra Vincent had done in this case. It was her failure to do so that caused the problem. In this case Ezra had filed the necessary form, but he failed to write a will so his child was out of luck. Justice Brennan then pointed to what for him was the fundamental problem, that Louisiana punished innocent children for the sins of their parents. He ended his decision by saying:

In my judgment, only a moral prejudice, prevalent in 1825 when the Louisiana statutes under consideration were adopted, can support Louisiana's discrimination against illegitimate children. Since I can find no rational basis to justify the distinction Louisiana creates between an acknowledged illegitimate child and a legitimate one, that discrimination is clearly invidious . . . I think the Supreme Court of North Dakota stated the correct principle in invalidating an analogous discrimination in that State's inheritance laws: "This statute, which punishes innocent children for their parents' transgressions, has no place in our system of government, which has as one of its basic tenets equal protection for all."[29]

The next year, in *Weber v. Aetna Cas. & Sur. Co.*, the Court struck down a Louisiana law which made it impossible for an illegitimate child to receive payments under worker's compensation insurance.[30] Between *Labine* and *Weber* Justices Black and Harlan had been replaced by Justices Powell and Rehnquist. All the justices except Justice Rehnquist agreed with the conclusion that *Levy*, not *Labine*, controlled this case. Illegitimate children could not be kept from receiving death benefits under the worker's compensation law. Justice Powell wrote the majority decision arguing that *Labine* was based on the "traditional deference" the Court gives to the state's power to regulate the disposition of property at death. He went on to say:

The status of illegitimacy has expressed through the ages society's condemnation of irresponsible liaisons beyond the bonds of marriage. But visiting this condemnation on the head of an infant is illogical and unjust. Moreover, imposing disabilities on the illegitimate child is contrary to the basic concept of our system that legal burdens should bear some relationship to individual responsibility or wrongdoing. Obviously, no child is responsible for his birth and penalizing the illegitimate child is an ineffectual—as well as an unjust—way of deterring the parent.[31]

Of course in the Hittite, Greek, and Roman eras illegitimacy was not a "condemnation of irresponsible liaisons." It was simply a way of guaranteeing that the legal wife got her share of the marriage bargain: faithfulness in exchange for property and status for her children alone.

In 1973 the Court struck down two more statutes that discriminated against illegitimate children. *Gomez v. Perez* involved a Texas law that granted "legitimate children a judicially enforceable right to support from their natural fathers and at the same time denied that right to illegitimate children."[32] In *New Jersey Welfare Rights Org. v. Cahill* the Court decided that New Jersey could not deny welfare benefits to children simply because they were illegitimate.[33] Only Justice Rehnquist dissented in that case.

In 1976, however, the Court upheld the federal Social Security statute which required illegitimate children to prove both that the deceased wage earner was in fact a parent and that the child was living with or being supported by that parent at the time of death.[34] Under that statute legitimate children were presumed to be dependent at the time of death while illegitimate children were not. A majority of the Court did not find this to be unreasonable given the probability that legitimate children are in fact dependent on their parents for support.

These decisions are typical of the rulings made during the Burger era. The Court could have left the law as it had been for thousands of years, and allowed states and the federal government to discriminate against illegitimate children. A majority of the Court, however, felt that to do so would violate the principle of Equal Protection embodied in the Fourteenth Amendment. At the same time the Court was not willing to simply say that from then on, for all purposes, illegitimate children (assuming they could prove their parentage) had to be treated just like legitimate children.

GRISWOLD

The *Griswold* decision, discussed at length in the last chapter, involved a doctor and a clinic administrator convicted of giving advice about contraception to a married woman. Five justices found this to be in violation of a constitutionally protected right to privacy. Two felt it violated accepted principles of "substantive due process" and two thought the law should not have been overturned.

Legal commentators at the time speculated on just how far the new right to privacy might go.[35] The answer, as the overview in the last chapter indicates, is that the right has mainly affected three areas: sex and marriage, abortion and the right to die, and search and seizure. The *Bowers v. Hardwick* decision is a key factor in deciding how extensive the "right to sex and marriage" is. It therefore makes sense to ask what the right to sex and marriage included before *Bowers*, what *Bowers* stands for, and what the right to sex and marriage may include after *Bowers*.

BEFORE BOWERS

After *Griswold* the U.S. Supreme Court decided that the right to privacy protects the right to marry people of a different race and the right of poor people to marry and divorce even if they cannot afford the required fee.[36] In 1972 in *Eisenstadt v. Baird*, the Court decided that single people have the same right to receive contraceptives as married people.[37] In 1977 the Court decided that the right to privacy includes the right to live with relatives who are not part of the nuclear family.[38] The major question at the end of the 1970s was: Does the right to privacy include the right to have sex, and if so what kind of sex? Legal commentators and state supreme court judges provided several different answers.

Two commentators who argued that these decisions did not necessarily lead to the "right to have sex" were Bruce Hafen and Thomas Grey. Bruce Hafen pointed out that the right to "prevent" conception does not necessarily include the right to "cause" conception. He referred to a decision by Justice Brennan where he spoke specifically about the "individual's right to decide to prevent conception."[39] Thomas Grey argued that these post-*Griswold* sex and marriage cases should be seen as supporting the right to have and control a family, not the right to have sex. They could be viewed not as a great liberal assault on laws controlling sex and marriage, but as a great conservative reaction in favor of "traditional institutions."[40]

On the other hand a number of judges concluded that this line of cases did lead inevitably to the right to have sex; at least normal, heterosexual sex, and possibly the right to commit sodomy, at least between consenting adults. *Griswold* and *Eisenstadt* read together protect the right of everyone, single or married, to receive contraceptives. But what good is a contraceptive if people cannot do anything with it? While these decisions could be limited to the right to "prevent" childbirth, surely if the point of all this is to protect traditional values of family, then the right to "cause" childbirth must also be protected.

Following this logic the Supreme Court of New Jersey held the New Jersey fornication law unconstitutional, at least as it applied to "consensual, noncommercial, heterosexual activity between adults."[41] In *State v. Saunders,* two men were charged with raping two women. The men stated that the women had consented to exchange sex for marijuana cigarettes. The jury acquitted the two men of rape but found them guilty of fornication. The New Jersey Supreme Court, citing *Griswold* and other U.S. Supreme Court decisions, found this statute unconstitutional because it infringed on the right of privacy protected by the U.S. Constitution. The court said it would be "anomalous" to hold that the right to privacy protects the right to receive contraceptives but not the right to have sex. The court relied particularly on *Eisenstadt v. Baird* for the proposition that the right to privacy protects both unmarried and married individuals. The court also found this statute violated the right to privacy protected by the New Jersey Constitution. The court examined the reasons put forward by the state to justify the statute— prevention of venereal disease, prevention of illegitimate childbirth, and protection of morality—but ruled that the right of privacy outweighs these considerations.

Before *Bowers* several state courts had concluded, based on *Griswold* and *Eisenstadt,* that state anti-sodomy statutes are unconstitutional, at least as applied to "consenting adults of the opposite sex." In the 1976 case of *State v. Pilcher* the Iowa Supreme Court held a sodomy statute unconstitutional to the extent it made "consensual sodomitical practices" a crime when performed "in private by adult persons of the opposite sex" even if the people in question were not married.[42]

In the 1986 case of *Post v. State* the Oklahoma Supreme Criminal Court came to the same conclusion.[43] It held that attempts to criminalize "anal sodomy and fellatio" when performed in private by consenting adults of the opposite sex violated the right to privacy. The U.S. Supreme Court refused to review this decision.

Also, before *Bowers* several courts had declared state sodomy laws unconstitutional whether they were applied to heterosexuals or homosexuals. In the 1980 case of *People v. Onofre*, the highest court of New York declared New York's sodomy law unconstitutional.[44] Several cases were before the court for simultaneous review: one involved males convicted of performing anal sodomy while the others involved males and females convicted of performing oral sex. The New York consensual sodomy law made all these acts illegal. The New York Attorney General argued that the *Griswold* line of cases only protected "marital intimacy" and "procreative choice," but the New York Court relied on *Eisenstadt v. Baird, Stanley*, and Justice Brandeis' dissent in *Olmstead* to reject this argument. The New York Court's decision is worth quoting at length:

In light of these decisions, protecting under the cloak of the right of privacy individual decisions as to indulgence in acts of sexual intimacy by unmarried persons and as to satisfaction of sexual desires by resort to material condemned as obscene by community standards when done in a cloistered setting, no rational basis appears for excluding from the same protection decisions—such as those made by defendants before us—to seek sexual gratification from what at least once was commonly regarded as "deviant" conduct, so long as the decisions are voluntarily made by adults in a noncommercial, private setting. Nor is any such basis supplied by the claims advanced by the prosecution—that a prohibition against consensual sodomy will prevent physical harm which might otherwise befall the participants, will uphold public morality and will protect the institution of marriage. Commendable though these objectives clearly are, there is nothing on which to base a conclusion that they are achieved by section 130.38 of the Penal Law. . . .

In sum, there has been no showing of any threat, either to participants or the public in general, in consequence of the voluntary engagement by adults in private, discreet, sodomous conduct. Absent is the factor of commercialization with the attendant evils commonly attached to the retailing of sexual pleasures; absent the elements of force or of involvement of minors which might constitute compulsion of unwilling participants or of those too young to make an informed choice, and absent too intrusion on the sensibilities of members of the public, many of whom would be offended by being exposed to the intimacies of others. Personal feelings of distaste for the conduct sought to be proscribed by section 130.38 of the Penal Law and even disapproval by a majority of the populace, if that disapproval were to be assumed, may not substitute for the required demonstration of a valid basis for intrusion by the State in an area of important personal decision protected under the right of privacy drawn from the United States Constitution—areas, the number and definition of which have steadily grown but, as the Supreme Court has observed, the outer limits of which it has not yet marked.[45]

The Court then distinguished this decision from those allowing the legislature to prohibit marijuana possession by observing that the legislature could at least make a case that marijuana is a "dangerous substance" that must be controlled. With these cases the highest court in New York changed the nineteenth-century definition of the "police power" of state governments. While the state could control people's behavior to protect their "health and safety," it could no longer impose the "morals" of the majority on everyone else. The U.S. Supreme Court refused to review this decision.

Also in 1980 the Supreme Court of Pennsylvania came to a similar conclusion in *Commonwealth v. Bonadio.*[46] In that case the defendants were males and females arrested in an adult pornographic theater on charges of deviate sexual intercourse. The statute defined deviate sexual intercourse as "sexual intercourse per os or per anus between human beings who are not husband and wife, and any form of sexual intercourse with an animal." The court ruled that to be a valid exercise of the police power a statute must: (1) serve a purpose beneficial to the general public, not one segment of society, (2) be reasonably necessary to the accomplishment of that purpose and (3) not be unduly oppressive to individuals. The court decided that, while it is legitimate to protect the public from offensive public displays and minors or animals from abuse, none of these goals were protected by this statute. It had only one purpose, to "regulate the private conduct of consenting adults," and the court found this to be beyond the power of the state as delegated by the people.

BOWERS

In 1986 the U.S. Supreme Court decided *Bowers v. Hardwick.*[47] In August 1982 Hardwick was charged with violating Georgia's sodomy law alleging that he had committed an act of sodomy with another adult male in his own bedroom. The District Attorney decided to drop the charges. Hardwick then sued in federal court challenging the constitutionality of the statute, arguing that, as a practicing homosexual, he was in imminent danger of arrest.

The legend of *Bowers* is that five justices were ready to find that the right to privacy includes the right to engage in homosexual sodomy in the privacy of one's own bedroom. Then Justice White passed around his dissenting opinion and Justice Powell changed his mind. Justice White's dissent became the majority opinion and the old majority opinion became a dissent. Since such activity is secret it will never be known for sure if this is what happened. Justice Powell did vote with Justice White and several years later it was reported that he wished he had voted the other way. The only way to fully understand this decision is to begin by quoting from Justice White's majority decision:

This case does not require a judgment on whether laws against sodomy between consenting adults in general, or between homosexuals in particular, are wise or desirable. It raises no question about the right or propriety of state legislative decisions to repeal their laws that criminalize homosexual sodomy, or of state-court decisions invalidating those laws on state constitutional grounds. The issue presented is whether the Federal Constitution confers a fundamental right upon homosexuals to engage in sodomy and hence invalidates the laws of the many States that still make such conduct illegal and have done so for a very long time. The case also calls for some judgment about the limits of the Court's role in carrying out its constitutional mandate.

We first register our disagreement with the Court of Appeals and with respondent that the Court's prior cases have construed the Constitution to confer a right of privacy that extends to homosexual sodomy and for all intents and purposes have decided this case. The reach of this line of cases was sketched in *Carey v. Population Services International* . . . *Pierce v. Society of Sisters* . . . and *Meyer v. Nebraska* . . . were described as dealing with child rearing and education; *Prince v. Massachusetts* . . . with family relationships; *Skinner v. Oklahoma ex rel. Williamson* . . . with procreation; *Loving v. Virginia* . . . with marriage; *Griswold v. Connecticut* . . . and *Eisenstadt v. Baird* . . . with contraception; and *Roe v. Wade* . . . with abortion. The latter three cases were interpreted as construing the Due Process Clause of the Fourteenth Amendment to confer a fundamental individual right to decide whether or not to beget or bear a child.[48]

Justice White went on to say that these cases involved "family, marriage or procreation" and could not be used to find a "fundamental right to engage in homosexual sodomy." After asserting that homosexual sodomy could be left out of the right to privacy without doing severe damage to the concept, Justice White turned to the general principles that have been used to support efforts at substantive due process decision-making since the demise of *Lochner*. He quoted from *Palco v. Connecticut* decided in 1937 for the proposition that the Fourteenth Amendment protects only "fundamental liberties that are implicit in the concept of ordered liberty."[49] He quoted from Justice Powell's opinion in *Moore v. East Cleveland* to the effect that the Fourteenth Amendment protects only "liberties . . . deeply rooted in this Nation's history and tradition."[50] He then pointed out that proscriptions against homosexual sodomy have ancient roots: It was a crime under British law and in all thirteen states when the Bill of Rights was ratified.

It is important to remember that Justice White, to get and hold a majority of the Court, had to speak in very limited terms. He stated the question narrowly: Does the U.S. Constitution provide for the right of "homosexuals" to engage in "sodomy?" He was not talking about heterosexuals and he was not talking about sex in any general sense. The very real question then becomes: what does the right to privacy protect in this area after *Bowers*?

AFTER BOWERS

Justice Stevens in his dissent in *Bowers* argued that the only way to make sense out of the privacy cases is to deem "private" the right of consenting adult homosexuals to engage in sodomy in their own bedrooms. After *Bowers* several commentators have gone to great lengths to argue that the right to privacy protects the right of heterosexuals to engage in the kind of sex that might lead to childbirth, as well as sodomy.[51] First they point out that after the Court decided *Bowers* it refused to review *Post v. State*, where the Oklahoma court voided a sodomy statute that prohibited sodomy between consenting adult heterosexuals.[52] If the Court had wanted to put sodomy outside the ambit of privacy, it could have done so by overturning that Oklahoma decision.

Another reason for arguing that *Bowers* only leaves homosexuals out of the right to privacy is that the statute in *Bowers* was a general one prohibiting all kinds of sodomy. While the particular individuals in the case were homosexuals, the entire statute was under review by the Court. Yet Justice White framed the question narrowly: Does the "Federal Constitution" confer a "fundamental right upon homosexuals to engage in sodomy?" Chief Justice Burger in his concurring opinion paraphrased Blackstone when he described homosexual sodomy as "the 'infamous crime against nature' . . . an offense of 'deeper malignity' than rape, a heinous act 'the very mention of which is a disgrace to human nature,' and 'a crime not fit to be named.' "[53] Even the Georgia attorney general in arguing in support of the statute said it would be unconstitutional to enforce it against married couples.[54] It must be stressed that the U.S. Supreme Court has never held that the Equal Protection Clause of the Fourteenth Amendment protects homosexuals from any kind of discrimination.

What about the right of heterosexuals, married and unmarried, to have normal heterosexual sex? *Eisenstadt v. Baird* established that both married and unmarried individuals have a right to buy contraceptives. If they have a right to buy contraceptives, it follows that they must have a right to use them. *Stanley v. Georgia* is instructive because it stood for the proposition that while a state may ban the sale of obscene material, it may not punish people for viewing such material in the privacy of their own home.[55] With *Griswold* and *Eisenstadt* the Court went a step further and protected the right to buy contraceptives. Surely if individuals, "married and unmarried," can buy contraceptives they have the right to use them in their own home without governmental interference. That means, at a minimum, the right of heterosexuals to use contraceptives for their original purpose, to prevent childbirth resulting from normal heterosexual sex.

A similar conclusion can be drawn from Justice White's opinion in

Bowers. The opinion talks about the right to privacy protecting "family relationships," "procreation," "marriage," "contraception," and "abortion." While homosexual sodomy is not covered by these terms, heterosexual intercourse is implicated in all of them. This would suggest that fornication statutes violate privacy rights even in view of *Bowers*.

In *Bowers* the Court stressed ancient prohibitions against homosexual sodomy. The same argument, however, cannot be made regarding heterosexual activity. The ancient Hittite law code outlawed sex with particular animals and between some family members, but sodomy between consenting, unrelated adults was not mentioned. The Puritan concern with sex between adults, particularly between consenting unmarried heterosexuals, is almost unique in Indo-European history. It was part of a desire by one religious group to impose, through the force of the state, its morality on the rest of society, outside the general historical tradition of that society.

That is not to say that a future conservative Court could not limit *Griswold* and *Eisenstadt* to their facts and find that while unmarried individuals may purchase contraceptive devices, they may use them only when they get married. The Court could also argue that by allowing married couples to use contraceptive devices the Court only intended them to have some general control over the timing of childbirth and was not condoning the practice of having heterosexual sex for fun, even for married couples.

In 1990 Maryland's highest court faced a criminal case involving private, noncommercial sexual acts between consenting heterosexual adults, specifically the performance of fellatio. The Court took note of the New York and Pennsylvania decisions discussed earlier, *Onofre* and *Bonadio*. It also discussed decisions by courts in Rhode Island, North Carolina, and Arizona that held the right to privacy does not give unmarried heterosexual adults the right to perform "unnatural copulation."[56] All three courts apparently believed that similar activity engaged in by married individuals could not be criminalized.

A majority of the Maryland court decided to take the coward's way out and decide that the statutory language, "unnatural or perverted sexual practices," does not mean the performance of fellatio "where it is not engaged in for commercial purposes and involves consenting adults of opposite sexes in the privacy of the home."[57] In this way the Maryland court avoided the constitutional question.

From the Hittite law code to Puritan New England laws were used to outlaw behavior engaged in by religions other than those supported by the state. The Hittites outlawed sex with certain animals, but not the horse, for example. Some scholars interpret that to mean the Hittites used the horse in some religious ceremonies in ways that most Americans probably would not approve of. The ancient Greeks and

Romans put blasphemers to death, but generally did not regulate sexual behavior with their law codes except where questions of inheritance were concerned. The ancient Greeks appear to have been particularly tolerant of homosexual behavior. When one looks back to the "tradition" of America, one has to remember that more people were put to death in Puritan New England for committing the crime of being a Quaker than for violating any particular sexual statute.

In the 1990 decision of *Employment Div. v. Smith*, the U.S. Supreme Court decided that it could not find a way to allow those following some religions to violate criminal laws that would otherwise apply to the rest of the population. At the same time, with the decisions concerning the right to privacy, the Court has made it clear that some things should be beyond the reach of government. These things include fundamental decisions concerning sex and marriage and certain behaviors conducted in the privacy of one's own home. It is still not clear how far the right to privacy goes in this regard, however.

Concerning sex and marriage, what is protected by the constitutional right to privacy? Heterosexual fornication? Probably. Heterosexual sodomy performed by married adults? Apparently. Heterosexual sodomy performed by unmarried adults? Maybe. Homosexual sodomy performed by adults? Generally not, but some state Supreme Courts have been willing to go that far.

NOTES

1. 98 U.S. 145 (1878).
2. Mormon Church v. United States, 136 U.S. 1 (1890).
3. Davis v. Beason, 133 U.S. 333, 341 (1890).
4. Cope v. Cope, 137 U.S. 682 (1891).
5. Hennington v. State of Georgia, 163 U.S. 299 (1896).
6. Sunday Closing Law Cases, 366 U.S. 420 (1961).
7. West Virginia Bd. of Ed. v. Barnette, 319 U.S. 624 (1943) overturning Minersville v. Gobitis, 310 U.S. 586 (1940).
8. Torcaso v. Watkins, 367 U.S. 488 (1961).
9. 310 U.S. 296 (1940).
10. Chaplinsky v. New Hampshire, 315 U.S. 568 (1942).
11. Martin v. City of Struthers, 319 U.S. 141 (1943); Murdock v. Pennsylvania, 319 U.S. 105 (1943) see also Follett v. Town of McCormick, 321 U.S. 573 (1944).
12. Marsh v. Alabama, 326 U.S. 501 (1946).
13. Cleveland v. United States, 329 U.S. 14 (1946).
14. 330 U.S. 1 (1947).
15. Engel v. Vitale, 370 U.S. 421, 437 (1962).
16. Tilton v. Richardson, 403 U.S. 672 (1971).

17. 406 U.S. 205 (1972).

18. 268 U.S. 510 (1925).

19. 406 U.S. 205, 215–6 (1972).

20. 110 S. Ct. 1595 (1990).

21. *Id.* at 1601, note 1.

22. *Id.* at 1603.

23. *Id.* at 1604.

24. Lochner v. New York, 198 U.S. 45, 75 (1905).

25. 391 U.S. 68 (1968).

26. 401 U.S. 532 (1971).

27. *Id.* at 539.

28. *Id.* at 541.

29. *Id.* at 558–9, citing In re Estate of Jensen, 162 N.W. 2d 861, 878 (1968).

30. 406 U.S. 164 (1972).

31. *Id.* at 175.

32. 409 U.S. 535 (1973).

33. 411 U.S. 619 (1973).

34. Mathews v. Lucas, 427 U.S. 495 (1976).

35. Dixon, *The Griswold Penumbra: Constitutional Charter for an Expanded Law of Privacy?*, 64 Mich. L. Rev. 197, 204 (1965).

36. Loving v. Virginia, 388 U.S. 1 (1967); Zablocki v. Rfedhail, 434 U.S. 374 (1978); Boddie v. Connecticut, 401 U.S. 371 (1971).

37. 405 U.S. 438 (1972).

38. Moore V. City of East Cleveland, 431 U.S. 494 (1977).

39. Hafen, *The Constitutional Status of Marriage, Kinship and Sexual Privacy— Balancing the Individual and Social Interests*, 81 Mich. L. Rev. 463, 530–1 (1983) quoting Carey v. Population Servs. Int'l, 431 U.S. 678, 688 (1977).

40. Grey, *Eros, Civilization and the Burger Court*, 43 Law & Contemp. Probs., Summer 1980, 83.

41. 381 A.2d 333 (N.J. 1977).

42. 242 N.W.2d 348, 358 (Iowa, 1976).

43. 715 P.2d 1105 (Okla. Crim. App.) cert. denied, 107 S. Ct. 290 (1986).

44. 415 N.E.2d 936 (N.Y. 1980), cert. denied 451 U.S. 987 (1981).

45. *Id.* at 940–2.

46. 415 A.2d 47 (Penn. 1980).

47. 478 U.S. 186 (1986).

48. *Id.* at 190.

49. 302 U.S. 319 (1937).

50. 431 U.S. 494, 503 (1977).

51. Note, *Constitutional Barriers to Civil and Criminal Restrictions on Pre- & Extramarital Sex*, 104 Harv. L. Rev. 1660 (1991); Note, *The Constitutional Privacy Doctrine After Bowers v. Hardwick: Rethinking the Second Death of Substantive Due Process*, 62 S. Cal. L. Rev. 1297 (1989); Note, *Chipping Away at Bowers v. Hardwick: Making the Best of an Unfortunate Decision*, 63 N.Y.U. L. Rev. 154 (1988).

52. 715 P.2d 1105 (Okla. Crim. App.), cert. denied, 107 S. Ct. 290 (1986).

53. Bowers v. Hardwick, 478 U.S. at 197 (Burger, C. J., concurring), quoting 4 W. Blackstone, Commentaries, 215.

54. Bowers v. Hardwick, 478 U.S. at 218 n. 10 (Stevens, J., joined by Brennan and Marshall, J.J., dissenting).

55. 394 U.S. 557 (1969).

56. State v. Santos, 413 A.2d 58 (R.I. 1980); State v. Poe, 252 S.E.2d 843 (N.C. App. 1979); State v. Bateman, 547 P.2d 6 (Ariz. 1976).

57. Schochet v. State, 580 A.2d 176, 186 (Md. 1990).

8

Life and Death

The rights to life and death have evolved through a series of five major Supreme Court decisions: *Roe v. Wade, City of Akron v. Akron Center for Reproductive Health, Thornburgh v. American College of Obstetricians & Gynecologists, Webster v. Reproductive Health Services,* and *Cruzan v. Director, Missouri Dept. of Health.* Although a few other decisions will be discussed briefly, these five are the key to understanding where the law stands on the fundamental issue of life and death.

ROE V. WADE

Roe v. Wade may be the most famous Supreme Court decision of the twentieth century.[1] It was not an easy decision for the Court to make. The case was originally argued before the Court in December 1971, reargued in October 1972, and decided in January 1973. The case was brought by an anonymous "pregnant, single woman" who was prevented from obtaining a legal abortion by a Texas law which allowed abortions only to save the life of the mother.

Justice Blackmun began the majority opinion by referring with approval to Justice Holmes' dissent in the *Lochner* case to the effect that the Court should not allow the fact that something is generally considered either "natural" or "shocking" to "conclude our judgment upon the question."[2] Justice Blackmun then surveyed the history of abortion. He pointed out that restrictions on abortions are of a relatively "recent vintage," and that abortions were legal in ancient Greek and Roman times. Under ancient English law an abortion performed before the fetus had "quickened" was not a criminal offense. American abortion statutes were a product of the nineteenth century. Gradually, the quickening distinction disappeared as all abortions came to be illegal. Blackmun suggested that when the Constitution was written "a woman enjoyed a substantially broader right to terminate a pregnancy" than she did in 1973.[3]

He believed states have two valid interests in controlling abortions: one in regulating medical procedures in general to make them safe and one in protecting potential life. He then discussed at length the development of the constitutional right of privacy and found that this right is "broad enough to encompass a woman's decision whether or not to terminate her pregnancy."[4] While he did not specifically state when life begins, he did trace the history of the concept of life and pointed out that throughout most of western history, life has generally been considered to begin at birth. He also said that the word "person" as used in the Fourteenth Amendment "does not include the unborn."[5] In other words, a fetus is not protected by the Bill of Rights or the Fourteenth Amendment.

He then developed the trimester system. He argued that during the first trimester of pregnancy a woman's right to privacy outweighs the state's right to regulate medical care to protect her safety, because it is an "established medical fact . . . that until the end of the first trimester mortality in abortion may be less than mortality in normal childbirth."[6] After that point the state may regulate abortions to protect the health of the mother. The state's second legitimate interest in protecting the "potential life" of the fetus does not become compelling until the beginning of the third trimester when the fetus is capable of life outside the mother's womb. At that point the state "may go so far as to proscribe abortion during that period, except when it is necessary to preserve the life or health of the mother."[7]

Only two justices, White and Rehnquist, dissented. Justice White could not agree that, prior to viability, the Constitution "values the convenience, whim, or caprice of the putative mother more than the life or potential life of the fetus."[8] He found the decision to be an "improvident and extravagant exercise" of judicial power. Justice Rehnquist had difficulty concluding that the right of privacy was even involved in this case. While he did believe a law that forbade an abortion even when the mother's life was threatened would be unconstitutional, he did not see how the Court could go much beyond that.

BETWEEN ROE AND AKRON

Roe v. Wade was followed by a series of decisions on abortions, most decided by either a five to four or six to three vote. In *Planned Parent-*

hood v. Danforth the Court struck down a Missouri law to the extent it required the woman's husband, or parent if she was not married, to consent to the abortion.[9] In *Maher v. Roe* the Court ruled that a state could limit the use of Medicaid funds to only those "first trimester abortions" that are "medically necessary."[10] In *Colaulti v. Franklin* the Court struck down a Pennsylvania law that required a doctor performing an abortion to do everything possible to save the life of a viable fetus.[11] The majority found the statute too vague to be enforceable. In *Bellotti v. Baird* the Court struck down a Massachusetts law that required an unmarried woman under the age of eighteen to get permission from a parent or judge before having an abortion.[12] In *Harris v. McRae*, however, the Court upheld the federal government's right to refuse to pay even for "medically necessary" abortions under the Medicaid program.[13] In *H.L. v. Matheson* the Court upheld the power of states to require physicians to notify the parents of "immature, dependent, unemancipated minors," if possible, before performing an abortion.[14]

CITY OF AKRON

By 1983 Justice O'Connor had been appointed to the Court, and it was she who wrote the dissenting opinion in the case of *City of Akron v. Akron Center for Reproductive Health* that was joined by Justices White and Rehnquist.[15] The case involved attempts by the City of Akron to regulate abortion clinics. A majority of the Court felt these regulations were unnecessary, did not serve the legitimate interests of the city and were simply attempts to prevent abortions. Justice O'Connor, the only woman ever to sit on the U.S. Supreme Court, did not see it that way. That she dissented, and the content of her dissent, gave hope to those who wanted to see *Roe v. Wade* limited in scope or even overturned. Justice O'Connor began her dissent by expressing her displeasure with the trimester system. She said:

neither sound constitutional theory nor our need to decide cases based on the application of neutral principles can accommodate an analytical framework that varies according to the "stages" of pregnancy, where those stages, and their concomitant standards of review, differ according to the level of medical technology available when a particular challenge to state regulation occurs.[16]

She then cited decisions handed down between *Roe v. Wade* and *City of Akron* for the proposition that abortion regulations are not unconstitutional unless they "unduly burden the right to seek an abortion."[17] Justice O'Connor felt this concept of "unduly burdensome" regulation should be applied throughout the pregnancy without reference to the particular trimester.

Justice O'Connor objected to the shifting sands that formed the foundation for the trimester system set down in 1973 in *Roe v. Wade*. She objected to the fact that the majority had decided in *Akron* that the first sixteen weeks (one trimester plus one month) was now the acceptable period during which the dilation and evacuation procedure could safely be used. Not only had the Court refused to provide a "bright line" to guide states and cities, but it had further blurred the already "blurred line" provided in *Roe v. Wade*. She objected to the idea that constitutional standards would change "every time the American College of Obstetricians and Gynecologists (ACOG) or similar group revises its views."[18] She argued that just as medical technology would increase the time during which a simple abortion could be performed safely (extending the length of the first trimester) so medical technology would improve the ability to save the premature infant and push back the time when a fetus is viable outside the womb (extending the length of the third trimester). When would they meet in the middle and create the need to speak of lengths of time different from those laid down in *Roe v. Wade?* She concluded that the trimester system was "clearly on a collision course with itself," and argued that judicial decisions should be capable of "continuity over significant periods of time."[19] It is the trimester system that makes *Roe v. Wade* particularly susceptible to major revision or abandonment. Justice O'Connor can argue that *Roe v. Wade* was not killed, it simply self-destructed.

She then turned to the basic logic of *Roe v. Wade*. There the Court had said that the state has two interests: one in seeing to it that an abortion, like any other medical procedure, is performed under circumstances that insure maximum safety for the patient, and one in protecting the potentiality of human life. Justice O'Connor argued that the state has these interests through the entire pregnancy and therefore the trimester system makes no logical sense. She could not see how the "potential for human life" is any less potential in the first weeks of pregnancy than in the last weeks. She also did not feel the regulations imposed by the city of Akron were unreasonable. Those regulations required abortions after the first trimester to be performed in a hospital; an unmarried minor under the age of fifteen had to have either parental consent or a court order; the doctor had to inform the woman of the status of the fetus, and of the physical and emotional complications that might result from an abortion; the doctor had to wait twenty-four hours after a woman signed a consent form to perform the abortion; and the doctor had to dispose of the fetal remains in a humane and sanitary way. The majority of the Court found these regulations to be unconstitutional; the dissenters did not agree.

THORNBURGH

While Chief Justice Burger voted with the majority in *Akron*, he joined the dissenters in the 1986 case of *Thornburgh v. American College of Obstetricians and Gynecologists*.[20] This case involved a Pennsylvania statute that required the doctor to obtain the woman's "informed consent," which meant giving her a great deal of information concerning both the risks of abortions and the existence of alternatives (and agencies willing to assist the mother before and after birth). The physician had to fill out elaborate reports for the state and have another doctor present at the abortion if the fetus might be viable. The majority viewed these simply as attempts to restrict a woman's right to have an abortion, not as necessary regulations to protect either the health of the mother or the potential life of the fetus.

Chief Justice Burger dissented along with Justices White, Rehnquist, and O'Connor. Chief Justice Burger's dissent is the most interesting because he voted with the majority in both *Roe v. Wade* and *Akron*. He said he thought when he voted with the majority in those cases that the Court rejected the idea of "abortion on demand." Now he had become convinced that this was exactly what a majority of the Court favored. He felt the majority had come a long way from *Roe v. Wade* and no longer really recognized the legitimate interests of the state. He was particularly distressed that a majority of the Court would not allow the state to require "that a woman contemplating an abortion be provided with accurate medical information concerning the risks inherent in the medical procedure which she is about to undergo and the availability of state-funded alternatives if she elects not to run these risks."[21] He ended his decision by calling for a "reexamination" of *Roe v. Wade*. Presumably he meant by this that he was ready to overturn that decision just a dozen years after it had been handed down.

WEBSTER

Finally in 1989, with the addition of Justices Scalia and Kennedy, the Court decided *Webster v. Reproductive Health Services*.[22] This decision upheld the right of the state of Missouri to forbid the use of public employees and facilities for the performance of "nontherapeutic abortions." It also upheld a statutory provision that stated that after twenty weeks of pregnancy a fetus would be presumed viable and a physician would have to overcome that presumption before performing an abortion. Justice O'Connor was the fifth vote in favor of the Missouri statute, but she did not feel the facts of this case warranted overturning either *Roe v. Wade* or the trimester system. Several states took that as an invitation to pass strict anti-abortion laws that would provide the Court with that opportunity.

CRUZAN

Cruzan v. Director, Missouri Dept. of Health is not an abortion case, it is a "right to die" case; nevertheless, it bears importantly on the questions of life and death discussed in this chapter.[23] Nancy Cruzan was left in a "persistent vegetative state" as the result of an automobile accident. She exhibited motor reflexes but no significant cognitive function. The Missouri Supreme Court ruled that there would have to be "clear and convincing" evidence of what her wishes would have been before she could be taken off the life support system.

Chief Justice Rehnquist wrote the majority decision in *Cruzan*. He could have said there is no "right to die" protected by the Fourteenth Amendment, but he did not; indeed only Justice Scalia argued for that result. This means eight of the nine justices agreed that a constitutional right to die exists, but disagreed on its foundation and its extent. Chief Justice Rehnquist scrupulously avoided the phrase "right to privacy," instead, he argued that people have a "protected liberty interest in refusing unwanted medical treatment" and that this "liberty" interest included the right to die. However, this "right to die" has to be balanced against the "relevant state interests." He was willing to "assume" that, for a competent person, the right to die would outweigh any contrary state interests and would allow "a competent person a constitutionally protected right to refuse lifesaving hydration and nutrition."[24] Of course, Nancy Cruzan was unconscious and the whole point of the case was the need to determine by what method her wishes could be established, given that she could not speak for herself. The Missouri Supreme Court had required that "the incompetent's wishes as to the withdrawal of treatment be proved by clear and convincing evidence," and a majority of the U.S. Supreme Court felt this was reasonable and did not violate the constitutionally protected "right to die."

Justice O'Connor's concurring opinion is of particular interest. She agreed that people have a "protected liberty interest" in refusing unwanted medical treatment. She then said, citing Justice Brandeis' dissent in the *New State Ice Co.* case, that it was time for states to "experiment" with appropriate procedures to safeguard the interests of "incompetents" in these kinds of situations. She made it clear, however, that the U.S. Supreme Court would reserve the right to review these "experiments" at a later date.

THE ISSUE BEFORE THE COURT

Soon after *Webster* several states passed very restrictive abortion statutes. In 1991 the Louisiana Legislature passed the most restrictive statute over the governor's veto. The Louisiana law makes it illegal for physicians to perform most abortions. Doctors face a possible ten years in prison and a $100,000 fine, but there is no penalty for the woman. Abortions are banned except to save the life of the mother and for some victims of rape and incest. The abortion must be performed within the first thirteen weeks of pregnancy. There is no provision for abortion of a deformed fetus and abortion is defined to include prescribing any drug or using any instrument to help a woman terminate a pregnancy. A Utah law passed in 1991 contains the same exceptions and also allows abortions to protect a woman's health and in cases of grave fetal deformities. A Pennsylvania law enacted in 1989 bans abortions after twenty-four weeks and requires spousal consent and a twenty-four-hour waiting period among other restrictions. At some point in the 1990s the U.S. Supreme Court will rule on the constitutionality of these new, very restrictive statutes. The Court has several options.

First, the Court could simply overturn *Roe v. Wade* and get out of the abortion regulation business entirely. It is doubtful that the Court will do so, however, because of the existence of one very realistic hypothetical situation. Suppose a majority of a state agreed with John Stuart Mill that people should not be allowed to have children unless they can support them. Certainly if the state has an interest in "protecting the potentiality of human life" it also has a very compelling interest in not being saddled with another indigent child which it will have to support and educate for two decades. While a century ago a state could not make this argument, the welfare state of today certainly can. What if that state forced poor women to have abortions against their will? Is the Supreme Court really willing to allow that to happen? And as to the argument that this would involve unfair discrimination against the poor, what if a majority of a state decided, as has China, that people will only be allowed to have one child because of overpopulation? And what if the state, as has China, engaged in forced abortions as a last resort when illegal pregnancy was discovered? Again, would a majority of the Court allow this kind of a law in the United States? If not, then the Court cannot get out of the abortion business.

At the same time, the Court has made it clear that *Roe v. Wade* cannot remain in its present form. Another alternative would be to abandon the trimester system and draw a fairly bright line at the point where a fetus is "capable of meaningful life outside the mother's womb." One legal commentator has suggested that until this point of viability the

Court should prevent undue interference in the decision to have an abortion; after this point, however, the state could prohibit abortions with a few obvious exceptions.[25]

There is a third alternative. The Court avoided making an explicit decision concerning when life begins in *Roe v. Wade*. The Court could do so now and decide that life begins at conception. In that case the state could control abortions as it sees fit, but it would not be able to require women to have abortions because that would interfere with the right of the fetus to live. This would take the Court from one end of the continuum, protecting women's rights, to the other, protecting fetus' rights.

As a fourth alternative, the Court could adopt what appears to be Justice O'Connor's standard, that the regulations should not be "unduly burdensome." This compromise position would keep abortions legal while allowing states to regulate them to a much greater extent than is currently the case.

Whatever the Court decides, that decision will be one of the most important in U.S. history. Will future generations look back on it as current generations do *Dred Scott* and *Lochner*, as a strange anachronism that led to great civil unrest and changed the political course of a nation, or will it simply modify past precedent in the face of new information? Only time will tell.

NOTES

1. 410 U.S. 113 (1973).
2. *Id.* at p. 117, quoting Justice Holmes' dissenting opinion in Lochner v. New York, 198 U.S. 45, 76 (1905).
3. *Id.* at 140.
4. *Id.* at 153.
5. *Id.* at 158.
6. *Id.* at 163.
7. *Id.* at 163–4.
8. *Id.* at 221.
9. 428 U.S. 52 (1976).
10. 432 U.S. 464 (1977).
11. 439 U.S. 379 (1979).
12. 443 U.S. 622 (1979).
13. 448 U.S. 297 (1980).
14. 450 U.S. 398 (1981).
15. 462 U.S. 416 (1983).
16. *Id.* at 452.
17. Maher v. Roe, 432 U.S. 464 (1977) quoting Bellotti v. Baird, 428 U.S. 132 (1977).

18. 462 U.S. 416, 456 (1983).
19. *Id.* at 458.
20. 476 U.S. 747 (1986).
21. *Id.* at 783.
22. 109 S. Ct. 3040 (1989).
23. 110 S. Ct. 2841 (1990).
24. *Id.* at 2852.
25. Note, *A Thorn in the Side of Privacy: The Need for Reassessment of the Constitutional Right to Abortion*, 70 Marq. L. Rev. 534 (1987).

9

Mind and Body

Recent years have seen a dramatic increase in "mind and body" testing of employees. Fearful of the risks posed by employees who are dishonest, impaired by illicit substances, or adversely affected by psychological or genetic traits, many employers are subjecting employees and job applicants to urine and other tests. Alarmed at the notion of losing a job because of a test, not to mention their bodily integrity and reputation, employees have attacked these tests as an invasion of privacy.

Unlike most of their private sector counterparts, public employees bent on challenging the legality of such testing programs may rely on the federal Constitution.[1] Claims typically advanced are that tests violate the Fourth Amendment ban on unreasonable search and seizure, Fourteenth Amendment requirements of equal protection and due process of law, and the constitutional right of privacy. Most of the litigation so far has involved the legality of drug testing—specifically, urine testing or "urinalysis"—but the legal principles developed in that area are generally applicable to other forms of workplace testing as well.

DRUG TESTING AND THE FOURTH AMENDMENT

The most often-litigated issue raised by urinalysis concerns its status under the Fourth Amendment, which provides:

The right of the people to be secure in their persons, houses, papers, and effects, against unreasonable searches and seizures, shall not be violated, and no warrants shall issue, but upon probable cause, supported by oath or affirmation, and particularly describing the place to be searched, and the person or things to be seized.

Whether a governmental investigation is a "search" is the initial issue in a Fourth Amendment analysis. If it is, whether the investigation was reasonable and required a warrant must be determined.

In 1989, the U.S. Supreme Court considered the "search" implications of workplace drug testing in *Skinner v. Railway Labor Executives' Ass'n.*[2] and *National Treasury Employees Union v. Von Raab.*[3] In doing so, the Court did not write on a clean slate, as scores of lower court precedents existed. These precedents agreed on many issues regarding drug testing but disagreed on some critical issues. To appreciate the impact of *Skinner* and *Von Raab*, it is important to understand what the lower court cases had said.

To decide whether a governmental investigation involves a search, the Supreme Court uses the test articulated by Justice John M. Harlan in his concurring opinion in *Katz v. United States.*[4] Under this test, a search occurs if the investigation invades a subjective expectation of privacy that society deems reasonable. Cases predating *Skinner* and *Von Raab* agreed that a urinalysis involves a search because it invades reasonable privacy expectations. Courts compared compulsory testing to a government taking of blood, which entails a search, and noted that tests intrude on privacy and dignity and allow both the discovery of medical data unrelated to drug use and the observation of off-duty employee activity. The cases further agreed that because drug levels fall over time, tests must be given promptly, which eliminates the need for a search warrant. In addition, because employees cannot, as a condition of employment, be forced to accept an illegal drug test, an unconstitutional test will not be redeemed by an employee's "consent" to it, although advance consent may lessen his or her expectation of privacy. Finally, because a urinalysis is a search, it must be conducted "reasonably." Reasonableness is assessed by balancing the extent of the test's intrusion on privacy against the degree to which it promotes valid government interests, taking into account the manner, place of and justification for the test.

The cases differed sharply, however, over when a test is justified and is conducted reasonably. The split centered on: (1) How significant is the nature of one's job (e.g., whether it affects the public welfare) in terms of privacy interests and the justification for testing? (2) Does it matter if there is a history of drug use in the industry or evidence of a current problem? (3) May tests be given randomly or only with reason to believe a certain worker is impaired, and if the latter, what level of suspicion is needed? (4) How important are testing mechanics and accuracy?

Likening urinalysis to an administrative search, which needs little

suspicion of wrongdoing, some courts held that individualized suspicion of impairment is not needed to justify testing if the industry has
a history of intense state regulation and privacy rights are protected.
In *Shoemaker v. Handel,*[5] for example, New Jersey was allowed to randomly test horse racing jockeys. The court stressed the need to preserve public confidence in racing, in which wagering is heavy and corruption is a threat; New Jersey's intense regulation of the racing industry
since 1939; the reduction of the jockeys' privacy expectations through
their advance knowledge of the tests, and the testing plan's safeguards, which protected privacy and limited the testers' discretion in
determining whether to test. Finding the police industry the most in-
tensely regulated in New Jersey, the court in *Policeman's Benevolent Ass'n
v. Township of Washington*[6] used this rationale in upholding random
testing of police.

Other cases upheld random drug testing deemed "reasonable" based
on an assessment of the relevant facts. In *Transportation Workers Local
234 v. SEPTA,*[7] the court held that a plan to test transportation workers
randomly was reasonable in light of the interest in insuring public safety;
documented cases of accidents involving workers impaired by, and applicants testing positive for drugs; the fact that the plan applied only
to jobs affecting the public safety; and the safeguards in the plan, including confidentiality and verification of results, chain-of-custody procedures, and a careful random selection process. *Rushton v. Nebraska
Public Power District*[8] upheld a nuclear power plant's testing plan,
stressing that it did not require the act of urination to be witnessed and
that the industry affects the public safety. *McDonell v. Hunter*[9] held that
individual suspicion is not needed if workers in sensitive jobs—prison
guards, in that case—are tested uniformly (e.g., in routine physical examinations or by systematic random selection) but that other tests require a suspicion of drug use within twenty-four hours.

Many courts, however, required the employer to have particularized
suspicion to test. In *Copeland v. Philadelphia Police Department*[10] a city
was allowed to test a policeman accused by a former girlfriend of using
drugs only on the basis of a "reasonable suspicion" that he had done
so. Relevant factors included the nature of the tip, the informant's reliability, and the degree of corroboration. The court found enough suspicion in Copeland's having been off his beat with a drug seller and
not so reporting in his patrol log, coupled with the girlfriend's claim.
Lovvorn v. City of Chattanooga[11] used this standard in voiding a random
testing plan for firefighters. While it acknowledged the interests at stake,
the court held that the plan required samples to be given under observation, and it stressed the privacy interest involved. It then said that
whether random testing is permissible depends not on whether an industry is heavily regulated, but on the nature of that industry and the
harm to society that would likely result if mandatory tests were forbid-

den. Finding the likelihood of damage to society because of an impaired firefighter to be relatively low, the court held that for random testing to be reasonable, there must be evidence of a department-wide drug problem or individual suspicion of impairment.

When *Skinner* and *Von Raab* appeared, therefore, the main question was whether urine tests require individualized suspicion of impairment. The Supreme Court answered in the negative. The outcomes of these cases were so tied to the particular facts, however, that it is unreasonable to conclude that across-the-board random testing is now permissible. The most that can be said is that random testing is now legal with respect to certain employees in certain instances and under certain conditions.

Skinner involved federal rules requiring railroads to test their workers' blood and urine in the event of accidents involving death, serious injury, or property damage. Specimens are obtained at a medical facility and sent to a laboratory for analysis, and employees are notified of the results and given a chance to respond before a final report is prepared. The rules also allow testing after certain rules violations or accidents if a supervisor reasonably suspects either impairment or that an employee's acts were a contributing factor. If results will be used to discipline, the employee must be allowed to have blood analyzed independently. The rules also seek to prevent sample tainting due to chain-of-custody problems.

The Supreme Court held seven-to-two that tests given in reliance on federal authority involve enough government action to trigger the Fourth Amendment, that the tests involve "searches," that neither a warrant nor "probable cause" is required to conduct them, and that their reasonableness depends on all the circumstances. But it declined to hold, as had the Ninth Circuit Court of Appeals, that individualized suspicion is needed to insure that tests will detect current impairment. Where privacy interests implicated by a search are minimal and vital governmental interests would be harmed by requiring individual suspicion, the Court said, the search may be considered reasonable despite its absence. Conceding that requiring the performance of an excretory function traditionally deemed private is not a minimal concern, the Court noted that the rules do not require urine to be given under observation and call for it to be analyzed in a laboratory; thus, the testing process is like that used in regular physical exams. Finally, the Court found the workers' privacy expectations lessened by their being in an industry pervasively regulated to ensure the public safety.

The Court also stressed that on-the-job intoxication is a major problem in the railroad industry and that workers, who discharge duties fraught with such risks that even a momentary lapse can be disastrous, can cause great loss before signs of impairment are noticeable. History also shows that even the threat of discharge for working while impaired is not an effective deterrent unless violators know they will be detected; by tying testing to a triggering event, the timing of which cannot be predicted, the rule increases the deterrent effect of its penalties. Also, given the chaos at accident sites, it would be hard for investigators to find evidence creating a suspicion of impairment in a particular employee. An individualized suspicion rule would thus bar testing in many cases, which could prevent the obtaining of clues as to the cause of an accident. Finally, the Court ruled that the inability of a test to measure drug intoxication is not a reason to void it. To be relevant evidence need not conclusively prove the fact at issue, but only tend to make its existence more or less likely. Even if a test disclosed only recent drug use, the Court said, this would justify further investigation to determine if the employee used drugs at the relevant times.

In *Von Raab* a five-to-four Court upheld the testing plan of the Customs Service. Tests were required for employees involved in drug interdiction or who handled classified material. Because the decision turned largely on the details of the plan, the lower court's detailed description of it is set out here:

After an employee qualifies for a position covered by the Customs testing program, the Service advises him by letter that his final selection is contingent upon successful completion of drug screening. An independent contractor contacts the employee to fix the time and place for collecting the sample. On reporting for the test, the employee must produce photographic identification and remove any outer garments, such as a coat or jacket, and personal belongings. The employee may produce the sample behind a partition, or in the privacy of a bathroom stall if he so chooses. To ensure against adulteration of the specimen, or substitution of a sample from another person, a monitor of the same sex as the employee remains close at hand to listen for the normal sounds of urination. Dye is added to the toilet water to prevent the employee from using the water to adulterate the sample.

Upon receiving the specimen, the monitor inspects it to ensure its proper temperature and color, places a tamper-proof custody seal over the container, and affixes an identification label indicating the date and the individual's specimen number. The employee signs a chain-of-custody form, which is initialed by the monitor, and the urine sample is placed in a plastic bag, sealed, and submitted to a laboratory.

The laboratory tests the sample for the presence of marijuana, cocaine, opiates, amphetamines, and phencyclidine. Two tests are used. An initial screening test uses the [EMIT]. Any specimen that is identified as positive on this initial test must then be confirmed using gas chromatography/mass spectrometry (GC/MS). Confirmed positive results are reported to a "Medical Review Officer," [a] licensed physician . . . who has knowledge of substance abuse disorders and has appropriate medical training to interpret and evaluate the individual's positive test result together with his or her medical history and any other relevant biomedical information. . . . After verifying the positive result, the Medical Review Officer transmits it to the agency.

Customs employees who test positive for drugs and who can offer no satisfactory explanation are subject to dismissal from the Service. Test results may not, however, be turned over to any other agency, including criminal prosecutors, without the employee's written consent.[12]

As in *Skinner*, the Court held that the tests involve a search and must be reasonable. It also ruled out warrants, noting that requiring one for each job-related intrusion would make it difficult for offices to function. It then turned to the individualized suspicion issue. Analogizing this search to building code inspections, which seek not to enforce the criminal law but to prevent hazardous conditions, and to suspicionless searches of airline passengers, the Court said that sometimes the government need to prevent harm justifies suspicionless searches. Searches of Customs workers are in this category: their safety is continually threatened by drug traffickers, and this coupled with their access to contraband and the chance of bribes necessitates their unimpeachable integrity.

Also relevant to a "reasonableness" inquiry, the Court said, is the degree of interference with personal liberty caused by a test. Conceding that the privacy intrusion involved in collecting urine could be substantial, the Court nonetheless said that the "operational realities" of the workplace justify job-related intrusions by supervisors that might be unreasonable in other contexts. Certain types of jobs, moreover, carry diminished privacy expectations for employees. The Customs workers' diminished expectations and the fact that the testing plan contains safeguards to minimize its intrusion on privacy made the plan reasonable.

The challenge to the plan involved two other claims: It was unjustified because there was no perceived drug problem among Customs workers; and because drug users can avoid detection through abstinence or adulterating samples, it was not sufficiently productive to justify its invasion of privacy. In reply, the Court said that the "extraordinary" safety and national security interests at stake justified attempts to ferret out even casual drug users, and the fact that most employees will test negative did not impugn the plan. If potential harm is substantial, the need to prevent it may justify reasonable searches designed to advance that goal. To the other argument the Court replied that addicts may be unable to abstain or unaware of the fade-away effect of some drugs. And because the time it takes for drugs to become undetectable in urine varies with the individual, no employee's pattern of elimination for a particular drug can be predicted.

Justices Brennan and Marshall dissented in *Von Raab* and *Skinner*. They made three points. First, they labeled "unprincipled" the notion that "special needs" justify ignoring the probable cause and warrant language in the Fourth Amendment. They felt the Court should abandon its balancing approach to search cases and apply the amendment as written. Second, they argued that random testing is illegal even under the special-needs or balancing approach, and that individualized suspicion should be a constitutional prerequisite to a test. Finally, they attacked the mechanics and accuracy of current testing methods, especially their inability to measure current impairment as opposed to past drug use.

Justices Scalia and Stevens voted with the majority in *Skinner*. While they rejected the claim that the interest in deterring drug use justified the searches involved, they felt the public interest in assessing the causes of railroad accidents supported the testing rules. The demonstrated frequency of drug use by railroad workers and the link between such use and the risk of substantial harm, moreover, made random testing a reasonable means of protecting society. They joined the dissenters in *Von Raab*, however, insisting that neither the frequency of drug use by Customs workers nor a connection with any harm was shown or even likely. To them, the Customs rules were nothing but an "immolation of privacy and human dignity in symbolic opposition to drug use"—a sign that the government meant to "get tough" on drug use, and to invade privacy to prove it, whether or not there was reason to suspect such use in the industry. In a sarcasm-laced dissent, Justice Scalia asserted that such a program is unacceptable in our society.

I do not believe for a minute that the driving force behind these drug-testing rules was any of the feeble justifications put forward by counsel here and accepted by the Court. The only plausible explanation, in my view, is what the Commissioner himself offered in the concluding sentence of his memorandum to Customs employees announcing the program: "Implementation of the drug screening program would set an important example in our country's struggle with this most serious threat to our national security." . . . What better way to show that the Government is serious about its "war on drugs" than to subject its employees on the front line to this invasion of their privacy and affront to their dignity? To be sure, there is only a slight chance that it will prevent some serious public harm resulting from Service employee drug use, but it will show to the world that the Service is "clean" and—most important—will demonstrate the determination of the Government to eliminate this scourge of our society! I think it obvious that this justification is unacceptable; that the impairment of individual liberties cannot be the means of making a point; that symbolism, even symbolism for so worthy of a cause as the abolition of unlawful drugs, cannot validate an otherwise unreasonable search.[13]

After *Skinner* and *Von Raab*, the following conclusions regarding "the law" of drug testing seemed warranted. (1) Public and some private employment testing involves a Fourth Amendment search. (2) If the Fourth Amendment applies to a drug test, neither a warrant nor probable cause to suspect impairment is needed to conduct it, but it must be "reasonable." This is determined by weighing its intrusion on privacy against its promotion of valid societal interests. (3) If an industry affects the public welfare or has a history of intense state regulation or a drug problem, random testing in that industry is legal. The less a job affects the public or is regulated by the state the more evidence of a drug problem is needed to randomly test; as the job's effect on the public, the amount of state regulation, and the evidence of a drug problem decrease, the basis for suspicionless testing does as well. (4) That tests cannot measure impairment and are not 100% accurate is no basis for automatically voiding them, although the more guarantees in a plan (e.g., chain-of-custody safeguards, procedures to ensure the confidentiality of results, back-up tests if an initial test is positive, and giving tests under laboratory conditions) the more likely that it will be upheld. (5) Neither advance notice nor employee consent will necessarily validate a test, but they increase the likelihood of its passing muster. The extent to which a plan limits the testers' discretion is also important. (6) The more a plan protects employee privacy, the greater its chances of surviving. The circumstances under which samples are taken will be crucial.

Post-*Skinner* and *Von Raab* cases bear out these conclusions. Using *Von Raab* as a guide, for example, the court in *Bluestein v. Skinner*[14] upheld a random testing plan of the Federal Aviation Administration as applied to employees who held safety-sensitive jobs, including flight crews and attendants, flight testing personnel, air controllers, and maintenance workers. *Seelig v. Koehler*[15] upheld the random testing of city correction officers, who, the court said, "voluntarily sacrifice certain cherished freedoms" by "choosing to" work in the paramilitary milieu of the City Correction Department." And in *Nat'l Fed'n of Fed. Employees v. Cheney*[16] the court held that employees in law enforcement, drug prevention programs, and aviation are subject to testing due to both the government's safety interest and their own diminished privacy expectations. But the court was unable to determine the reasonableness of testing employees in a Personnel Reliability Program since that category included positions ranging from nuclear reactor operators to animal caretaker; thus, it remanded that issue to the lower court. The court did hold that laboratory technicians could not be randomly tested.

In *Brown v. Winkle*,[17] the court, borrowing language from *Von Raab*, approved the testing of firefighter candidates, since that job, the court said, depends on judgment and dexterity "far more than does drug interdiction and the carrying of firearms." Safety concerns and diminished privacy expectations in a highly regulated industry were reasons given for rejecting a bus driver's challenge to a transit authority testing plan in *Moxley v. Regional Transit Service*.[18] But in *Amer. Postal Workers Union v. Frank*[19] the court refused to permit the testing of job applicants at the postal service. Without the safety concerns posed by jobs dealing with drug interdiction or involving firearms or public transportation, and given that the postal service is not a highly regulated industry in the traditional sense, the proposed screening was stopped.

THE FOURTEENTH AMENDMENT

The Fourteenth Amendment requires state and local governments to give "due process of law" before denying people life, liberty, or property. Procedurally, deprivations must be preceded by notice of the alleged violation and an appropriate hearing. Government workers fired or disciplined in connection with a urinalysis may have a due process claim if a property or liberty interest is thereby infringed.

Whether employees have a property interest in their job depends on its nature. "At-will" employees, who serve at their employer's pleasure for an indefinite period, may be dismissed at any time; they have no expectation of continued employment and hence no property interest in their job. But if the law, agency policy, a contract, or even verbal assurances create a reasonable expectation of job security, they have a property interest in the job and may not be fired without notice and a hearing.

The cases say little about the due process implications of urinalysis, but standards can be gleaned from other sources, especially *Cleveland Board of Education v. Loudermill*,[20] which involved the firing of an Ohio civil service employee, without a hearing, for lying on his job application. Noting that Ohio statutes allowed the man to keep his job absent good cause for dismissal, the Court said he had a "property" interest in continued employment, and that absent a need for his immediate removal from the workplace, he was thus entitled to a preremoval hearing. In *Fraternal Order of Police, Lodge No. 5 v. Tucker*,[21] the court applied these standards in finding that the plaintiffs were denied due process because, although they were told they were to be disciplined, they were not given specifics of the charges against them; thus, they had no meaningful chance to rebut the evidence of their drug use.

Given the possibility of a due process challenge stemming from a urine test, public employers have been cautioned to: (1) Remember that even at-will employees may have a property or liberty interest in their job, and thus be entitled to due process in a disciplinary context, if the law, agency policy, their contract, or verbal assurances have created a reasonable expectation of job security. (2) Advise workers of agency rules, including those governing on- or off-the-job substance use. (3) Advise workers that they are subject to testing periodically or in certain instances, and if the latter, specify them. (4) Give workers notice of the charges against them before firing or disciplining for drug use or for other reasons. (5) Where feasible, afford employees an opportunity for a hearing before a dismissal. (6) Ensure that testing mechanisms are as reliable as possible. (7) Avoid making remarks while administering or implementing the results of a test which may be construed as infringing on an employee's liberty interests.

THE CONSTITUTIONAL RIGHT OF PRIVACY

The federal constitutional right of privacy has two parts: an interest in autonomy, or freedom from unwanted government intrusions in decisions about one's life, and a right to be protected from public disclosure of intimate facts about oneself. While they say little about the autonomy implications of urinalysis, cases like *Schmerber v. California* and *Rochin v. California*[22] indicate that minor bodily intrusions will be tolerated and that a balancing approach that considers the nature of and need for a test, its reliability and test conditions, and whether less intrusive options were available will be used to decide privacy claims. Random tests given to detect drug use stand a better chance of violating privacy rights than tests accompanying physical examinations or based on reasonable suspicion.

The right to keep private facts private is limited, however, and whether employers who divulge drug test results or insist that employees reveal personal data (e.g., medicine being taken) violate it depends on whether the interest in disclosure outweighs the intrusion. In *Shoemaker v. Handel*, the court found that the testing plan did not violate disclosural rights because it had been amended to provide that test results would not be disclosed, even to law enforcement authorities. The court stated that although privacy rights in medical information exist, governmental concerns may support the access to such data if it is protected from unauthorized disclosure. Because the racing commission's concern for racing integrity justified its access to test data, the jockeys' privacy concern was limited to preserving the confidentiality of the test results, and the rule did this. If the commission ceased to comply with the rule, said the court, "the jockeys may return to court with a new lawsuit."

OTHER "MIND AND BODY" TESTS

Drug testing is the most prevalent employment screening test, but other workplace "mind and body" tests are increasing in popularity. For example, until 1988, when Congress enacted the Employee Polygraph Protection Act[23] forbidding the use of polygraph tests and their results in most job settings, there had been a vast increase in the use of such tests to try to gauge employee honesty. With roughly two million Americans having been identified as seropositive for AIDS, testing to learn which employees and job applicants are infected with the Human Immunodeficiency Virus (HIV) is more frequent. Some employers engage in genetic testing to determine who might be susceptible to particular disease and thus riskier in terms of disability benefits, absenteeism, and the like. And significant amounts of intelligence and ability testing has been occurring since World War II.

Most challenges to such testing have been based on state tort, contract, constitutional law, or on federal statutory law. Where attacks have been based on the federal Constitution, the same principles developed in drug testing litigation have controlled the disposition of the cases.

Regarding AIDS tests, for example, the constitutional guarantees most directly applicable in the workplace are those of privacy as well as due process and equal protection of the law. The validity of a test may also be challenged under the Fourth Amendment, as taking blood to be tested for HIV antibodies clearly would involve a search. For a test to be legal, an employer would have to show that the interests to be served by testing outweigh privacy expectations. Two court decisions on this issue have come out differently; one finding that the government's interests in testing were paramount,[24] the other holding to the contrary.[25]

Privacy issues could also surface in contexts other than testing. Once an employer learns about an employee's or applicant's HIV status, whether through employment-based antibody tests, self disclosure, or other methods, constitutional, statutory, or common law privacy principles may dictate what may be done with that data. Laws controlling the confidentiality of medical and personnel records, and specifically HIV test results, may also come into play. If an employer keeps this information, he must safeguard access to it. In *Cronin v. New England Telephone Co.*, a company supervisor asked Cronin why he took time off for doctor's visits. After receiving assurances of confidentiality, Cronin said he was being treated for symptoms of ARC. Despite these assurances, the supervisor told his superiors of Cronin's condition, and they organized meetings with all employees who had worked with him to tell them he had AIDS. Cronin sued under state privacy law, and his claim survived a motion to dismiss before being settled out of court.

Courts are sympathetic to employers who want to conduct "mind and body" testing, but they have not simply allowed tests under any conditions. On the contrary, they have recognized that testing invades privacy, which they have sought to ensure is at least minimally protected. In assessing the legality of a testing plan, courts will consider the extent to which the industry affects public welfare, has been regulated by the state, and has a history of drug use among workers; how adequately the plan protects privacy and seeks to safeguard both the collection process and the samples obtained; whether employees had notice of the tests; whether there is reason to suspect impairment among particular employees; and whether efforts have been made to ensure test accuracy. Where employers have addressed these issues, their plans have generally withstood challenges involving both privacy- and non-privacy-based claims.

NOTES

1. The amendments to the Constitution generally constrain only government employers. Private employers, however, may be found to have engaged in "state action," if, for example, the state has assisted them in abridging a constitutional right, they exercise power usually reserved to the government, the extent of governmental involvement in their activities so blurs the line between them and the government as to make their conduct state action for all practical purposes, they implement a program prescribed by a federal entity, or state control of their acts is deemed sufficient effectively to make those acts the state's responsibility.

2. 109 S. Ct. 1402 (1989).
3. 109 S. Ct. 1384 (1989).
4. 389 U.S. 347 (1967).
5. 795 F.2d 1136 (3rd Cir. 1986).
6. 850 F.2d 133 (3rd Cir. 1988).
7. 863 F.2d 1110 (3rd Cir. 1988), *aff'd on rehearing*, 884 F.2d 709 (1989).
8. 844 F.2d 562 (8th Cir. 1988).
9. 809 F.2d 1302 (8th Cir. 1987).
10. 840 F.2d 1139 (3rd Cir. 1988).
11. 846 F.2d 1539 (6th Cir. 1988).
12. 109 S. Ct. 1402, 1404–05 (1989).
13. 109 S. Ct. at 1399–1401.
14. 908 F.2d 451 (9th Cir. 1990).
15. 556 N.E.2d 125 (N.Y. Ct. App. 1990).
16. 884 F.2d 603 (D.C. Cir. 1989), *cert denied*, 110 S. Ct. 864 (1990).
17. 715 F.Supp. 195 (N.D. Ohio 1989).
18. 772 F.Supp. 977 (W.D.N.Y. 1989).
19. 725 F.Supp. 87 (D. Mass. 1989).
20. 107 S. Ct. 1487 (1985).

21. 4 IER Cases 168 (3rd Cir. 1989).

22. 384 U.S. 757 (1966); 342 U.S. 165 (1952).

23. Pub. L. 100–347, 102 Stat. 646.

24. Local 1812 Am. Fed'n of Gov't Employees v. U.S. Dept. of State, 662 F.Supp. 50 (D. D.C. 1987).

25. Glover v. Eastern Neb. Community Office of Retardation, 686 F.Supp. 243 (D. Neb. 1988).

PART III

Beyond Constitutional Privacy

10

Who Owns History?

Who owns history? When people hear that question they usually reply: no one. If pressed they suggest that people who lived the history might have some claim. No one has yet answered that historians own history. Of course asking the question in that way almost compels the answer "no one." Few people who have laid claim to history have put it in those terms. They have hidden their claim in the laws of privacy and copyright.

For the purposes of this chapter, assume this situation: Celebrity, a movie star, has lived a very interesting life, and Writer has written and published the definitive unauthorized biography of Celebrity. A movie studio in Hollywood called Studio has a screenplay written based on Writer's book and comes out with a movie entitled "Celebrity, the True Story" which is very successful at the box office. Studio did not get permission from either Celebrity or Writer to make the movie and does not intend to share any of the profits from the movie with either of them. There is nothing in the movie or the book that would justify a lawsuit for defamation (given the present state of defamation law involving "public figures" this is a reasonable assumption).[1]

Both Celebrity and Writer would like to sue Studio and get some of the money Studio made on this movie. The question is: What chance does either of them have?

At the outset one point is certain: Celebrity has no chance of stopping the movie's release. That was made clear in the case of *Rosemont Enterprises, Inc. v. McGraw-Hill Book Co.*, when Howard Hughes tried to stop the publication of Clifford Irving's admittedly fictional biography of Mr. Hughes. The Court said "It is a well-settled principle of law that prior restraint is illegal censorship . . . And it has been held that prior restraint may not issue even as against a publication alleged to be false or scandalous."[2]

CELEBRITY VERSUS STUDIO

Does someone have a property interest in their own life story? *Corliss v. Walker Co.*, decided in 1893, was the first case on that question.[3] The widow of George H. Corliss, a famous inventor, tried to stop the sale of an unauthorized biography of Mr. Corliss. The court could have dealt with this case, which alleged an invasion of privacy, by saying either that only Corliss could bring this lawsuit, and since he was dead no action existed, or that Corliss was a public figure and thus had nothing to complain about. Instead, the court stated its reason for ruling against the widow in broader terms:

But whether Mr. Corliss is to be regarded as a private or public character (a distinction often difficult to define) is not important in this case. Freedom of speech and of the press is secured by the constitution of the United States and the constitutions of most of the states. This constitutional privilege implies a right to freely utter and publish whatever the citizen may please, and to be protected from any responsibility for so doing, except so far as such publication, by reason of its blasphemy, obscenity, or scandalous character, may be a public offense, or by its falsehood and malice, may injuriously affect the standing, reputation, or pecuniary interests of individuals.[4]

For federal judge Colt the answer was obvious: The rights of free speech and press do not tolerate allowing individuals to stop publications about their own lives, or the lives of their ancestors, unless they violate the obscenity laws or constitute defamation of character.

The first legal commentator to discuss the implications of a case like Celebrity's wrote in *Law Notes* in 1922.[5] The deposed king of Germany, William Hohenzollern, brought suit in Germany to stop the production of a play entitled *Bismarck's Dismissal*, in which he figured as a leading character. The American commentator could find no similar case in American law. He suggested that the fact that the person selected for representation on the stage would ordinarily be a "public character" would go far "to destroy any right of privacy which the law might otherwise recognize."[6] He went on to ask if the law should make any distinction between magazine articles and stage dramas and concluded "the right to depict historical events on the stage seems no less than the right to describe them in books, and certainly the latter right is not postponed until the death of all the actors in the event."[7]

The first American case in which the plaintiff claimed a property interest in her own life story was the California case of *Melvin v. Reid*.[8] Gabrielle Darley spent her early years as a prostitute and was tried and acquitted of murder in 1918. She gave up her "life of shame," married Bernard Melvin, and from then on led a "virtuous, honorable, righteous life."[9] In 1925 a movie company released a motion picture entitled "The Red Kimono" based on Gabrielle Darley's past life and using the name Gabrielle Darley for the main character. The publicity for the film made it clear that Gabrielle Darley was now Mrs. Melvin, a respected member of California society. Gabrielle's friends found out about her past and, according to Gabrielle, "scorned and abandoned her."[10] She sued for invasion of privacy and conversion of a property interest in her own life story. The court denied her actions based on the idea that she owned her life story, saying that it could find "no authorities sustaining such a property right in the story of one's life."[11] The court also ruled that "the use of the incidents from the life of appellant in the moving picture is in itself not actionable."[12]

The court did conclude, however, that she had a cause of action for invasion of privacy. The court defined the right of privacy as a "right to be let alone" and allowed Mrs. Melvin to recover because her right to "seclusion" had been violated when her present name was used to advertise the film. The court also said that the right to "seclusion" would be considered waived if the person involved had become prominent.

The court cited Section 1, Article 1 of the California Constitution, which says all California citizens have "certain inalienable rights" that include the right to pursue and obtain "happiness." It felt the use of Gabrielle Darley's true name was "unnecessary and indelicate" and interfered with society's goals of rehabilitating "the fallen." It also violated all the standards of "morals" and "ethics" known to the court. Gabrielle Darley, now Mrs. Melvin, would receive damages for this invasion of her privacy.

The only other case in which a property interest in one's own life story was seriously argued is *Rosemont Enterprises, Inc. v. McGraw-Hill Book Co.*[13] There, the New York court said that "Howard Hughes is no different from any other person in that he cannot have a monopoly, nor can he give a monopoly to any entity, with respect to works concerning his life."[14]

While American courts have not welcomed the idea of a property interest in one's own life story, that is not the end of the matter. Most plaintiffs do not explicitly claim such an interest, but instead disguise the action in terms of an invasion of privacy. Professor Prosser has divided the tort of invasion of privacy into four parts.[15] One is "intrusion," where the defendant invades the plaintiff's solitude or seclusion. The second is "false light," which has been used to allow recovery for such things as putting an honest person's face in a rogue's gallery of criminals or filing suit for someone without permission.[16] The other parts of privacy are "public disclosure of private facts" and "appropriation."

Public Disclosure of Private Facts

This tort began with the publication in 1890 of the now classic law review article by Louis Brandeis and Samuel Warren entitled "The Right to Privacy," discussed at length in Chapter Five.[17] The authors were shocked by the proclivity of the newspapers of the time for publishing intimate details about people's private lives. They felt the law should allow such people to recover for invasion of privacy. At the same time they recognized that the right of privacy should be limited by the public's right to know about things of general interest and suggested that public figures and public officials would have a very limited right of privacy.[18]

By the time of *Melvin v. Reid* in 1931 the right of privacy had evolved sufficiently that the court was able to summarize it as follows:

(1) The right of privacy was unknown to the ancient common law. (2) It is an incident of the person and not of property—a tort for which a right of recovery is given in some jurisdictions. (3) It is a purely personal action, and does not survive, but dies with the person. (4) It does not exist where the person has published the matter complained of, or consented therto. (5) It does not exist where a person has become so prominent that by his very prominence he has dedicated his life to the public, and thereby waived his right to privacy. There can be no privacy in that which is already public. (6) It does not exist in the dissemination of news and news events, nor in the discussion of events of the life of a person in whom the public has a rightful interest, nor where the information would be of public benefit, as in the case of a candidate for public office. (7) The right of privacy can only be violated by printings, writings, pictures, or other permanent publications or reproductions, and not by word of mouth. (8) The right of action accrues when the publication is made for gain or profit.[19]

In *Melvin* the court allowed Gabrielle Darley to recover for an invasion of privacy, based on California's constitutional guarantee of the right to pursue happiness.

The other leading case concerning dramatizations is *Mau v. Rio Grande Oil Inc.*[20] The plaintiff was a chauffeur who, on March 22, 1937, was held up by a robber and shot. The incident was dramatized on the CBS radio show "Calling All Cars." The plaintiff was allowed to recover for an invasion of privacy after arguing that the show had caused him so much mental anguish that on the day following the broadcast he was too upset to drive and was promptly discharged by his employer.

As can be seen from the rather singular facts in *Melvin* and *Mau*, Celebrity doesn't fit into the "public disclosure of private facts" category. The court made clear in *Melvin* that areas of general public interest and information about public figures are privileged. This privilege has expanded through the twentieth century to the point where it is difficult to see how Celebrity could hope to recover.[21]

Celebrity might try to argue that she was an "involuntary" public figure and thus entitled to some special consideration. A long list of cases suggest, however, that even then Celebrity would be out of luck. Consider, for example, the case of *Sidis v. F-R Pub. Corp.*[22] The *New Yorker* magazine searched out and found James Sidis, who at age eleven had lectured distinguished mathematicians, and at sixteen had graduated from Harvard. The magazine found Sidis two decades later, living in a one room apartment in a run-down section of Boston and working as a clerk. The court held that even after two decades Sidis was still enough of a public figure, and his activities were still enough a matter of public interest, that he could not recover for invasion of privacy. Other involuntary public figures who have lost in their attempts to claim an invasion of privacy include the wife of a man stabbed to death on the street, the daughter of a man arrested for real estate fraud, and the family of a woman who committed suicide.[23]

The U.S. Supreme Court dealt with this issue in *Time Inc. v. Hill*.[24] The case involved the Hill family who were held hostage by escaped convicts for nineteen hours in September 1952. Their ordeal was turned into a novel, a play, and ultimately a movie starring Humphrey Bogart. *Life* magazine did a story about the play in which they searched out the Hill family and exposed them to unwanted publicity. The Hill family sued and won, but the U.S. Supreme Court reversed and remanded, ruling that because they were public figures they could only recover if there had been "knowing or reckless falsity" in the article.[25] In other words they could not sue for simple invasion of privacy, but only for defamation of character or "false light" invasion of privacy.

It seems clear that if the Hill family, certainly involuntary public figures, cannot recover for an invasion of privacy without a showing of "knowing or reckless falsity," then Celebrity is going to be out of luck.[26]

Appropriation

Appropriation means using someone's name or picture to sell a product. Legal history reveals that most of the battles between people who did not want their life stories told, and the people who wanted to tell them, have been fought in the appropriation arena.

The earliest case in this area was *Roberson v. Rochester Folding Box Co.*[27] At the beginning of the twentieth century a young girl found her picture being used without her permission in advertisements for a particular brand of flour. She sued, but the highest court in New York held that she had no cause of action. The New York legislature passed a statute in response to this decision which made it a misdemeanor to use, for advertising or purposes of trade, the name, portrait or picture of a living person without obtaining written consent, and allowing the injured party to sue for damages as well.

The next important case in this area is *Binns v. Vitagraph Co. of America.*[28] In 1909 the steamships *Republic* and *Florida* collided at sea. Jack Binns began sending a distress signal using "wireless telegraphy" (a new invention called the radio). The Vitagraph Company made a movie entitled "C.Q.D. or Saved by Wireless: A True Story of the Wreck of the Republic," which was a complete dramatization using actors. The movie was so successful that the company went on to make a whole series of movies starring the same actor in the role of "Jack Binns." Jack Binns sued under the New York law and was allowed to recover, but the court did not clarify whether this was because the company made a movie about his life and used his real name, thus putting movies in the same category as flour, or because the later movies had little to do with the wreck of the *Republic* and were nothing more than an exploitation of Jack Binns' name and reputation. For forty years the New York courts struggled with that question.

In 1919, in *Humiston v. Universal Film Mfg. Co.*, the New York court ruled that newsreel movies did not violate the New York law saying it was "unable to see any practical difference between the presentation of these current events in a motion picture film and in a newspaper."[29] While the court was unanimous in this holding, it split three to two over the question of whether posters with plaintiff's picture on them used to advertise the film were a violation. The majority felt that to allow recovery for that would keep the movie makers from advertising at all, so they denied recovery completely.

Over the years New York courts limited *Binns* to its special facts. Recovery was denied, for example, in *Sarat Lahiri v. Daily Mirror, Inc.*, where the plaintiff sued because his picture had been used to illustrate a magazine article that had nothing to do with him; in *Freed v. Loew's Inc.*, where the plaintiff had posed for a Navy recruiting poster which was used in a movie set; and in *Levy v. Warner Brothers Pictures Inc.*, where the former wife of George M. Cohan sued because of her portrayal in a movie with James Cagney called "Yankee Doodle Dandy."[30]

The case of *Molony v. Boy Comics Publishers* involved an accident in

1945 in which an Army bomber crashed into the Empire State Build-ing.[31] All the occupants of the plane were killed. Molony, a young assistant pharmacist's mate in the U.S. Coast Guard, was the hero of the day, evacuating victims and administering first aid. Six months later a magazine entitled *Boy Comics* came out with a comic strip account of the event. Molony sued under the New York law, forcing the court to decide what *Binns* really meant. May people recover if their lives have been dramatized, or does appropriation occur only if a movie or comic strip has nothing to do with reality and only uses someone's name to attract customers? The court took the second, narrower view of *Binns* and denied recovery, arguing that the key to *Binns* was that the plain-tiff had been impersonated (which was true of the later films) and that recovery had been based on that fact alone.

In *Youssoupoff v. CBS Inc.*, the plaintiff was a Russian prince who participated in the murder of Rasputin.[32] CBS made a television show about the events surrounding Rasputin's death. CBS admitted that the show was a fictional dramatization but claimed to have stayed as close to the facts as possible. The court held that the use of drama did not change the fact that the purpose of the show was to convey informa-tion, much like a magazine or newspaper. It ruled that the prince could not recover unless he could show "that the portrayal . . . by the actor who impersonated him, or the dialogue employed, tended to outrage public opinion or decency in respects other than those produced by the admitted historical facts."[33]

After *Roberson* and the passage of the New York statute, New York courts tried to draw a line between daily newspapers, which were not covered by the law, and advertisements on sacks of flour, which were. It was suspected after *Binns* and *Humiston* that the line fell between movie newsreels (to be treated like newspapers) and dramatic factual movies (to be treated like sacks of flour). Over the decades that fol-lowed the U.S. Supreme Court made it clear that movies, even enter-tainment movies, are protected by the First Amendment's freedom of the press.[34] With the decision in the *Youssoupoff* case, the line had ob-viously moved, but where is it today? Most likely between news post-ers (press) and entertainment posters and board games (flour). In *Fac-tors Etc. Inc. v. Pro Arts, Inc.*, for example, the heirs of Elvis Presley were allowed to recover against the maker of a poster of Elvis put out in memory of Elvis' death.[35] The court held that this constituted using Elvis' name and picture for the purposes of trade. The courts also ap-pear to have decided that board games that use the names, biographi-cal data, and pictures of famous people are nothing more than com-mercial products and have allowed the celebrities involved to recover damages.[36]

All of this seems to leave Celebrity out in the cold, at least in New

York. What if she sued in California? The leading California case is *Stryker v. Republic Pictures Corp.*[37] That case involved the motion picture "Sands of Iwo Jima," made in 1949. John Wayne played Sergeant Stryker, a tough but heroic marine who got his men through the battle of Iwo Jima and in some scenes appeared to win the battle single-handed.[38] The studio advertised that the movie re-enacted certain incidents in the life of the real Sergeant Stryker, who sued claiming that his privacy had been violated. Citing *Sidis,* the California Appeals Court affirmed the dismissal of the case, observing that Stryker was to some extent a public figure and that his complaint did not allege any falsehoods or that he had suffered any mental anguish.

What if the movie is not a biography at all but a work of fiction? In *Spahn v. Messner, Inc.,* the author of a so-called biography had not interviewed any of former professional baseball player Warren Spahn's teammates or done much research of any kind.[39] The highest court in New York found that the author had basically written a novel about a baseball player and put Spahn's name and picture on it to sell copies. The court found this to be an act of appropriation and allowed Spahn to recover. The U.S. Supreme Court remanded the case for reconsideration in light of *Time Inc. v. Hill,* but the New York court held that the "knowing or reckless falsity" test had been met. Although there is no case on this point, it seems clear that if a movie were strictly a work of fiction which used the name of a celebrity to sell tickets, that celebrity would be allowed to recover.

Can the relatives of famous deceased personalities sue and claim ownership of their life stories? The widows of both Jesse James and Al Capone tried and were unsuccessful.[40]

What if the names have been changed but the movie is advertised as being based on real people and real events? Can the real people sue and recover damages? The courts have uniformly held that they cannot. The case of *Waters v. Moore* is illustrative.[41] Francis Waters and Edward Egan participated in one of the greatest drug busts in New York history. Robin Moore wrote a book entitled *The French Connection* that was a true account of those events. Twentieth Century Fox bought the movie rights to the book and made the movie "The French Connection," using fictitious names. Everyone knew the movie was based on the book in which the real names appeared. Francis Waters sued under the New York law but was not allowed to recover. The court said that "New York's privacy statute strikes a delicate balance between the free dissemination of ideas and individual privacy. The former is paramount. The latter, though applied liberally to achieve its laudatory purpose, is subordinate to the principle of a free press."[42]

This is the result that one would expect; yet one cannot help but sympathize with Mr. Waters. Edward Egan became an actor in Hollywood and a television consultant for police shows. Robin Moore was paid a lot of money for the right to use his name and his book title. Francis Waters got nothing, even though he took the risks in real life. That brings us to the other major question of this chapter: Did Twentieth Century Fox have to pay Robin Moore to make a movie about that drug bust? What if they had not wanted to use Robin Moore's name and book title but had simply used his book as a major source of information in writing a screenplay for a movie? Could Robin Moore have successfully sued? To answer that question requires an examination of some basic concepts of American copyright law.

WRITER VERSUS STUDIO

The basic distinction in copyright law is between ideas and original expression. As the U.S. Supreme Court said in the 1899 case of *Holmes v. Hurst*, the copyright law does not protect the "right to the use of certain words because they are the common property of the human race," or the right to own ideas; rather it protects the right to "that arrangement of words which the author has selected to express his ideas."[43] In our hypothetical case, if the Studio had made a copy of Writer's book and sold it on the street that would violate the copyright law. They did not do that. The most they could be considered to have taken is the plot of Writer's book which is the life story of Celebrity. Can the taking of a plot ever be considered a copyright violation?

The 1936 case of *Sheldon v. Metro-Goldwyn Pictures Corp.* was a suit to stop the showing of the movie "Letty Lynton" as an infringement of the plaintiff's copyrighted play, "Dishonored Lady."[44] Both the movie and the play were based on an historical event. In 1857 a Scottish girl, Madeleine Smith, was tried for poisoning her lover. As recently as 1927 the whole proceedings had been published in book form. The playwright used the event as the basis for his play, but he also added a great deal in the way of plot, characters, events, and dialogue. The judge in the case, Learned Hand, outlined in the decision all the fictional details the playwright had added to the historical facts. He then discussed how much of this *added* plot the movie-makers had stolen and found that they had taken more than the idea, the basic historical facts; they had taken the original expression of the playwright in the form of added plot and characters.

In another case, *Nichols v. Universal Pictures Corp.*, Judge Hand was faced with a play, "Abie's Irish Rose," and a movie made after the play entitled "The Cohens and the Kellys."[45] Both are about a Jewish boy and an Irish girl living in New York City who are secretly married and the trouble they go through in trying to get their families to accept their marriage. Judge Hand pointed out that the playwright's copyright did not extend to ideas and went on to discuss the many differences in plot and characters between the play and the movie. He held:

In the two plays at bar we think both as to incident and character, the defendant took no more—assuming that it took anything at all—than the law allowed. The stories are quite different . . . The only matter common to the two is a quarrel between a Jewish and an Irish father, the marriage of their children, the birth of grandchildren and a reconciliation . . . A comedy based upon conflicts between Irish and Jews, into which the marriage of their children enters, is no more susceptible of copyright than an outline of Romeo and Juliet.[46]

In our hypothetical case the Studio took no more than the historical facts of the biography. The Writer added no plot, characters, or dialogue that were products of his imagination. His original expression consisted in the words he chose to express the facts, which were not taken by the movie. As will be seen, however, that no original expression was taken did not mean there could be no recovery for copyright infringement, at least until recently. This is because of an idea British judges developed to interpret British copyright law that was taken up by American judges.

The standard copyright analysis in the United States (hereafter Category One) is simple. To recover in a copyright case plaintiffs have to prove that the defendant has copied their work. This could be difficult if plaintiffs had to find an eyewitness to the copying, but this is not required; instead, the court simply compares the two works. If the expression of the first appears in the second the court will presume copying. While courts say that proof of access plus similarity of expression are needed to prove copying by inference, courts have been known to infer access from the similarity of expression alone.[47]

This analysis is fine for the standard case involving two novels or two plays in which the expression is substantially similar. Where there are millions of ways of expressing an idea, it is reasonable to presume that if the same expression is found in the second work it was probably copied from the first. However, there are not always millions of ways of expressing an idea.

As early as 1879 in *Baker v. Selden* the U.S. Supreme Court had to deal with a very different situation.[48] Baker had invented a new bookkeeping system and published a copyrighted book explaining it and displaying the forms needed to use it. Selden wrote a book about Baker's system and included copies of Baker's forms. Baker sued, claiming that Selden had copied his forms, which he had. The Supreme Court began with the proposition that only expression, not ideas, can be protected by copyright. It found that Baker's idea and its expression (the forms) were so intertwined that protecting the expression would mean protecting the idea, and held that Selden had not infringed on Baker's copyright. This will be called Category Three analysis: where the idea and the expression of that idea cannot be separated, the expression can be copied. Later courts have used this Category Three analysis to deny copyright protection to books which explained a new method of selling pianos, a new shorthand system, and the bylaws of a mutual burial association.[49]

Between Category One (so many ways to express the idea that copying will be inferred from the similarity alone) and Category Three (so few ways to express the idea that to stop the copying of expression would give a monopoly of the idea itself) is Category Two. In Category Two the court cannot infer copying from similarity of expression because there are too few ways of expressing the idea to make that reliable; instead, the court inquires further to see if there is actual evidence of copying.

This analysis was first used in England to deal with claims of copyright infringement involving maps. Obviously, two maps of the same area will look alike if they are accurate. British courts took testimony from the parties involved as to the methods used in making the second map. As one British judge put it, the second map maker "must count the milestones for himself."[50] An early American court used this method in *Brightley v. Littleton*.[51] Both plaintiff and defendant had published forms to be used as liquor licenses. The judge recognized that there are only a few ways the requirements of the statute can be met in a legal form so he inquired further to find out if there was proof of actual copying. The judge found such proof and held for the plaintiff. Both British and American judges, however, have had difficulty deciding where Category Two ends and Category Three begins. The American cases can be divided into two groups: the directory cases and the history cases.

Directory Cases

Having invented Category Two analysis for cases involving maps, British courts proceeded to fit other "fact" works into that category. When American courts considered whether a mere compilation of facts could be protected by copyright, they accepted the British answer and crammed fact compilations into Category Two. The classic case is *Sampson & Murdock Co. v. Seaver-Radford Co.* decided in 1905.[52] The plaintiff published a copyrighted city directory of Boston. The defendant "evidently constructed portions of its directory by simply reproducing corresponding portions" of the plaintiff's directory.[53] The American court cited a number of English cases for the proposition that such directories could be copyrighted and that actual copying would constitute infringement. The defendant was found guilty of copyright infringement. Other American courts followed this lead.

In the 1922 case of *Jeweler's Circular Pub. Co. v. Keystone Pub. Co.* both companies had published books illustrating the trademarks used by various jewelry companies.[54] There was actual proof that the defendant copied from the plaintiff's book (rather than gathering the trademarks itself, i.e. counting the milestones itself) and the court, after discussing several British cases and the *Sampson* case, found the first company's copyright had been infringed. One member of the *Jeweler's Circular* panel dissented, however, saying:

I dissent from the treatment of trade-marks in their relation to copyright. If (as is true) John Doe cannot copyright his own trade-mark, he evidently cannot copyright a thousand other trade-marks belonging to as many other owners. Nor is this truth avoided by the fact that he calls his list of trade-mark reproductions a directory. Assuming now (what no one doubts) that Doe can copyright a directory . . . of matters and things in themselves incapable of copyright, what is such a copyright worth? Nothing at all, as a copyrighting per se of such things as trade-marks; but it does protect the selection, ordering, and arrangement of the pictured or printed material; and infringement of such copyright consists, and consists only, in the copying of a material part of such selection, etc. In this case there was no such material copying . . . I think this plain error of law, in that it gave to an advertising trade list maker a proprietary interest in whatever trade-mark he chose to list. It makes the trade-mark owner, who thereafter reproduces his own trade-mark (using plaintiff's book for copy) an infringer.[55]

Not all American courts have allowed copyright protection to be used in this way.[56] In fact the first American court to face this question in 1829 came to the opposite conclusion. In the case of *Clayton v. Stone* the plaintiff wanted to protect his daily list of current market prices.[57] The court denied copyright protection, finding that Congress did not intend copyright to extend to such works. The court did not really explain the result and the case is generally not cited by later directory cases.

The lengths to which American courts went is illustrated by the 1937 case of *Leon v. Pacific Telephone & Telegraph Co.*[58] The plaintiff telephone company put out a telephone directory which the defendant used to create a reverse directory where people could look up the number and find the name. The Court found this to be copyright infringement.

In short, American courts, following the lead of British courts, placed into Category Two (a few ways of expressing the idea) cases that should have been in Category Three (so few ways to express the ideas (facts) that to stop the copying of expression would be to give a monopoly of the ideas (facts) themselves). Yet, even in Category Two, there must be more than mere similarity (all that is required in Category One). Obviously, such directories are going to look alike. How does anyone prove actual copying? The compilers of such directories handled that problem by using trap-information: putting in false information to trap the copier. In *No-Leak-O Piston Ring Co. v. Norris*, for example, the plaintiff published a directory of piston rings which allowed its customers to look up the model of the car and tell what type of piston ring to use.[59] In the 1919 edition of this copyrighted work they also included twelve fictitious models. The defendant's book came out in 1920 and contained ten of the twelve fictitious models. Faced with that evidence the defendant admitted copying but claimed that such facts could not be copyrighted. The court dismissed that contention quickly by pointing out that even phone directories can be copyrighted!

With these directory cases the copyright law had been pushed to the point where some writers had been given what amounted to ownership of the *facts* contained in their directories.

History Cases

This brings us to the cases dealing more directly with history and biography. In these cases some courts refused to allow the writers to obtain any kind of ownership of the facts they wrote about, but others did not.

In the 1935 case of *Echevarria v. Warner Bros. Pictures*, for example, the plaintiff had written a story based on the Philippines' war for independence from the United States; Warner Brothers put out a movie called "Across the Pacific" based on the same events.[60] There were many differences in characters and plot. The Court ruled that "one cannot build a story around a historical incident and then claim exclusive right to use of the incident."[61] The 1937 case of *Caruthers v. R.K.O. Radio Pictures Inc.*, involved a manuscript called "The Sooners," which dealt with the early days of the Oklahoma territory.[62] The defendant movie company had produced a movie entitled "Cimmarron" based on the novel by the same name which also dealt with the early days of the Oklahoma territory. In finding for the defendant the court said: "ideas as such are not copyrightable. This is also true of the supposed facts of history which necessarily must be dealt with in a similar manner by all historians."[63]

In 1939 Judges Learned and Augustus Hand were part of a three-judge panel for the Second Circuit Court of Appeals in the case of

Collins v. Metro-Goldwyn Pictures Inc.[64] The plaintiff had written a book entitled *Test Pilot* and the defendant movie company had made a movie by the same name about the same subject. The court found no copyright infringement. The court stated that: "the series of events portrayed in the book purports to represent real occurrences which, aside from the form of expression, are not protected by the Copyright Act."[65]

The history and biography cases generally remained separated from the directory cases. In *Funkhouser v. Loews, Inc.* the Court found no copyright infringement of the book *Cupid Rides the Rails* by the movie "The Harvey Girls" even though they were both about the same historical incidents.[66] In *Lake v. CBS* the Court found that a radio show about Wyatt Earp did not infringe on the copyrighted book *Wyatt Earp, Frontier Marshall.*[67]

Not every court agreed with this interpretation, however. In 1950 the Seventh Circuit Court decided *Toksvig v. Bruce Pub. Co.*[68] In that case the plaintiff had spent many years doing research for a book about the life of Hans Christian Anderson. The defendant wrote a novel and used much of the factual information in the plaintiff's book. The court found this to be a violation of the first author's copyright.

Other federal circuit courts did not accept this logic. In *A. A. Hoehling v. Universal City Studios, Inc.* decided by the Second Circuit Court in 1980, Chief Judge Kaufman began his decision with this statement:

A grant of copyright in a published work secures for its author a limited monopoly over the expression it contains. The copyright provides a financial incentive to those who would add to the corpus of existing knowledge by creating original works. Nevertheless, the protection afforded the copyright holder has never extended to history, be it documented fact or explanatory hypothesis. The rationale for this doctrine is that the cause of knowledge is best served when history is the common property of all.[69]

The case involved a movie about the Hindenburg tragedy. Hoehling published his book *Who Destroyed the Hindenburg* in 1962. There he presented the theory that the explosion had been caused by Eric Spehl, a crew member. Ten years later Mooney published his book *The Hindenburg.* Universal City Studies bought the movie rights to Mooney's book and had a screenplay written. Hoehling sued for copyright infringement, claiming that both Mooney and Universal City Studios copied the essential plot of his book—that Eric Spehl sabotaged the Hindenburg. The Second Circuit Court held that Hoehling's copyright extended only to his expression, not to his ideas and the surrounding historical facts.

The Second Circuit Court continued to hold this position. In 1986 it decided *Walker v. Time Life Films Inc.*[70] Thomas Walker wrote a book entitled *Fort Apache*, published in 1976, about his true experiences as a police officer in the forty-first precinct of New York City located in the South Bronx. The film, "Fort Apache: The Bronx" was released in 1981. The Court ruled that the facts of Walker's book were not protected by copyright and if the movie producers took anything, it was facts, not expression. The Court also rejected the idea that, because of similar titles, people would believe wrongly that the movie was based on the book. This precinct had been called Fort Apache long before Walker published his book.

In 1990 it looked as if even the Seventh Circuit Court had finally come to a similar conclusion in these kinds of cases in *Nash v. CBS, Inc.*[71] This case involved the question of whether John Dillinger, Public Enemy Number One, really died in a hail of bullets at the Biograph Theater in Chicago on a hot July night in 1934. Writer Jay Robert Nash did not think so and wrote two books, *Dillinger Dead or Alive?* (1970) and *The Dillinger Dossier* (1983), in an effort to prove that Dillinger learned of the trap set by the FBI and sent another hoodlum to die in his stead. Nash pointed to facts such as Dillinger had blue eyes while the corpse had brown, and Dillinger's father had the body encased in concrete before burial. CBS produced an episode of the "Simon and Simon" detective television show that turned on the idea that Dillinger might not have died that night. The court found that CBS had taken nothing other than the facts as Nash had presented them and this did not violate the copyright law.

THE FEIST PUBLICATIONS CASE

In 1991 the U.S. Supreme Court finally cleared up this confusion with a unanimous decision in *Feist Publications v. Rural Telephone Services Co.*, which involved the publication of a telephone directory by Rural Telephone Service Company.[72] The directory listed names and telephone numbers in alphabetical order. Feist Publications published a large area-wide phone directory and included the information in Rural's directory in its larger compilation. Feist tried to purchase the information from Rural as it had done with other phone companies but Rural would not sell. Rural proved copying by showing that some fictitious names it had included in its directory were contained in Feist's directory.

Justice O'Connor began the opinion by pointing out that for over a century the law had been clear as mud: facts are not copyrightable, compilations of facts are copyrightable. She recognized an "undeniable tension" between these two positions. She pointed out that the key is "originality." A compilation can have originality because the author "chooses which facts to include, in what order to place them, and how to arrange the collected data so that they may be used effectively by readers."[73] However, copyright protection extends only to those aspects of the work that are original. She went on to say: "notwithstanding a valid copyright, a subsequent compiler remains free to use the facts contained in another's publication to aid in preparing a competing work, so long as the competing work does not feature the same selection and arrangement."[74] Selection and arrangement of facts are copyrightable, facts themselves are not. Justice O'Connor discussed at length the *Jeweler's Circular* case, siding with the dissent, and argued that the Copyright Act of 1976 made this all clear. Finally, she ruled that Rural's alphabetical listing of names with phone numbers was not "original" and therefore could not be protected by copyright. She did not care that false facts had been copied because the copying of facts was not forbidden by the copyright law.

The argument had been made that in some cases historical facts were copyrightable because even phone numbers were copyrightable. But phone numbers are not copyrightable after all. Justice O'Connor pointed approvingly to the decisions made by the Second Circuit Court discussed above. It turns out that even writers cannot own history.

PRIVACY VERSUS FREE SPEECH

While it seems clear that a Celebrity or anyone else does not own the facts of their life, the question still remains whether anyone could sue a media defendant for invasion of privacy because a "truthful" fact had been revealed about them and the revelation caused them great mental anguish. The whole point of the 1890 *Harvard Law Review* article by Brandeis and Warren was that in some cases such damages should be allowed. During the twentieth century both the right of privacy and the right of free speech (and press) grew. In several cases the U.S. Supreme Court has faced the question whether the right of privacy can outweigh the right of free speech and has in every instance answered in the negative. The two most important cases are *Cox Broadcasting Corp. v. Cohn* and *Florida Star v. B.J.F.*[75] Both involved the publication of the names of rape victims by newspapers in violation of state law. In both a majority of the Court felt that the right of the people to receive accurate information outweighed any right of privacy enjoyed by the rape victims.

In the 1975 *Cox* case Justice White, writing for the majority, said everyone is surrounded by a zone of privacy which the State may protect from intrusion by the press.[76] However, Justice White made it clear that this was not a case of appropriating a name for commercial purpose, physical intrusion into seclusion, or publication of information tending to put an individual into a false light. It was instead a case of the publication of private facts which would be offensive to a person of ordinary sensibilities. He pointed out that this kind of claim directly confronts the constitutional freedoms of speech and press. Justice White declined to answer the broad question: whether truthful publications may ever be subjected to civil or criminal liability without violating the First and Fourteenth Amendments. Instead he focused on the narrow question: whether the state may impose sanctions on the accurate publication of the name of a rape victim obtained from legally available public records. The answer was no.

Florida Star (1989) was a similar case.[77] Florida law made public records containing this kind of information private. Nevertheless a policeman mistakenly left such information in the press room of the police department, where a reporter learned the name of a rape victim and a newspaper subsequently published it. The newspaper was prosecuted under a law similar to the one in the *Cox* case. A majority of the Court ruled that the newspaper had a constitutional right to publish the information it had obtained. The majority again refused to say whether every publication of "truthful" information is protected by the First Amendment.

Justice White wrote a stinging dissent, joined by Chief Justice Rehnquist and Justice O'Connor. He argued that in this case, because the information was not in a record generally available to the public, the state should have been able to punish a newspaper for publishing it. He asked: If the name of a rape victim is not protected by the right of privacy, what is? This dissenting opinion is somewhat puzzling. Justices White, O'Connor and Chief Justice Rehnquist have maintained all along that there is no constitutional right of privacy. If that is true, how can this nonexistent right ever be held to be greater than the right of free speech, a right generally acknowledged to be the most important right protected by the Bill of Rights?

Cox and *Florida Star* leave open the still unanswered question: Can a private person (not a public figure or public official) ever sue a newspaper for the truthful publication of intimate facts that do not place the individual in a false light but would be highly offensive to anyone of ordinary sensibilities, or would such a lawsuit infringe on the right of free speech and free press protected by the First Amendment? The U.S. Supreme Court may never give a definitive answer to that question.

NOTES

1. New York Times v. Sullivan, 376 U.S. 254 (1964); Curtis Pub. Co. v. Butts, 388 U.S. 130 (1967); Gertz v. Robert Welch Inc., 418 U.S. 323 (1974).

2. 85 Misc. 2d 583, 586, 380 N.Y.S.2d 839, 842–3 (Sup. Ct. 1975).

3. 57 F. 434 (D. Mass. 1893).
4. *Id.* at 435.
5. Comment, *Right to Privacy*, 26 Law Notes 102 (1922).
6. *Id.*
7. *Id.*
8. 297 P. 91 (Cal. App. 1931).
9. *Id.* at 91.
10. *Id.* at 91.
11. *Id.* at 94.
12. *Id.* at 93.
13. 380 N.Y.S.2d 839 (Sup. Ct. 1975).
14. *Id.* at 844.
15. W. Prosser, TORTS (4th ed. 1971) Ch. 20.
16. Itzkovitch v. Whitaker, 39 So. 499 (La. 1905); Steding v. Battistoni, 208 A.2d 559 (Conn. Cir. 1964).
17. Warren and Brandeis, *The Right of Privacy*, 4 Harv. L. Rev. 193 (1890).
18. *Id.* at 214–5.
19. 297 P. 91, 92–3 (Cal. App. 1931).
20. 28 F. Supp. 845 (N.D. Cal. 1939).
21. Comment, *Public Interest as a Limitation of the Right of Privacy*, 41 Ky. L. J. 126 (1952); Spiegel, *Celebrity's Right to Privacy*, 30 So. Calif. L. Rev. 280 (1957).
22. 113 F.2d 806 (2d Cir. 1940).
23. Jones v. Herald Post Co., 18 S.W.2d 972 (Ky. 1929); Hillman v. Star Pub. Co., 117 P. 594 (Wa. 1911); Metter v. Los Angeles Examiner, 95 P.2d 491 (Cal. App. 1939).
24. 385 U.S. 374 (1967).
25. *Id.* at 397.
26. Hemingway v. Random House Inc., 23 N.Y.2d 341, 244 N.E.2d 250 (1968) (Hemingway's wife refused recovery); Nimmer, *The Right to Speak from Times to Time: First Amendment Theory Applied to Libel and Misapplied to Privacy*, 56 Calif. L. Rev. 935 (1968); Bartelsman, *The First Amendment and Protection of Reputation and Privacy—New York Times Co. v. Sullivan and How it Grew*, 56 Ky. L. J. 718 (1968); Comment, *Privacy—Privilege to Report Matters of Public Interest*, 21 S. Ca. L. Rev. 92 (1968); Kalven, *Privacy in Tort Law—Were Warren and Brandeis Wrong?*, 31 Law & Cont. Problems 326 (1966); Bloustein, *Privacy, Tort Law, and the Constitution: Is Warren and Brandeis' Tort Petty and Unconstitutional as Well*, 46 Tex. L. Rev. 611 (1968); Pember and Teeter, *Privacy and the Press Since Time Inc. v. Hill*, 50 Wash. L. Rev. 57 (1974); Giglio, *Unwanted Publicity, the News Media, and the Constitution: Where Privacy Rights Compete with the First Amendment*, 12 Akron L. Rev. 229 (1978); Woito and McNulty, *The Privacy Disclosure Tort and the First Amendment: Should the Community Decide Newsworthiness?* 64 Iowa L. Rev. 185 (1978); Ashdown, *Media Reporting and Privacy Claims—Decline in Constitutional Protection for the Press*, 66 Ky. L. J. 759 (1978); Comment, *The First Amendment Privilege and Public Disclosure of Private Facts*, 25 Cath. U. L. Rev. 271 (1975); Beytagh, *Privacy and a Free Press: A Contemporary Conflict in Values*, 20 New York L. Forum 453 (1975); Treece, *Commercial Exploitation of Names, Likenesses and Personal Histories*, 51 Tex. L. Rev. 637 (1973).
27. 171 N.Y. 538, 64 N.E. 442 (1902).

28. 210 N.Y. 51, 103 N.E. 1108 (1913).

29. 189 App. Div. 467, 474; 178 N.Y.S. 752, 757 (1919).

30. 162 Misc. 776, 295 N.Y.S. 382 (Sup. Ct. 1937); 175 Misc. 679, 24 N.Y.S.2d 679 (Sup. Ct. 1940); 57 F. Supp. 40 (S.D.N.Y. 1944).

31. 277 App. Div. 166, 98 N.Y.S.2d 119 (1950).

32. 41 Misc. 2d 42, 244 N.Y.S.2d 701 (Sup. Ct. 1063) *aff'd mem.* 19 App. Div. 2d 865, 244 N.Y.S.2d 1 (N.Y. App. 1963).

33. *Id.* at 47–8, 244 N.Y.S.2d at 707.

34. Winters v. New York, 333 U.S. 507 (1948); Burstyn v. Wilson, 343 U.S. 495 (1952); Kingsley Pictures Corp. v. Regents, 360 U.S. 684 (1960).

35. 579 F.2d 215 (2d Cir. 1978).

36. Palmer v. Schonhorn Enterprises Inc., 96 N.J. Super. 72, 232 A.2d 458 (Ch. 1967); Uhlzaender v. Henricksen, 316 F. Supp. 1277 (D. Minn. 1970).

37. 108 Cal. App. 2d 191, 238 P.2d 670 (1951).

38. The authors have seen the movie several times.

39. 18 N.Y.2d 324, 274 N.Y.S.2d 877, 221 N.E.2d 543 (1966), *remanded* 387 U.S. 239 (1967), *reaffirmed* 21 N.Y.2d 124, 286 N.Y.S.2d 832 (1967).

40. James v. Screen Gems, Inc., 174 Cal. App. 2d 650, 344 P.2d 799 (1959).

41. 70 Misc. 2d 372, 334 N.Y.S.2d 428 (Sup. Ct. 1972).

42. *Id.* at 377, 334 N.Y.S.2d at 434.

43. 174 U.S. 82, 86 (1899).

44. 81 F.2d 49 (2d Cir. 1936), *cert. denied* 298 U.S. 669 (1936).

45. 45 F.2d 119 (2d Cir. 1930), *cert. denied* 282 U.S. 902 (1930).

46. *Id.* at 121–2.

47. Arnstein v. Porter, 154 F.2d 464 (2d Cir. 1946); Smith v. Little, Brown & Co., 245 F. Supp. 451 (S.D.N.Y. 1965), *aff'd* 360 F.2d 928 (2d Cir. 1966); Heim v. Universal Pictures Co., 154 F.2d 480 (2d Cir. 1946); Miller Studio, Inc. v. Pacific Import Co., 147 U.S.P.Q. 388 (S.D.N.Y. 1965).

48. 101 U.S. 99 (1879).

49. Stone & McCarrick v. Dugan Piano Co., 210 F. 399 (E.D.La. 1914), *aff'd* 220 F. 837 (5th Cir. 1915).

50. Kelly v. Morris, L.R. 1 Eq. 697, 701 (1866).

51. 37 F. 103 (E.D.Pa. 1888).

52. 140 F. 539 (1st Cir. 1905).

53. *Id.* at 540.

54. 281 F. 83 (2d Cir. 1922), *cert. denied* 259 U.S. 581 (1922).

55. *Id.* at 96–7.

56. Edward Thompson C. v. American Law Book Co., 122 F. 922 (2d Cir. 1903).

57. 5 Fed. Cas. No. 2,872 (S.D.N.Y. 1829).

58. 91 F.2d 484 (9th Cir. 1937).

59. 277 F. 951 (4th Cir. 1921).

60. 12 F. Supp. 632 (S.D.Ca. 1935).

61. *Id.* at 638.

62. 20 F. Supp. 906 (S.D.N.Y. 1937).

63. *Id.* at 907.

64. 106 F.2d 83 (2d Cir. 1939).

65. *Id.* at 86.

66. 208 F.2d 185 (8th Cir. 1953).
67. 140 F. Supp. 707 (S.D.Ca. 1956).
68. 181 F.2d 664 (7th Cir. 1950).
69. 618 F.2d 972, 974 (2d Cir. 1980).
70. 784 F.2d 44 (2d Cir. 1986).
71. 899 F.2d 1537 (7th Cir. 1990).
72. 111 Sup. Ct. 1282 (1991).
73. *Id.* at 1289.
74. *Id.*
75. 420 U.S. 469 (1975); 491 U.S. 524 (1989).
76. 420 U.S. 469 (1975).
77. 491 U.S. 524 (1989).

11

State Constitutional Privacy

The preceding chapters have examined the historical, philosophical, and legal underpinnings, as well as the creation, evolution, and present contours of the right of privacy that the U.S. Supreme Court has said exists in the federal Constitution. From this discussion it could be inferred that this right has become so ingrained in American law as to preclude the Court from seriously limiting its scope or denying its existence. To so conclude, however would be a grievous error. As has been stressed, the right is entirely Court-created, and what the Court gives, it can take away.

Bolstered as the Court now is with very conservative, young justices—Presidents Reagan and Bush appointed Justices Thomas, O'Connor, Kennedy, Scalia, and Souter, and holdovers Justice White and Chief Justice Rehnquist are from the same mold—many think it is poised to assault many of the federal constitutional rights that prior Courts have recognized. A prime candidate is the abortion right that the 1973 Court said is part of a woman's Fourteenth Amendment "liberty." Another target may be the whole notion of "constitutional privacy" itself.

Two decades ago, when President Nixon began replacing the liberal justices of the Warren Court with far more conservative justices, some lower court judges, alarmed about the implications of those appointments in terms of individual rights, began seeking alternative ways to protect those rights. The movement they launched, which acquired the name "New Federalism," was spearheaded by Oregon Supreme Court Justice Hans Linde. New Federalists argued that state courts wanting to preserve, if not expand, existing federal civil rights should view their state constitutions as vehicles for doing so. Many state constitutions, they noted, have provisions similar to those in the federal Bill of Rights; if state courts were to hold that these provisions protect individual rights even more than the Bill of Rights, the U.S. Supreme Court would be powerless to say otherwise. This was affirmed by the Court itself when it held that "[i]f a state court decision indicates clearly and expressly that it is alternatively based on *bona fide* separate, adequate, and independent [*i.e.* state] grounds, we, of course, will not undertake to review the action."[1]

As the years passed this movement gained momentum as conservatives were increasingly appointed to the federal bench. Abortion, school funding, and sex discrimination are just three areas in which the New Federalism has maintained and even expanded federal constitutional rights based on state constitutional law, while the U.S. Supreme Court has chipped away at those rights. Indeed, in 1990 it was estimated that in twenty years state high courts had issued more than 600 opinions going beyond the federal minimum standards on individual rights issues.[2]

Given the magnitude of this effort and its potential for individual rights—especially now, when, with the replacement of Justices Brennan and Marshall with Justices Souter and Thomas, the Court is more conservative than it has been in decades—it deserves some treatment here.

Each state has a choice of methods by which it can protect a federal constitutional right.[3] When it is claimed that a federal right is protected by both the federal and state constitutions, some state courts analyze the latter claim before the former; if they accept it, there is no need to look at federal law. Other states turn first to the claim that a right is protected by the federal constitution and examine the state claim only afterward, if at all. The last group looks concurrently at the federal and state constitutional claims and makes a decision based on both. As noted, states that look at and accept state-based claims independently, by examining them first or as an alternative to a federal claim, can provide protection for civil rights which is immune from review by the federal courts.

State guarantees of civil liberties can be more expansive than those offered by the U.S. Supreme Court. In an important First Amendment decision, for example, that Court agreed California could go farther in protecting speech rights than the Court was willing to go.[4] And freedom of speech is not the only right with which states have chosen to deal independently.

Ten states have explicit provisions in their constitutions that protect privacy or the right to be left alone.[5] Even more have interpreted other provisions in their constitutions as creating a penumbra-based privacy right. Whatever the basis, many states have designated themselves as the last bastion for privacy rights due to a culmination of political and legal events which have kept the federal courts from being aggressive or even maintaining the *status quo* in this area. An examination of selected key decisions affords a notion of the direction states seem headed on this issue.

POLYGRAPHS AND THE TEXAS RIGHT TO PRIVACY

In September 1983 the Texas Department of Mental Health and Mental Retardation adopted a policy stating that employees were subject to mandatory polygraph testing if an investigation of wrongdoing was warranted. The policy called for "adverse personnel action" against any employee who declined to take a test. The Texas State Employees Union sued the Department claiming the policy violated the right of privacy of state employees. In a battle that ended in the Texas Supreme Court, a new state-based constitutional right of privacy was created.

Although a lower court had found a privacy right based on state common law, it did not award the plaintiff attorney fees and court costs.[6] This ruling was appealed, affording the Texas Supreme Court an opportunity to review the case to decide the fee issue as well as to comment on the privacy concerns. The court ruled on the case in October 1987.

After hearing arguments, the court reversed the fee ruling. More importantly, the court discussed the privacy issue not in common law terms, as Texas courts had previously done, but rather in terms of the Texas Constitution. Although the Texas Constitution contains no explicit privacy guarantee, the court held that one is implied in several parts of the Texas Bill of Rights. For example, the court noted that freedoms of speech and of the accused not to testify against themselves are protected, as are citizens from unreasonable intrusion in their homes. Religious freedom is also protected. In the court's view, these provisions reflect a general tendency of the Texas Constitution to value privacy. Citing the introduction to the Texas Bill of Rights, the court held that "[w]e do not doubt, therefore, that a right of individual privacy is implicit among those general, great and essential principles of liberty and free government" that were established by the Texas Bill of Rights.

Having created this right, the court established a standard under which to judge the validity of state intrusions on it. The court held that citizens can be denied privacy only if the state has a "compelling" interest in achieving an objective and there is no other reasonable way to achieve it.

With this new privacy right it appeared that Texas courts were positioned to extend significant personal protection to Texans. But in fact, courts have done little with this right. For example, a Houston school teacher who felt her rights were violated when her classroom performance was videotaped was denied recovery, on the ground that the behavior was performed in public.[7] Nonetheless, the powerful language of the *Texas State Employees Union* case has most commentators convinced that Texans are now shielded from unwarranted governmental incursion into their lives.[8]

ABORTIONS AND THE FLORIDA RIGHT TO PRIVACY

As was noted in Chapter 8, in 1989 the U.S. Supreme Court decided *Webster v. Reproductive Health Services.*[9] That case involved the constitutionality of a Missouri statute which restricted a woman's right to obtain an abortion. Declining to reexamine *Roe v. Wade*, despite Justice Scalia's protest that the Court should do just that, the majority decided to defer to the states. As Justice Blackmun said in his dissent, "the plurality . . . would return to the states virtually unfettered authority to control the quintessentially intimate, personal, and life-directing decision whether to carry a fetus to term. . . ."[10]

Shortly after this decision, several state legislatures attempted to pass tough new laws restricting abortion rights. If, however, privacy issues like abortion were to be left to the states to decide, it soon became clear that lawmakers would not be the only ones involved. Besides granting legislators leeway to manipulate privacy, the Court also opened the door for state courts to analyze how privacy should be understood in a local context. The Florida Supreme Court lost little time in accepting this invitation.

In *In re T.W.*,[11] that court invalidated several statutes which restricted access to abortion, in the process winning an overnight national reputation as a protector of women's rights. The court did so based on Florida's explicit constitutional right of privacy. In 1980 Floridians amended the constitution by stating that everyone has the "right to be let alone and free from governmental intrusion into his private life. . . ."[12] Using this provision as authority, the court held that in Florida there is a right of privacy which extends further than any such right under the U.S. Constitution.

The case involved parental consent statutes, and the court held that a woman's right to decide extends to minors. While the victory was important to Florida's pro-choice contingency, it was also significant to those interested in how states handle privacy. This is because the court reemphasized the method by which states can provide wider protection for civil liberties than the federal government can. As the opinion notes, "the [Florida constitutional] amendment embraces more privacy interests, and extends more privacy protection to the individual in those interests, than does the federal Constitution."[13] Finally, the court examined the standard by which to judge government intrusions on a citizen's privacy. Following the lead of the Texas Supreme Court in 1987, the court allowed such infringements only if there is a "compelling state interest." By adopting this standard, the Florida court strengthened the notion that states have their own power over privacy.

The Florida Supreme Court has used the compelling interest standard in several non-abortion cases. In 1990, for example, the court decided *In re Guardianship of Estelle M. Browning v. Herbert*,[14] which relied on *In re T.W.* in holding that there is a state right of privacy which protects the "right to die" decision of the terminally ill. There the court discussed whether the state had a compelling interest in infringing on this decision and found that it did not; in so doing, it stressed that the guarantee of privacy in the Florida Constitution is a powerful guardian of individual liberties and that it is willing to use that guarantee to protect those liberties. Other state privacy cases have involved blood transfusions, backyard helicopter searches, government phone tapping, and a luggage search on a South Florida bus.[15]

SEX AND THE NEW JERSEY RIGHT TO PRIVACY

Many states have laws which attempt to control the sexual activity of consenting adults. For example, over twenty states have laws banning sodomy. When the U.S. Supreme Court refused to invalidate state anti-sodomy laws in 1986 in *Bowers v. Hardwick*,[16] it effectively allowed courts in each state to be the final arbiter of the constitutionality of such laws.

One frequent basis for attacking sexual behavior laws is that they violate privacy.[17] New Jersey courts have, in a series of cases, effectively taken away from the legislature the power to criminalize sexual behavior between adults. While New Jersey has no explicit constitutional right of privacy, one has been understood to exist since 1976 when, in *In re Quinlan*,[18] the New Jersey Supreme Court held that this right protected a parental decision to terminate the life of their comatose daughter.

The next year, two men were indicted under a rarely used New Jersey fornication law banning intercourse between unmarried consenting adults. The men appealed on the basis that the statute violated their privacy, as there was no compelling interest in discouraging this type of sexual relationship. The New Jersey Supreme Court agreed.[19] Arguing that the right to be left alone is the right most cherished by civilized men, the court held that in New Jersey such sexual behavior is beyond the realm of legitimate state interference. Importantly, the court did not rely solely on the federal privacy concept in reaching its decision; instead, it cited the state privacy right that it had recognized in *Quinlan*.

With this foundation, a New Jersey appeals court found itself faced with the validity of the state anti-sodomy law. The holding was somewhat inevitable given the strength of the existing privacy right. Remarking that "[p]rivate personal acts between two consenting adults are not to be lightly meddled with by the State" and that the "right of personal autonomy is fundamental to a free society," the court struck down the New Jersey sodomy laws on privacy grounds.

The New Jersey approach demonstrates a direct, powerful way to set precedent and then use it to guard against intrusions into the private lives of citizens. Several states which have privacy provisions in their constitutions now have sodomy statutes and other sexual behavior laws on the books. The New Jersey approach shows that a consistent judiciary can reconcile the public policy distinction between these kinds of laws and the right of privacy.

In 1992 a Texas Appeals Court ruled that the Texas sodomy law was a violation of the Texas constitutional right to privacy. The decision has been appealed to the Texas Supreme Court.

As noted in previous chapters, the modern notion of privacy was for all practical purposes created in 1890 in the Warren and Brandeis article in the *Harvard Law Review*.[20] In that seminal article, the authors recognized a need for constant refinement and development of this right. "That the individual shall have full protection in person and in property is a principle as old as the common law; but it has been found necessary from time to time to define anew the exact nature and extent of such protection." Perhaps the framers of the U.S. Bill of Rights intended decisions on privacy and other rights not specifically mentioned to be left to the states; whether or not they did is the subject of much scholarly debate. What no one disputes, however, is that under the current trend of Supreme Court decisions, states seem to have been handed—and many have welcomed—the responsibility to define privacy's role in society. How different states handle this responsibility has and will continue to have a tremendous effect on the citizens of that state, and eventually on all citizens.

NOTES

1. Michigan v. Long, 463 U.S. 1032, 1041 (1983).
2. National Law Journal, May 28, 1990.
3. *See generally*, Silverstein, *Privacy Rights in State Constitutions: Models for*

Illinois, 89 U. Ill. L. Rev. 215 (1989), Collins & Galie, *Models of Post-Incorporation Judicial Review: 1985 Survey of State Constitutional Individual Rights Decisions,* 55 U. Cin. L. Rev. 317 (three models).

4. Robins v. Pruneyard Shopping Center, 447 U.S. 74 (1980).

5. Alaska, Arizona, California, Florida, Hawaii, Illinois, Louisiana, Montana, South Carolina, and Washington.

6. Texas State Employees Union v. Texas Dep't of Mental Health and Mental Retardation, 708 S.W.2d 498 (Tex. App.-Austin 1986), *rev'd in part, aff'd in part,* 746 S.W.2d 203 (Tex. 1987).

7. Roberts v. Houston Ind. School District, 788 S.W.2d 107, 111 (Tex. App.-Houston [1st Dist.] 1990).

8. *See, e.g.,* Johnson, *Abortion, Personhood and Privacy,* 68 Tex. L. Rev. 1521 (1990).

9. 109 S. Ct. 3040 (1989).

10. *Id.* at 3067 (Blackmun, J., dissenting).

11. 551 So.2d 1186 (Fla. 1989).

12. Fla. Const. art. I, sec. 23.

13. *Id.* at 1192.

14. 568 So.2d 4 (Fla. 1990).

15. Public Health Trust of Dade County v. Wons, 541 So.2d 96; Riley v. State, 511 So.2d 282; Shaktman v. State, 553 So.2d 148; Bostick v. State, 554 So.2d 1153.

16. 478 U.S. 186 (1986).

17. For a good general discussion of sexual privacy and the states, *see* Morris, *Challenging Sodomy Statutes: State Constitutional Protections for Sexual Privacy,* 66 Ind. L. J. 609 (1991).

18. 355 A.2d 647 (N.J. 1976), *cert. denied,* 429 U.S. 922 (1976).

19. State v. Saunders, 381 A.2d 333 (N.J. 1977).

20. Warren and Brandeis, *The Right to Privacy,* 4 Harv. L. Rev. 193 (1890). *See* Chapter 5.

12

Conclusion

On October 15, 1991, the citizens of the United States were treated to a televised roll call vote of the United States Senate on the confirmation of Clarence Thomas to the Supreme Court. As each Senator stood to vote the television flashed the count at the bottom of the screen. Finally it was official: by a vote of fifty-two to forty-eight Clarence Thomas was a justice of the United States Supreme Court. This marked a major milestone in the history of the United States. America began the twentieth century with a Supreme Court much more conservative than the average citizen and will end the twentieth century the same way. In between, the New Deal and Warren Courts redefined the concepts of individual rights and governmental power over business. The Burger Court tried to reach a compromise on many of the important issues of the day but too often ended up with fuzzy lines that gave little guidance to the judges of America on important constitutional questions.

It was almost forgotten in the last few days of special hearings on sexual harassment that the major focus of the Thomas confirmation hearings had been the right to privacy. Clarence Thomas said he believed the Constitution protects a general right to privacy, but declined to say if that right included the right to have an abortion. As Thomas was sworn in by Chief Justice Rehnquist on October 23, 1991, the new make-up of the Court became obvious. Chief Justice Rehnquist, who had often been the lone voice of extreme conservatism on the Burger Court, swears in a fellow conservative. Of the seven justices that voted in favor of the right to obtain an abortion in the 1973 decision of *Roe v. Wade*, only two remain on the Court. Of the remaining seven justices, all have either expressed a desire to overrule *Roe v. Wade* or are believed to be willing to do so.

But the America these justices will make decisions for is very different from the America of a century ago. In a very real sense America has evolved further down the road Locke and Montesquieu imagined. When Thomas Jefferson, James Madison, and others found themselves victors after the revolutionary war they set out to rid America of what they considered outmoded legal concepts that would have no place in a modern liberal democratic society. No longer would punishment fall on both the wrongdoer and his descendants. No longer would houses be searched without a warrant, taxes be levied without the consent of the legislature, and soldiers be billeted in private homes without the owner's consent. Church and state would be separate, meaning there would no longer be an "established" church and that all religious beliefs would be tolerated. But this was just the beginning. The slaves would have to be freed and women would have to achieve the equal status Locke (followed by Mill) suggested. Montesquieu's concept that law should not be used to enforce a particular moral code would have to be fulfilled. Rousseau's new people and new institutions would have to be created. The line Mill hoped to draw between the freedom of the individual and the power of the government would have to be drawn, and redrawn as concepts of freedom progressed.

From natural law to natural rights to substantive due process to the right to privacy, the problem of finding the proper line between governmental power and individual liberty is still present. As each new generation has been raised with an ever greater sense of their "rights" as "citizens" of the first free country, America has had to ask over and over again what it means to be free. As countries in Eastern Europe move to replace the "established" religion of Communism with a new "established" religion of Catholicism, Americans are reminded of why their ancestors left Europe in the first place. Most of them came for freedom first, democracy second. As the soldiers left for Operation Desert Storm, Americans were reminded of the price that has been paid and will be paid again to protect the "unalienable" rights of "life, liberty and the pursuit of happiness."

After the American Revolution Thomas Jefferson was ambassador to France. Reading his letters to the United States it becomes clear that the Europeans he met thought the United States was a unique experiment not because it was a democracy but because it was a democracy dedicated to the protection of individual liberty. History was full of democracies where the majorities had used their power to control or even enslave a minority. The idea that both democracy and liberty would be supreme values was new and many wondered if such an experiment could succeed. The particular aspect of this concept that intrigued the Europeans the most was the idea that church and state would be separated. The United States wanted to be a "secular" state that would allow the worship of many different religions within its borders and would avoid using the power of the state to enforce religious beliefs. At the same time the Americans who fought the revolutionary war knew their English history. They knew the Puritan Commonwealth failed precisely because it refused to grant individual liberty and to tolerate other religions.

Two centuries ago the United States began this experiment in the creation of a state that would neither "establish" religion nor interfere with the "free exercise" of religion. Today the United States and the U.S. Supreme Court is faced with the logical consequences of that decision. During the nineteenth century the Court spoke often of the "police power" of states. This was seen as the power to promote the public "health, safety and morals." While John Stuart Mill had called for an end to laws that outlawed behavior which did not do any harm to anyone else, most legislators and judges have felt that such laws are legitimate. Now the question before the Court and the society is the extent to which it is appropriate for the state to tell people what their "morals" will be.

There are those who argue that laws against polygamy, sodomy, and fornication are almost impossible to enforce so society should not worry about them. The problem with that argument, however, is that such laws can be enforced in particular situations when the state decides it wants to "get someone." The Mann Act makes it a federal crime to transport women across a state line for immoral purposes (which include the purpose of cohabitation). How many college students violate that law during spring break every year? Generally courts strike down laws which define a criminal offense so that most people cannot tell what kinds of behavior are prohibited. What does "immoral purpose" or "crime against nature" mean to the average American at the end of the twentieth century? In a world in which the average teenager has experienced sexual relations, what good are laws designed to limit teenage promiscuity by withholding access to contraceptives?

Justice Rehnquist in his dissenting opinion in *Carey* argued that the soldiers who fought in the Revolutionary and Civil Wars would be horrified to learn that their efforts went to protect the right to have contraceptive vending machines in truck stop rest-rooms. That may or may not be true but would it not be more relevant to ask what the soldiers, male and female, who fought in Operation Dessert Storm thought they were protecting? How many of them would be shocked to discover that such a right was not protected by the Constitution?

The United States is a strange society in that everyone from the president to a private in the army has to take an oath to "preserve, protect and defend the Constitution of the United States." Everyone owes allegiance to a document, not an individual, and its meaning has to change over time for it to remain relevant. Justice Black in *Katz* argued that it was not the Supreme Court's job to bring the Constitution "into harmony with the times" but a majority of the Court has always felt that this was exactly their role, and a role that only the Court could fulfill. The Constitution is a social contract that Americans sign every morning when they get up and decide to be law abiding, tax paying, citizens for that day. While the intent of the drafters is certainly relevant, so is the understanding of those everyday signers two centuries later. How many of them think they have a right to privacy?

If *Roe v. Wade* is overturned and the other privacy decisions are interpreted in a limited way, the right to privacy will protect little else besides the right to purchase contraceptives. Will history view *Griswold* and *Roe v. Wade* in the decades to come the same way *Lochner* is viewed today, as an example of where the Court took a wrong turn down the road of constitutional interpretation?

Some might argue that this would not be a bad result if it meant the U.S. Supreme Court would once and for all stop second guessing state legislatures. However, except for Justice Scalia, the justices do not seem headed in that direction. Chief Justice Rehnquist's decision in *Cruzan* acknowledges that the Court has a right to interpret the Due Process Clause of the Fourteenth Amendment in a "substantive" way to overturn legislation which a majority of the Court finds "unreasonable." There is a very real fear that the conservative Rehnquist Court will simply use that power to enforce its own particular "prejudices" in the same way the conservative *Lochner* Court did a century ago.

There is another issue that must be considered. Who should decide these questions? Why should the U.S. Supreme Court be the institution that turns the United States into a secular state and gets government out of the business of regulating sexual morality? It would come as a great surprise to most of the authors of both the Constitution and the Fourteenth Amendment to learn that the Court had assumed that role in American society at the end of the twentieth century. They would have assumed that such questions would be dealt with by state legislatures and state supreme courts interpreting state constitutions.

The Court made its decision in *Roe v. Wade* in part to keep such an emotional and divisive issue out of the political process. Why should that be the Court's role? Abortion raises very difficult questions concerning when life begins and how the rights of the unborn should be weighed against the rights of the mother. Thousands of years ago in the most ancient Indo-European societies the decision of whether the newborn child would live or die was strictly up to the father. Then it became a question for the state and the church. Now, in the twentieth century, the U.S. Supreme Court has decided it should be up to the mother alone. It is hard to imagine a more significant departure from the traditions of the society than this one.

On the other hand, there is something very unsettling about a world in which there is one abortion law in Catholic states, another in Mormon states, and still another in states where a religious minority is unable to gain control of the legislature. If *Roe v. Wade* is overturned, will ministers and priests run for office arguing that only they can be trusted to carry out the wishes of their religious constituents? Will state legislatures come to look more like the parliament of Iran than the parliament of a secular state? It is ironic that the descendants of the Episcopalians and Presbyterians who gave up their rights as members of the "established" churches of most American colonies two centuries ago find their right to obtain an abortion constrained at the request of sects that would be illegal if their ancestors had not been so tolerant. Has Rousseau's warning about the dangers of tolerating intolerant sects come to pass?

Throughout the twentieth century justices arguing against Court action in the "substantive due process" area have favored allowing the states to "experiment" with new social institutions. But how far is America prepared to allow those experiments to go? How much diversity can a nation stand? It could not exist "half slave and half free." Will it be able to exist "half abortion-on-demand, half abortion-as-felony?" While some might feel this is an exaggeration, there is probably no issue that has divided the country more since the Civil War than abortion.

There is also the policy issue. On September 11, 1991, the front page of the *San Jose Mercury News* contained two stories: one involved the confirmation hearings for Justice Thomas, and the other was about two fourteen-year old boys who performed an abortion on a fourteen-year old girl using an air rifle and a vacuum cleaner. They began by punching her in the stomach "very hard" and ended with a "lot of blood." The article talked about the confusion that surrounds this issue. These teenagers apparently elected to perform a home abortion because they believed abortions were illegal or not available to teenagers. The state involved was California and nothing could have been further from the truth. Regardless of whether the Court overturns *Roe v. Wade* or significantly modifies it, it is time to provide clear guidance for everyone. Until it does so, the blood of this and hundreds of other little girls will be on its conscience.

It could be said that beginning in the 1960s American society experienced both a civil rights and a sexual revolution and that the Supreme Court acknowledged both in its decisions in the 1960s and 1970s. In the 1980s and 1990s the Court has retreated in both areas. It has refused to take past decisions to their logical conclusions. This has left the law in both areas uncertain and to some extent engendered a disrespect for the law. Cynical people can say that the ideal of a government of law, not of men, is not realized when every new Supreme Court appointment brings major changes in such important areas of the law.

This book has been an attempt to present the current state of the law in an objective fashion. We do not urge the Court to decide the abortion issue one way or the other. We do urge the Court to come to a conclusion that is logical and can be explained to the average American with a straight face. After a quarter of a century the American people deserve at least that from the highest court in the land. We also urge the Court not to reject the concept of a "right to privacy" entirely if it does overturn *Roe v. Wade*. If abortion is beyond the reach of such a right, there are clearly many areas of life that should fall within its protection. While the right to privacy is vague, it is no vaguer than many rights explicitly protected by the Bill of Rights. At the same time it is not as all-encompassing as the power to declare laws passed by state legislatures unconstitutional because they do not conform to the prejudices of five members of the U.S. Supreme Court.

This book began by looking at the historical and philosophical foundations of the right to privacy. It must end by returning to Locke and Montesquieu. Indo-European society has changed more over the last three centuries than it did over the preceding three millennia. This is due in no small part to the ideas expressed by these two men. When Locke spoke of the rights of mothers to equal respect he was setting in motion concepts that would ultimately lead to today's equal rights for women and bring into question who should be allowed to regulate abortions. When Montesquieu said that they have no bastards where polygamy is permitted and this "disgrace" is only known in countries where a man is allowed only one wife, he was poking fun at a concept that he could not see any reason to uphold. When the U.S. Supreme Court tried to lessen the permissible burdens that states may place on illegitimate children, it did so in part as a logical consequence of a general attempt to end the idea that the sins of the parents should be visited on the children.

When both Locke and Montesquieu spoke of the need for religious toleration, they set in motion ideas that Thomas Jefferson and others turned into reality. America has been wrestling with the consequences of that reality ever since. When Justice Scalia and a majority of the Court refused in *Employment Division v. Smith* to make one law for the religious and another for everyone else they were facing up to the logical consequences of that idea. If it is not practical to exempt the religious from the enforcement of some laws which infringe on their religious conduct, should there still not be some areas of life which are beyond the power of the state to control?

Justice Brandeis in his famous dissenting opinion in *Olmstead* spoke of the need to protect people's "spiritual nature," their "feelings" and their "intellect," their "beliefs . . . thoughts . . . emotions and . . . sensations." He felt that the whole point of the Constitution was to confer on individuals "the right to be let alone—the most comprehensive of rights and the right most valued by civilized men." While it may be difficult in many cases to decide where to draw the line between the power of government and "the most comprehensive of rights" it is important that such a line be drawn and that the U.S. Supreme Court take the lead in drawing it.

Appendix

A BILL FOR ESTABLISHING RELIGIOUS FREEDOM IN VIRGINIA

Section I. Well aware that the opinions and belief of men depend on their own will, but follow involuntarily the evidence proposed to their minds; that Almighty God hath created the mind free, and manifested his supreme will that free it shall remain by making it altogether insusceptible of restraint; that all attempts to influence it by temporal punishments, or burthens, or by civil incapacitations, tend only to beget habits of hypocrisy and meanness, and are a departure from the plan of the holy author of our religion, who being lord both of body and mind, yet chose not to propagate it by coercions on either, as was in his Almighty power to do, but to exalt it by its influence on reason alone; that the impious presumption of legislature and ruler, civil as well as ecclesiastical, who, being themselves but fallible and uninspired men, have assumed dominion over the faith of others, setting up their own opinions and modes of thinking as the only true and infallible, and as such endeavoring to impose them on others, hath established and maintained false religions over the greatest part of the world and through all time: That to compel a man to furnish contributions of money for the propagation of opinions which he disbelieves and abhors, is sinful and tyrannical; that even the forcing him to support this or that teacher of his own religious persuasion, is depriving him of the comfortable liberty of giving his contributions to the particular pastor whose morals he would make his pattern, and whose powers he feels most persuasive to righteousness; and is withdrawing from the ministry those temporary rewards, which proceeding from an approbation of their personal conduct, are an additional incitement to earnest and unremitting labours for the instruction of mankind; that our civil rights have no dependence on our religious opinions, any more than our opinions in physics or geometry; and therefore the proscribing any citizen as unworthy the public confidence by laying upon him an incapacity of being called to offices of trust or emolument, unless he profess or renounce this or that religious opinion, is depriving him injudiciously of those privileges and advantages to which, in common with his fellow-citizens, he has a natural right; that it tends also to corrupt the principles of that very religion it is meant to encourage, by bribing with a monopoly of worldly honours and emoluments, those who will externally profess and conform to it; that though indeed these are criminals who do not withstand such temptation, yet neither are those innocent who lay the bait in their way; that the opinions of men are not the object of civil government, nor under its jurisdiction; that to suffer the civil magistrate to intrude his powers into the field of opinion and to restrain the profession or propagation of principles on supposition of their ill tendency is a dangerous fallacy, which at once destroys all religious liberty, because he being of course judge of that tendency will make his opinions the rule of judgment, and approve or condemn the sentiments of others only as they shall square with or suffer from his own; that it is time enough for the rightful purposes of civil government for its officers to interfere when principles break out into overt acts against peace and good order; and finally, that truth is great and will prevail if left to herself; that she is the proper and sufficient antagonist to error, and has nothing to fear from the conflict unless by human interposition disarmed of her natural weapons, free argument and debate; errors ceasing to be dangerous when it is permitted freely to contradict them.

Section II. We the General Assembly of Virginia do enact that no man shall be compelled to frequent or support any religious worship, place, or ministry whatsoever, nor shall be enforced, restrained, molested, or burthened in his body or goods, or shall otherwise suffer, on account of his religious opinions or belief; but that all men shall be free to profess, and by argument to maintain, their opinions in matters of religion, and that the same shall in no wise diminish, enlarge, or affect their civil capacities.

Section III. And though we well know that this Assembly, elected by the people for their ordinary purposes of legislation only, have no power to restrain the acts of succeeding Assemblies, constituted with powers equal to our own, and that therefore to declare this act to be irrevocable would be of no effect in law; yet we are free to declare, and do declare, that the rights hereby asserted are of the natural rights of mankind, and that if any act shall be hereafter passed to repeal the present or to narrow its operations, such act will be an infringement of natural right.

THE FIRST FIFTEEN AMENDMENTS OF THE UNITED STATES CONSTITUTION

Amendment I

Congress shall make no law respecting an establishment of religion, or prohibiting the free exercise thereof; or abridging the freedom of speech, or of the press; or the right of the people peaceably to assemble, and to petition the Government for a redress of grievances.

Amendment II

A well regulated Militia, being necessary to the security of a free State, the right of the people to keep and bear Arms, shall not be infringed.

Amendment III

No Soldier shall, in time of peace be quartered in any house, without the consent of the Owner, nor in time of war, but in a manner to be prescribed by law.

Amendment IV

The right of the people to be secure in their persons, houses, papers, and effects, against unreasonable searches and seizures, shall not be violated, and no Warrants shall issue, but upon probable cause, supported by Oath or affirmation, and particularly describing the place to be searched, and the persons or things to be seized.

Amendment V

No person shall be held to answer for a capital, or otherwise infamous crime, unless on a presentment or indictment of a Grand Jury, except in cases arising in the land or naval forces, or in the Militia, when in actual service in time of War or public danger; nor shall any person be subject for the same offence to be twice put in jeopardy of life or limb; nor shall be compelled in any criminal case to be a witness against himself, nor be deprived of life, liberty, or property, without due process of law; nor shall private property be taken for public use, without just compensation.

Amendment VI

In all criminal prosecutions, the accused shall enjoy the right to a speedy and public trial, by an impartial jury of the State and district wherein the crime shall have been committed, which district shall have been previously ascertained by law, and to be informed of the nature and cause of the accusation; to be confronted with the witnesses against him; to have compulsory process for obtaining witnesses in his favor, and to have the Assistance of Counsel for his defense.

Amendment VII

In Suits at common law, where the value in controversy shall exceed twenty dollars, the right of trial by jury shall be preserved, and no fact tried by jury, shall be otherwise reexamined in any Court of the United States, than according to the rules of the common law.

Amendment VIII

Excessive bail shall not be required, nor excessive fines imposed, nor cruel and unusual punishments inflicted.

Amendment IX

The enumeration in the Constitution, of certain rights, shall not be construed to deny or disparage others retained by the people.

Amendment X

The powers not delegated to the United States by the Constitution, nor prohibited by it to the States, are reserved to the States respectively, or to the people.

Amendment XI

The Judicial power of the United States shall not be construed to extend to any suit in law or equity, commenced or prosecuted against one of the United States by Citizens of another State, or by Citizens or Subjects of any Foreign State.

Amendment XII

The Electors shall meet in their respective states and vote by ballot for President and Vice-President, one of whom, at least, shall not be an inhabitant of the same state with themselves; they shall name in their ballots the person voted for as President, and in distinct ballots the person voted for as Vice-President, and they shall make distinct lists of all persons voted for as President, and of all persons voted for as Vice-President, and of the number of votes for each, which lists they shall sign and certify, and transmit sealed to the seat of the government of the United States, directed to the President of the Senate;—The President of the Senate shall, in the presence of the Senate and the House of Representatives, open all the certificates and the votes shall then be counted;—The person having the greatest number of votes for President, shall be the President, if such number be a majority of the whole number of Electors appointed; and if no person have such majority, then from the persons having the highest numbers not exceeding three on the list of those voted for as President, the House of Representatives shall choose immediately, by ballot, the President. But in choosing the President, the votes shall be taken by states, the representation from each state having one vote; a quorum for this purpose shall consist of a member or members from two-thirds of the states, and a majority of all the states shall be necessary to a choice. And if the House of Representatives shall not choose a President whenever the right of choice shall devolve upon them before the fourth day of March next following, then the Vice-President shall act as President, as in the case of the death or other constitutional disability of the President.—The person having the greatest number of votes as Vice-President, shall be the Vice-President, if such number be a majority of the whole number of Electors appointed, and if no person have a majority, then from the two highest numbers on the list, the Senate shall choose the Vice-President; a quorum for the purpose shall consist of two-thirds of the whole number of Senators, and a majority of the whole number shall be necessary to a choice. But no person constitutionally ineligible to the office of President shall be eligible to that of Vice-President of the United States.

Amendment XIII

Section 1. Neither slavery nor involuntary servitude, except as a punishment for crime whereof the party shall have been duly convicted, shall exist within the United States, or any place subject to their jurisdiction.

Section 2. Congress shall have the power to enforce this article by appropriate legislation.

Amendment XIV

Section 1. All persons born or naturalized in the United States, and subject to the jurisdiction thereof, are citizens of the United States and of the State wherein they reside. No State shall make or enforce any law which shall abridge the privileges or immunities of citizens of the United States; nor shall any State deprive any person of life, liberty, or property, without due process of law; nor deny to any person within its jurisdiction the equal protection of the laws.

Section 2. Representatives shall be apportioned among the several States according to their respective numbers, counting the whole number of persons in each State, excluding Indians not taxed. But when the right to vote at any election for the choice of electors for President and Vice President of the United States, Representatives in Congress, the Executive and Judicial officers of a State, or the members of the Legislature thereof, is denied to any of the male inhabitants of such State, being twenty-one years of age, and citizens of the United States, or in any way abridged, except for participation in rebellion, or other crime, the basis of representation therein shall be reduced in the proportion which the number of such male citizens shall bear to the whole number of male citizens twenty-one years of age in such State.

Section 3. No person shall be a Senator or Representative in Congress, or elector of President and Vice President, or hold any office civil or military, under the United States, or under any State, who having previously taken an oath, as a member of Congress, or as an officer of the United States, or as a member of any State legislature, or as an executive or judicial officer of any State, to support the Constitution of the United States, shall have engaged in insurrection or rebellion against the same, or given aid or comfort to the enemies thereof. But Congress may by a vote of two-thirds of each House, remove such disability.

Section 4. The validity of the public debt of the United States, authorized by law, including debts incurred for payment of pensions and bounties for services in suppressing insurrection or rebellion, shall not be questioned. But neither the United States nor any State shall assume or pay any debt or obligation incurred in aid of insurrection or rebellion against the United States, or any claim for the loss or emancipation of any slave; but all such debts, obligations and claims shall be held illegal and void.

Section 5. The Congress shall have power to enforce, by appropriate legislation, the provisions of this article.

Amendment XV

Section 1. The right of citizens of the United States to vote shall not be denied or abridged by the United States or by any State on account of race, color, or previous condition of servitude.

Section 2. The Congress shall have power to enforce this article by appropriate legislation.

Index

A. A. Hoehling v. Universal City Studios Inc., 166
Abbé du Bos, 45
"Abie's Irish Rose," 161–162
Abortion, 1, 3, 7, 12, 17, 37, 102, 116, 122, 127–134, 173–174, 176–177, 181–187
Academy of Bordeux, 43
Academy of Dijon, 47–48
Academy of France, 43
"Across the Pacific," 165
Adair v. United States, 70–71
Adam, 39–40
Adultery, 17–29, 40–42, 98, 113
Afroasiatic languages, 18–22
Agnostics, 7
AIDS, 147
Akkadians, 18
Akron, 127–134
Alabama, 82
Alcoholic beverages, 29, 54, 68, 92
Allgeyer v. Louisiana, 68
American College of Obstetricians and Gynecologists, 130
American Postal Workers Union v. Frank, 145
American Revolution, 2, 3, 59, 102, 182–183

Amish, 110–111
Anderson, Hans Christian, 166
Anet, Claude, 47
Anglican Church, 28–30. *See also* Episcopacy
Anglo-Saxons, 27
Ann of Bohemia, 36
Appropriation, 78–85, 156–161, 168–169
Aquinas, Thomas, 41
Arabic, 18
Arizona, 112, 122
Army, 159, 183
Articles of Confederation, 59
Assemble, right to, 2. *See also* First Amendment
Atheism, 48. *See also* Agnostics
Athens, 22–24. *See also* Greece
Augustus, Emperor, 1
Autobiography of John Stuart Mill, 50–52

Babylonia, 18–21
Babylonian Law Code, 1. *See also* Hammurabi's Law Code
Baker, Mr., 162–163
Bakers, 11, 69
Baker v. Selden, 162–163

Balliol College, 35
Baltimore, 65
Baltimore, Lord, 37
Barron v. Mayor and City Council of Baltimore, 65
Baseball, 160
Bastard. *See* Illegitimate children
Bastille, 45
Bellotti v. Baird, 129
Bentham, Jeremy, 51–56
Bentham, Samuel, 50–51
Bible, 1, 36, 39–42
Bigamy, 17, 28, 107–108
Bill of Rights, 49–51, 59; American, 2–4, 11, 35, 60–65, 67, 72–73, 95–97, 120, 169, 174, 178, 186; British, 2–3, 38; State, 175–178
Binns, Jack, 81, 158–159
Binns v. Vitagraph Corp. of America, 81, 158–159
Biograph Theater, 167
Biography, 77–79, 153–161
Birmingham, 83
Birth control, 51–55, 59, 96–104. *See also* Contraception
Bismarck's Dismissal, 154
Black, Justice, 73, 98–99, 113–114, 184
Blackmun, Justice, 12, 102, 114, 127–128, 176
Blackstone, 51, 121
Blood money, 22, 25, 27
Blood transfusion, 177
Bluestein v. Skinner, 144
Board games, 159
Boddie v. Connecticut, 101
Bogart, Humphrey, 157
Bookkeeping, 162–163
Bookmaking, 99
Bordeaux, 43
Boston, 2, 91, 157, 163–164
Bowers v. Hardwick, 103, 116–123, 177
Boy Comics Publishers, 158–159
Brainwashing, 54, 60. *See also* Education
Brandeis, Justice, 2, 71–73, 75–80, 83, 91–95, 99, 118, 132, 156, 168, 178, 187

Brennan, Justice, 12, 97, 101–102, 107, 114, 116, 143, 174
Brightley v. Littleton, 163
British copyright law, 162–164
Bronx, 167
Brown v. Winkle, 144
Bureaucracy, 54
Burger, Chief Justice, 12, 102–103, 110, 114, 121, 131, 181
Burger Court, 102–103, 110, 181
Bush, President George, 12, 173
Buston, Dr., 96

Cagney, James, 158
Calder v. Bull, 64–65
California, 81, 155, 160, 174, 185
California v. Greenwood, 100
"Calling All Cars," 81, 156
Calvin, 37, 47
Campari liquer, 84
Cantwell v. Connecticut, 109
Capital punishment, 27–28
Capone, Al, 160
Carey v. Population Services International, 101, 120, 183
Caruthers v. R.K.O. Radio Pictures Inc., 165
Catholic, 7, 25–26, 29–30, 35–38, 43–50, 95, 110, 182, 185
CBS, 156, 159, 166–167
"C.Q.D. or Saved by Wireless," 158
Chain of horrors argument, 7
Charlemagne, 26, 30
Charles I, 30, 37–38
Charles II, 37–38
Charter, 3, 4, 108
Chase, Justice, 64–65
Chattanooga, 139
Chicago, 167
Child labor, 71
China, 1
Chinese Communists, 7
Christ, 18, 38
Christ Church College, 37
Christianity, 12, 26, 36, 38, 43–44, 48. *See also* Catholic; Protestant; Religion
Church. *See* Religion

"Cimmarron," 165
Citizenship, 66–67
City of Akron v. Akron Center for Reproductive Health, 127–134
Civilization, 48, 66
Civil rights, 11–12, 61–63, 67, 83, 174
Civil War: American, 11, 62, 65–69, 102, 183, 185; English, 37–38
Clark, Justice, 96
Clayton v. Stone, 164
Cleveland Bd. of Ed. v. Loudermill, 145
Coast Guard, 159
Cohabitation, 21, 183
Cohan, George M., 158
"Cohens and the Kellys, The," 161–162
Colaulti v. Franklin, 129
Collins v. Metro-Goldwyn Pictures Inc., 166
Colony, 9
Colorado, 112
Colt, Judge, 154
Common law, 8, 69, 77, 82, 156, 175
Common Law, The, 69
Commonwealth v. Bonadio, 119, 122
Communism, 7, 182
Comte, 52, 54
Concubines, 23, 36
Conductor, 79
Confederacy, 63, 67
Connecticut, 64, 96, 98, 101, 109
Consent, 76
Considerations on the Causes of Roman Greatness and Decadence, 43
Constantine VI, 26
Constantinople, 26
Contraception, 17, 51–55, 59, 96–102, 116–117, 121–122, 183–187
Copeland v. Philadelphia Police Department, 139
Copyright, 76, 161–168
Corliss, George H., 77–79, 154
Corliss v. Walker Co., 77–79, 154
Cow, 20, 30
Cowardice, 23
Cox Broadcasting Corp. v. Cohn, 168–169
Crete, 23

Crime of moral turpitude, 5
Cromwell, Oliver, 37
Cronin v. New England Telephone Co., 147
Cruzan, Nancy, 132
Cruzan v. Director, Missouri Dept. of Health, 127–134, 184
Cuneiform, 18
Cupid Rides the Rails, 166
Custom Service, 104, 141–144

Darley, Gabrielle, 81, 155–156
Death. See Right to die
De Civili Dominio, 35
Declaration of Independence, 8, 10, 34, 59–60
Deed, 3
Defamation, 24, 76–77, 82–86, 153, 157
Defense of the Spirit of the Laws, 43
Democracy in America, 52
Democratic liberalism, 33–35, 45, 49–56
Denmark, 37
Desert Storm, 182–183
Despotic government, 46, 52
Dickler, Gerald, 79–80, 82
Diderot, 47–48
Dijon, Academy of, 47–48
Dillinger, John, 167
Dillinger Dead or Alive?, 167
Dillinger Dossier, The, 167
Directories, 163–168
Disclosure, 76–86, 156–157, 168–169
Discourse on the Origin of Inequality, 48
Discourse on the Sciences and the Arts, 47–48
"Dishonored Lady," 161
Divine right of kings, 1, 30, 39–40, 45
Divorce, 17, 19–20, 22–23, 27, 29, 44, 116
Dog, 20, 30
Door-to-door selling, 109
Douglas, Justice, 91, 95–97, 100, 107, 109–110, 113–114
Dover, K. J., 23
Dowry, 22–23, 43
Drakon, 22

Dramatization, 81, 154–169
Dred Scott v. Sandford, 11, 65–66, 134
Drugs, 3, 54, 100–104, 111–112, 137–146
Drug testing, 137–148
Dual federalism, 64
Due process clause, 62–69, 96, 120, 145–146, 184. *See also* Fourteenth Amendment; Procedural due process; Substantive due process

Earp, Wyatt, 166
East Cleveland, 102–103, 120
East India Company, 51
Ecclesiastical courts, 27–28
Echevarria v. Warner Bros. Pictures, 165
Economics, 38, 50, 70
Education, 33, 42, 48–55, 94–96, 98, 109–110, 174, 176
Egan, Edward, 60
Egypt, 17–18
Eisenhower, President Dwight D., 11
Eisenstadt v. Baird, 101, 116–118, 120–122
Electronic eavesdropping, 100
Eleventh Amendment, 6–7
Émile, 48–49
Emotional distress. *See* Mental anguish
Empire State Building, 159
Employee Polygraph Protection Act, 147. *See also* Polygraph
Employment Div. v. Smith, 111–112, 123, 186
Encyclopedia, 47
England, 1, 3, 8–9, 27–28, 37, 46, 50–56, 59, 67, 127, 183
Episcopacy, 28–30, 37, 185
Equal protection, 10, 67, 70, 101, 112–115, 121. *See also* Fourteenth Amendment
Equal rights, 12
Essay Concerning Human Understanding, 38, 41–42
Essay on Toleration, 38
Establishment of religion. *See* Religion

Establishment of the French Monarchy in Gaul, 45
Europe, 17
Eve, 42
Everson v. Bd. of Ed., 110
Excommunication, 46
Existentialism, 49
Exposure, 23, 26, 39

Factions, 60
Factors Etc. Inc. v. Pro Arts, Inc., 159
False light, 82–86, 155–157, 168–169
Falwell, Jerry, 84
Falwell v. Flynt, 84
Fathers, 39–43
Federal Aviation Administration, 144
Federalist papers, 60–61
Federation, 9, 60–61
Feist Publications, 167–168
Feist Publications v. Rural Telephone Services Co., 167–168
Fellatio, 117, 122
Fences, 9
Feudalism, 25–26, 30, 46
Field, Justice, 68
Fifteenth Amendment, 62, 66
Fifth Amendment, 64, 97, 199
Filmer, Sir Robert, 38–40, 42, 45
Firefighters, 139–140, 144
First Amendment, 10, 82, 85, 96–100, 107–112, 159, 168–169, 174. *See also* Free speech; Religion
Florida, 84–85, 100, 168–169, 176–177
Florida Star v. B.J.F., 84–85, 168–169
Florida Steamship, 158
Florida v. Riley, 100
Fornication, 17, 28–29, 102–103, 117, 122–123, 177–178, 183
Fort Apache, 167
"Fort Apache, The Bronx," 167
Fortas, Justice, 114
Fourteenth Amendment, 2, 11, 62–73, 93–104, 112, 120, 128, 132, 137–148, 169, 173, 184
Fourth Amendment, 92–95, 97–100, 103–104, 137–145
France, 8, 26, 37, 43–50, 114, 182
France, Academy of, 43

Franklin, Marc, 82
Franks, 26, 45
Fraternal Order of Police, Lodge No. 5 v. Tucker, 145
Fredum, 25
Freedom of the press, 2, 51, 61, 72. *See also* First Amendment
Freed v. Loew's Inc., 158
Free enterprise, 33, 50–56. *See also* Laissez-faire
Free exercise of religion. *See* Religion
Free speech, 2, 51, 53, 61, 72, 78–86, 97, 154, 168–169, 174–175. *See also* First Amendment
French Connection, The, 160–161
F-R Pub. Co., 157, 160
Funkhouser v. Loews, Inc., 166

Garbage, 100
Garden of Eden, 42
Gaul, 45. *See also* France
General will, 49, 52
Geneva, 37, 47
Georgia, 6, 29, 78–79, 99, 108, 118–121
Germanic Europe, 25–26, 45
Germany, 94, 154
Goddess culture, 22
Goldberg, Justice, 97–98
Gomez v. Perez, 115
Goodwill, 76
Grain elevators, 68
Gravity, 34, 48, 55
Great Depression, 62, 71
Great Law of 1682, 29
Greece, 3, 20–24, 30, 45, 67, 115, 122, 127
Greek, 17, 50
Grey, Thomas, 116
Griswold v. Connecticut, 96–104, 116–118, 120–122, 184

Hadley, Herbert S., 77–79
Hafen, Bruce, 116
Hamilton, Alexander, 60–61
Hammer v. Dagenhart, 71
Hammurabi's Law Code, 18–21

Hand, Augustus, 165–166
Hand, Learned, 161–162, 165–166
Happiness, 8, 34, 41–42, 48–56, 59, 81, 93, 155–156, 182
Hardwick, Mr., 119–120
Harlan, Justice, 69, 98–99, 113, 138
Harris v. McRae, 129
Harvard Law Review, 2, 75, 93, 168, 178
Harvard Law School, 69, 91
Harvard University, 157
"Harvey Girls, The," 166
Hatti, 18
Hattusa, 18
Hebrew, 18
Helicopter, 100, 177
Héloïse, The New, 48
Henry, Patrick, 2, 61
Henry VIII, 27, 37
Heretics, 27
Hieroglyphics, 18
Hill family, 83, 157, 160
Hillman, Ms., 79
Hindenburg, 166
Hindenburg, The, 166
History, 17–30, 50, 60, 64, 128, 153–169, 182, 186
Hittite Law Code, 1, 20–30, 122
Hittites, 17, 20–30, 67, 115, 122
H. L. v. Matheson, 129
Hobbes, Thomas, 30
Hoehling, A. A., 166
Hohenzollern, William, 154
Holland, 37–38, 43
Hollywood, 153, 160–161
Holmes, Justice, 69–72, 93–95, 112, 127
Holmes v. Hurst, 161
Holy Roman Empire, 37
Homer, 20, 22
Homosexuality, 17, 23, 98, 103
Hooker, Richard, 41
Horse, 21, 30, 122, 139
House of Commons, 51
Houston, 176
Hubbard v. Journal Pub. Co., 82
Hughes, Howard, 153–155
Huguenots, 37

Human Immunodeficiency Virus (HIV), 147
Humiston v. Universal Film Mfg. Co., 158–159
Huss, John, 36
Hustler magazine, 84
Hypothetical arguments, 7

I Claudius, 1
Iliad, 22
Illegitimate children, 17, 22, 24, 27, 108–117, 186
Illinois, 66, 68
Immigration, 66
Immunities, 36
Inalienable rights. *See* Unalienable rights
Incest, 17–22, 25, 27–29, 40–42, 46, 84
Inclusion of one excludes the other rule, 5
India, 17
Indo-Europeans, 17–29, 113, 122, 184, 186
Indulgences, 36
Industrial Revolution, 68
In re Guardianship of Estelle M. Browning v. Herbert, 177
In re Quinlan, 177–178
In re T. W., 176
Insurance, 68–69
Intangible property, 76, 78
Intent of the legislature rule, 5–6
Intercourse. *See* Fornication
Interstate commerce, 4, 62, 68, 70, 108
Intestate succession, 113
Introduction to the Principles of Morals and Legislation, An, 51
Intrusion. *See* Seclusion
Iowa, 117
Iradell, Justice, 65
Iran, 18
Ireland, 17
Irving, Clifford, 153
Islamic Fundamentalists, 7
Italy, 45
Iwo Jima, 160

James, Jesse, 160
James II, 1, 38, 42
Jay, Chief Justice, 11, 60
Jefferson, Thomas, 2, 10, 34–35, 61, 67, 182, 186
Jehovah's Witnesses, 109
Jesus. *See* Christ
Jeweler's Circular Pub. Co. v. Keystone Pub. Co., 164, 168
John, King, 1
Journal Pub. Co., 82
Judiciary Act, 65
Jury, 1, 27, 61, 63, 84

Katz v. United States, 99, 138, 184
Kaufman, Judge, 166
Kennedy, Justice, 131, 173
Kentucky, 9, 80, 91
Keynes, Lord, 73
Keystone Pub. Co., 164, 168
Knox, John, 37

Labine v. Vincent, 113–114
Labor, 40, 52, 69–71
Laissez-faire, 68, 70, 72. *See also* Free enterprise
Lake v. CBS, 166
Larremore, Wilbur, 78–79, 82
Latin, 17, 50. *See also* Rome
Law Notes, 154
Leon v. Pacific Telephone & Telegraph Co., 164
Letter Concerning Toleration, 42
Letter of the law, 5
Letters on the Blind, 47
"Letty Lynton," 161
Leviathan, 30
Levy v. Louisiana, 113–114
Levy v. Warner Brothers Pictures Inc., 158
Libel. *See* Defamation
Liberty, 9, 11, 33–34, 40–42, 46, 49, 52–55, 59–62, 69, 97, 182. *See also* Fourteenth Amendment
Life magazine, 83, 157
Linde, Justice Hans, 173
Liquor license, 163
Lochner Court, 11, 69–73, 91–96

Lochner v. New York, 11, 69–70, 95–96, 98, 112, 120, 127, 134, 184
Locke, John, 33–35, 37–43, 49, 52, 55, 59, 60, 64, 182–187
Loews, Inc., 158, 166
Lollards, 36
London, 38
Lotteries, 70–71
Loudermill, Mr., 145
Louis XIV, 43
Louisiana, 7–9, 66–68, 113–114, 133
Louisville, 72, 91
Loving v. Virginia, 101, 103, 120
Lovvorn v. City of Chattanooga, 139
Luther, Martin, 36

Macedonians, 24
Madison, James, 60–62, 97, 182
Magna Carta, 1
Maher v. Roe, 129
Malice, 83, 86
Malthus, Thomas, 51
Mann Act, 109–110, 183
Maps, 163
Marbury v. Madison, 11, 65
Marijuana, 100, 117–119, 141
Marines, 160
Marriage, 17, 18, 23–27, 44, 97, 101–103, 107–123
Marshall, Justice, 12, 99, 102, 114, 143, 174
Martial law, 37
Maryland, 37, 122
Massachusetts, 28–29, 35, 69, 120, 129
Masterpiece Theater, 1
Matriarchal society, 17
Mau v. Rio Grande Oil Co., 81, 156–157
McDonell v. Hunter, 139
McGraw Hill Book Co., 153–155
McReynolds, Justice, 94–96
Medicaid, 129
Melvin, Bernard, 155
Melvin v. Reid, 81–82, 155–157
Mensa et toro, 27
Mental anguish, 76–77, 79, 83, 85, 160

Mesopotamia, 18
Metro-Goldwyn Pictures Corp., 161, 166
Meyer v. Nebraska, 72, 94, 96–98, 103, 120
Middle East, 17, 26
Mill, John Stuart, 33–34, 50–56, 70, 111–112, 133, 182–187
Minimum wage, 71–72
Miscarriages, 19–20
Mississippi River, 9
Missouri, 78–79, 129, 131–132, 176
Missouri Compromise, 11, 65–67
Mittani, 18
Model Penal Code, 30
Molony, Mr., 158–159
Molony v. Boy Comics Publishers, 158–159
Monarchy, 46, 50
Money, 40
Monopoly, 61, 67, 93
Montesquieu, Baron, 25, 33–35, 43–47, 49–56, 59, 60, 182–187
Mooney, Mr., 166
Moore, Mrs. Inez, 103
Moore, Robin, 160–161
Moore v. City of East Cleveland, 102–103, 120
Morality, 10, 12, 22, 25, 29, 34, 41–42, 45–55, 66, 68–69, 114, 117–118, 155, 183
Mormon, 7, 107–110, 113, 185
Moses, 23
Moslems, 26
Mothers, 39–43, 46
Moxley v. Regional Transit Service, 145
Mule, 21–22
Muller v. Oregon, 71
Munn v. Illinois, 68
Murder, 18–22, 24, 27, 155, 159
Murphy, Justice, 109

Nash, Jay Robert, 167
Nash v. CBS, Inc., 167
National Fed'n of Fed. Employees v. Cheney, 144
National Prohibition Act, 92
National Recovery Act, 95

National Treasury Employees Union v. Von Raab, 103–104, 138–144
Naturalization, 66
Natural law, 8–9, 33–57, 64–65, 182–187
Natural rights, 8–9, 10, 33–59, 61, 64–65, 68, 182–187
Nature, state of, 40
Navy, 158
Nebraska, 72, 94, 139
Netherlands, 37. *See also* Holland
Nevada, 29
New Deal, 11, 72, 95
New Deal Court, 11, 91, 100, 181
New England, 29–30, 37, 123
New England Telephone, 147
New Federalism, 173
New Jersey, 115, 117, 139, 177–178
New Jersey Welfare Rights Org. v. Cahill, 115
New Mexico, 82, 112
New Orleans, 9, 67
Newspapers, 2, 76, 79, 80, 82, 84–85, 156, 168–169
New State Ice Co. v. Liebmann, 93–94, 132
New York, 11, 29, 60, 68–69, 71, 78, 83, 101–102, 118–119, 122, 155, 158–162
New Yorker, 157
New York Times, The, 82–84
New York Times v. Sullivan, 82–84
Nichols v. Universal Pictures Corp., 161
Ninth Amendment, 4, 35, 62, 97–100
Nixon, President, 12, 173
Nizer, Louis, 81–82
Noah, 39
No-Leak-O Piston Ring Co. v. Norris, 165
Normans, 27
North Africa, 18
North Carolina, 84, 122
North Dakota, 114
Nuisance, 76

Oath of allegiance, 109
Obscenity, 99, 118, 121, 154
O'Connor, Justice, 129–132, 167–169, 173

Oedipus, 23
Ohio, 129–130, 145
Oklahoma, 93, 117, 121, 165
Olmstead v. United States, 92–93, 99, 118, 187
On Liberty, 52–54
Onofre, Mr., 118–119, 122
Oregon, 71, 95, 111–112, 173
Oxen, 19–20
Oxford University, 35, 51

Pacific Telephone & Telegraph Co., 164
Palco v. Connecticut, 120
Paris, 43, 47, 61
Parliament, 2, 35, 37, 43, 51
Patriarcha, 38, 42
Patriarchal society, 18–21, 41–43
Patricians, 24
Patterson, Lou Bertha, 113–114
Pavesich, 78
Peasant's Revolt, 36
Pennsylvania, 29, 119, 122, 129, 131, 133, 139
Penumbras of privacy, 97–98, 100
People v. Onofre, 118–119, 122
Persia, 43–45
Persian Letters, 43–45
Petition of Right, 37
Peyote, 10, 111–112
Pharmacist, 101, 159
Philadelphia, 139
Philippines, 165
Photographic Co., 77, 79
Photography, 76–79, 154
Pierce v. Society of Sisters, 95–98, 110, 120
Pig, 20, 30
Plain meaning rule, 4–6
Planned Parenthood v. Danforth, 128–129
Plato, 94
Plebeians, 24
Pledge of allegiance, 109
Policeman's Benevolent Ass'n v. Township of Washington, 139
Police power, 66, 69, 108, 119, 183
Pollard v. Photographic Co., 77, 79
Polygamy, 107–110, 113, 183, 186

Polygraph, 147, 175
Pope, 26–27, 36, 43
Pope Clement VII, 36
Population Services International, 101, 120, 183
Posters, 158–159
Post Office, 70
Post v. State, 117, 121
Powell, Justice, 102–103, 111, 114, 119–120
Presbyterian, 37, 185
Presley, Elvis, 159
Press. *See* First Amendment; Newspapers
Primogeniture, 22, 26–28, 39, 44–45
Prince v. Massachusetts, 120
Printing press, 37
Prison guards, 139
Privileges or immunities clause, 63, 67–68. *See also* Fourteenth Amendment
Pro Arts Inc., 159
Probable cause, 92, 103, 137
Procedural due process, 63, 67. *See also* Fourteenth Amendment
Prohibition, 92
Prosser, Dean William, 82–86, 155
Prostitution, 17, 23, 36, 44, 112, 155, 183
Protestant, 2, 7, 27, 30, 35–37, 43, 46, 56, 112
Psychology, 38
Public disclosure of private facts, 76–86, 156–157, 168–169
Public figure, 76, 82–86, 153–157, 160
Publius, 60
Pullman compartment, 9
Puritans, 17, 28–30, 35, 37, 42, 122–123, 183

Quakers, 28–29, 35, 123
Queen's College, 51
Quinlan, Ms., 177–178

Racial discrimination, 67. *See also* Civil rights
Radio, 81–82, 156–158
Railroads, 9, 68, 70, 79, 93, 103, 108, 140–141

Railway Labor Executives' Ass'n, 103–104, 138–144
Rape, 5, 23, 82, 84, 117, 168–169
Rasputin, 159
Reagan, President, 12, 173
Reasonableness of Christianity as Delivered in the Scriptures, 38
Reconstruction, 67
Red Kimono, The, 81, 155
Reformation, 1, 3. *See also* Protestant
Regional Transit Service, 145
Rehnquist, Chief Justice, 12, 84, 102–103, 111, 114, 128–132, 169, 173, 181–187
Relativism, 34, 41–42
Religion, 9–10, 17–30, 35–37, 43–46, 61, 95–96, 107–112, 182–187
Reproductive Health Services, 127–134, 176
Republic Pictures Corp., 160
Republics, 45–46
Republic Steamship, 158
Restatement (Second) of Torts, 82
Restoration, 38
Revolutionary War. *See* American Revolution
Reynolds v. United States, 107–108
Rhode Island, 122
Richard II of England, 36
Right of publicity. *See* Appropriation
Right of seclusion. *See* Seclusion
Right to die, 8, 116, 132, 177
"Right to Privacy," 2, 75–78, 83, 87, 156, 168, 178
Right to receive knowledge, 96
Riley, Mr., 100
Rio Grande Oil Co., 81, 156–157
R.K.O. Radio Pictures Inc., 165
Roberson, Ms., 78, 83, 158
Roberson v. Rochester Folding Box Co., 78, 83, 158–159
Rochester Folding Box Co., 78, 83, 158–159
Rochin v. California, 146
Roe v. Wade, 102, 120, 127–134, 176, 181–187
Rome, 1, 3, 21, 24, 26–27, 30, 36, 44–45, 67, 114–115, 123, 127
"Romeo and Juliet," 162

Romulus, 23
Roosevelt, President Franklin D., 11–12, 71–73, 95
Roosevelt, President Theodore, 69
Rosemont Enterprises, Inc. v. McGraw-Hill Book Co., 153–155
Rousseau, Jean Jacques, 33–34, 47–50, 52, 54–56, 59, 182–187
Rules of statutory construction, 3–7
Rural Telephone Services Co., 167–168
Rushton v. Nebraska Public Power District, 139
Russia, 17, 54, 159

Saint Peter's, 36
St. Simon, 51
Sampson & Murdock Co., v. Seaver-Radford Co., 163–164
San Jose Mercury News, 185
Sanskrit, 17
Sarat Lahiri v. Daily Mirror, Inc., 158
Sardinia, King of, 47
Saxons, 26
Scalia, Justice, 111–112, 131–132, 143, 173, 176, 184, 186
Schmerber v. California, 146
Schwyz, 37
Scotland, 37, 161
Search and seizure. *See* Fourth Amendment
Seaver-Redford Co., 163–164
Seclusion, 77–86, 155, 168–169
Secondat, Charles Louis. *See* Montesquieu, Baron
Securities and Exchange Commission, 91
Seduction, 23
Seelig v. Koehler, 144
Seldon, Mr., 162–163
Separation of church and state, 9–10, 107–112, 182–187. *See also* Religion
SEPTA, 139
Sex, 2, 17, 19–30, 107–123, 177–178
Shaftesbury, Lord, 38
Sheep, 20, 26, 30
Sheldon v. Metro-Goldwyn Pictures Corp., 161

Shoemaker v. Handel, 139, 146
Sidis, James, 157
Sidis v. F-R Pub. Corp., 157, 160
"Simon and Simon," 167
Skinner v. Oklahoma ex rel. Williamson, 120
Skinner v. Railway Labor Executives' Ass'n, 103–104, 138–144
Slander, 24. *See also* Defamation
Slavery, 20–21, 24, 39, 66–67, 182, 185
Slaughter-House Cases, 67, 93
Smith, Adam, 73
Smith, Madeleine, 161
Snakes, 18, 20
Social contract, 49–50, 64, 184
Social Contract, The, 49–50
Socialism, 51–52
Social Security, 115
Sodomy, 17–22, 25, 27–30, 40–42, 103, 112, 116–123, 177–178, 183
Solon, 22–24
Some Thoughts Concerning Education, 38
"Sooners, The," 165
Sorcery, 19–20
Souter, Justice, 173–174
South Carolina, 6, 29
Spahn, Warren, 160
Spahn v. Messner, Inc., 160
Spain, 8, 26, 45
Sparta, 23, 94
Specifics reveal the general rule, 5
Spehl, Eric, 166
Spencer, Herbert, 73, 112
Spirit of the law, 5
Spirit of the Laws, The, 25, 43–47
Stanley v. Georgia, 99, 118, 121
State v. Pilcher, 117
State v. Saunders, 117
Statutory construction rules, 4
Sterilization, 98
Stevens, Justice, 12, 102–103, 121, 143
Stewart, Justice, 98–99, 102–103, 113
Stone, Justice, 72
Strict construction, 6–7, 12
Stryker, Sergeant, 160

Stryker v. Republic Pictures Corp., 160
Substantive due process, 63–73, 95, 98–100, 116, 120, 182–187. *See also* Fourteenth Amendment
Suburbs, 9
Subversion, 23
Suicide, 22, 28, 43–45, 157
Sullivan, Commissioner, 83
Sumerians, 18
Sunday laws, 53, 70, 108
Sun-goddess, 17
Suspicion, 103, 139–144
Sutherland, Justice, 95
Sweden, 37
Switzerland, 37
Syria, 17
Système de Politique Positive, 52

Taney, Chief Justice, 66
Taylor, Mrs., 52
Telephone directories, 163–168
Ten Commandments, 39–40
Terentilius, 24
Test Pilot, 166
Texas, 115, 127–128, 175–176
Texas Constitution, 175–176
Texas Dept. of Mental Health and Mental Retardation, 175–176
Texas State Employees Union, 175–176
Thebes, 24
Theft, 19–20, 25, 39
Thérèse, 47
Third Amendment, 97, 100
Third Letter for Toleration, 38
Thirteenth Amendment, 62, 66
Thomas, Justice, 12, 34, 55, 94, 102, 173–174, 181, 185
Thornburg v. American College of Obstetricians & Gynecologists, 127–134
Time, 83–84, 157, 160
Time Inc. v. Hill, 83–84, 157, 160
Time Life, 166
Tocqueville, Alexis de, 52
Toksvig v. Bruce Pub. Co., 166
Totalitarianism, 49
Trademark, 76, 164
Trade secrets, 76

Transportation Workers Local 234 v. SEPTA, 139
Treason, 21, 23, 28
Treaty of Verdun, 26
Trespass, 92, 100, 109
Trimester system, 128–134
"True Crime Inspires Tense Play," 83
Truman, President, 11–12
Truth, 76, 80, 85
Turin, 47
Turkey, 18, 20
Twelve Tables, 24. *See also* Rome
Twentieth Century Fox, 160–161
Two Treatises of Government, 38–43

Unalienable rights, 8, 34–35, 56, 59, 62, 64, 68, 155, 182
Unenumerated rights, 4, 35, 62. *See also* Ninth Amendment
Unions, 70–71
Universal City Studios, Inc., 166
Universal Pictures Corp., 161
Urinalysis. *See* Drug testing
Usury laws, 70
Utah, 7, 69, 107–108, 112–113, 133
Utilitarianism, 34, 41–42, 51–56

Venereal disease, 117
Vikings, 26
Vincent, Ezra, 113–114
Vincent, Rita, 113–114
Virginia, 10
Virginia Bill for Religious Freedom, 10, 35
Virtue, 48–50
Vitagraph Company, 81, 158

Walker, Thomas, 166–167
Walker v. Time Life Films Inc., 166–167
Walters, Francis, 160–161
Walters v. Moore, 160–161
Warens, Madam de, 47
Warner Brothers Pictures Inc., 158, 165
Warren, Chief Justice, 11, 97, 114, 173, 181
Warren, Samuel, 2, 75–80, 83, 156, 168, 178

Warren Court, 11, 181
Washington, 91
Washington, D.C., 63, 67
Washukanni, 18
Wayne, John, 160
Weber v. Aetna Cas. & Sur. Co., 114
Webster v. Reproductive Health Services,
    127–134, 176
Welfare, 115
White, Justice, 12, 98, 100, 102–103,
    114, 119–121, 128–132, 168–169,
    173
Who Destroyed the Hindenburg, 166
Wichita, 37
William the Conqueror, 27
William of Orange, 2, 38, 43
Wilson, President, 91
Wiretapping, 80, 86, 92–93, 99, 177

Wisconsin, 110
Wisconsin v. Yoder, 110
Witches, 27
Words in context rule, 5
World War II, 110
Wrongful death, 113–114
Wyatt Earp, Frontier Marshall, 166
Wycliffe, John, 35–36, 38

Yakima, 91
"Yankee Doodle Dandy," 158
Youssoupoff v. CBS Inc., 159

Zablocki v. Redhail, 101
Zion Parochial School, 94
Zoning, 102–103
Zurich, 37
Zwingli, Ulrich, 37

About the Authors

DARIEN A. MCWHIRTER is an attorney and consultant. He received his Ph.D. in political science from Yale University and his J.D. from the University of Texas Law School. He is the author of *Your Rights at Work* (1989), and co-author of *Privacy in the Workplace* (Quorum, 1990).

JON D. BIBLE is an Associate Professor of Business Law at Southwest Texas State University. He received his M.A. in American Studies and his J.D. from the University of Texas. He has published numerous articles on the law and is a co-author of *Privacy in the Workplace* (Quorum, 1990).

MAY 9 3!

WITHDRAWN

Middlesex County College Library

3 9320 00056838 3

AF